+ The Offi

Contents

Letter to Student 2
Letter to Parent/Guardian 3

Chapter One: What Is the SSAT? 4-6
- What Is the Purpose of the SSAT? 4
- How Is the SSAT Designed? 4
- The SSAT Is Reliable 4
- The SSAT Is a Norm-Referenced Test 4-5
- The SSAT Is a Standardized Test 5
- Should I Guess on the SSAT? 5
- SSAT Practice Online 6

Chapter Two: About the Middle Level SSAT 7-60
- The Sections of the Middle Level Test 7-9
- Test Overview 9
- The Writing Sample 10-11
- The Quantitative Section 12-13
  - Sample Questions: Quantitative 14-39
- The Reading Comprehension Section 40-43
  - Sample Questions: Reading Comprehension 44-46
- The Verbal Section: Synonyms 47-48
  - Prefixes, Suffixes, and Roots 49-52
  - Sample Questions: Synonyms 53
- The Verbal Section: Analogies 54-56
  - Sample Questions: Analogies 57-58
- Summing It Up 59

Chapter Three: Scores 61-66
- What Your Scores Mean 61
- Formula Scoring 61
- The Score Report 62-64
- Supporting the Test Taker 65

Chapter Four: The Character Skills Snapshot 67-72
- What Is the Character Skills Snapshot? 67
- How Was the Snapshot Designed? 67
- What Does the Snapshot Measure? 68
- The Sections of the Snapshot 69
- How Is the Snapshot Administered? 69
- Is the Snapshot Reliable? 69
- The Snapshot Is a Norm-Referenced Assessment 70
- Strategies for Taking the Snapshot 70
- Sample Questions 71-72

Middle Level Practice Tests 73-214
- Trying Out the Middle Level SSAT 74-76
- Practice Test I 77-112
- Practice Test II 113-144
- Practice Test III 145-178
- Practice Test IV 179-214

Evaluating Your Middle Level SSAT 215-230
- How Did You Do? 216
- Scoring the Practice Tests 216
- Computing Your Raw Score 217
- Answer Keys 218-229
- Equating Raw Scores to Scaled Scores 230

Dear Student,

The private schools you'll find in books and on television may be interesting, but the real world of private schools is even more amazing. You're reading this guide because you think that a private school might be right for you, and you're ready for one of the first steps — taking the SSAT.

This book will introduce you to the SSAT, the test format, and what to expect on test day. It contains practice tests that resemble the one you'll be taking, plus preparation tips to help you do your best on the SSAT and the Character Skills Snapshot.

The Official Study Guide for the SSAT gives you:

- The definition of an admission test
- Descriptions of the test sections
- Test-taking strategies
- An introduction to the Character Skills Snapshot
- Plenty of sample questions to practice
- Full-length practice tests
- Information about how to interpret scores
- Registration and test day checklists

What won't you find here? Shortcuts, tricks, or gimmicks. This is the only book that contains sample questions and practice tests written by SSAT test writers and the test-taking strategies to help you to do your best. There are some valuable hints that can help you stay on track and maximize your time. But when it comes down to it, getting familiar with the test format and scoring, studying specific content types covered on the test, and solving practice questions is the best way to prepare for the SSAT. In addition to this guide, we offer an online practice program (see page 6) that provides even more sample questions, subject quizzes, and practice tests.

The path ahead will be exciting, and you'll probably learn a lot about yourself on the way. We wish you the best as you prepare for this journey, which will help you apply to a school that can change your life.

The SSAT Test Development and Research Team

Dear Parent/Guardian,

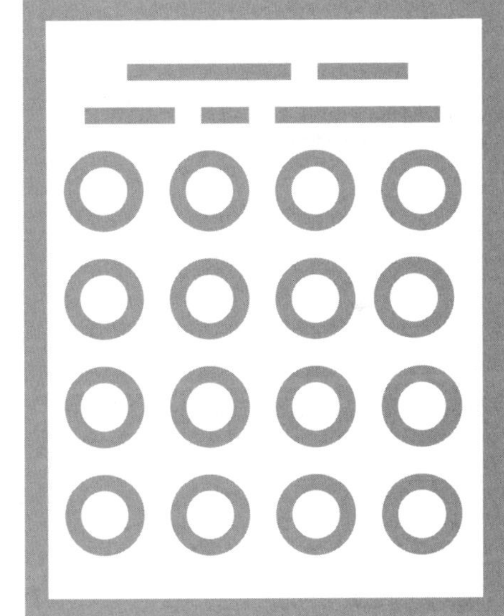

Congratulations on your decision to explore a private school education for your child! For more than 50 years, the SSAT has been the gold standard in admission testing for the world's best private schools. We know that the process of taking the SSAT can be fraught with concern and distress, but it needn't be. The SSAT is one important step on the road to a private school education — one that should be taken seriously but should not cause undue anxiety.

The results of admission testing, while integral to an application, are just one of many factors considered by admission officers when determining if your child and their school make a great match. The degree of emphasis placed on scores depends on the school and on other information, such as transcripts and teacher recommendations. For the vast majority of schools, students with a wide range of SSAT scores are admitted.

Here are a few questions that admission officers contemplate when reviewing an applicant's scores:

- Are the scores consistent with the student's academic record?
- Do the scores highlight areas of academic strength or weakness?
- How do these scores compare with those of other students in the applicant pool?
- How do these scores compare with students who have enrolled over the last few years?

As a parent, you have a central role to play in helping your child to succeed in the school application process by reminding them to keep the SSAT in perspective. Schools are most interested in finding out who your child is.

There are a multitude of sources, both on- and offline, that promise to prepare your child for the SSAT and increase their test score. This guide was created by our test development team to support your child's preparation efforts with legitimate information, test-taking strategies, and practice tests. We encourage you to use this guide as your official source for SSAT preparation and the Character Skills Snapshot information. On page 65, we share tips to help you support your student during this important preparation for taking the SSAT.

Finally, we urge you to use the ssat.org website not only to register your child for the test but also to access information about the private school application process, search for schools that are the right fit for your child and your family, and take advantage of our online practice program.

We hope *The Official Study Guide for the Middle Level SSAT* will help to make your family's experience of testing and applying to private school a successful and enjoyable one.

Good luck!

Heather Hoerle

Heather Hoerle, Executive Director & CEO, The Enrollment Management Association

Chapter One: What Is the SSAT?

What Is the Purpose of the SSAT?

The SSAT is designed for students who are seeking entrance to private schools worldwide. The purpose of the SSAT is to measure the verbal, quantitative, and reading skills students develop over time — skills that are needed for successful performance in private schools. The SSAT provides private school admission professionals with meaningful information about the possible academic success of potential students at their institutions, regardless of background or experience.

The SSAT is not an achievement test, although knowledge of a certain amount of mathematical content is necessary to do well on the quantitative sections of the test. Your most recent classroom math test, for example, was probably an achievement test: Your teacher designed it to evaluate how much you know about what was covered in class. The SSAT, on the other hand, is designed to measure the overall verbal, quantitative, and reading skills you have acquired, instead of focusing on your mastery of specific course materials.

SSAT tests are not designed to measure other characteristics, such as initiative, resilience, or teamwork, that may contribute to your success in school. As a complement to the SSAT's assessment of cognitive skills, we also offer the Character Skills Snapshot, which was designed expressly to measure character skills valued by private schools. To learn more about the Snapshot, visit ssat.org/snapshot.

How Is the SSAT Designed?

The SSAT measures three constructs: verbal, quantitative, and reading skills that students develop over time, both in and out of school. It emphasizes critical thinking and problem-solving skills that are essential for academic success.

The overall difficulty level of the SSAT is built to be at 50%–60%. This means that on average, 50%–60% of the test takers can answer the questions correctly. The distribution of question difficulties is set so that the test will effectively differentiate among test takers, who vary in their level of abilities.

To develop the SSAT, The Enrollment Management Association convenes content committees composed of content experts and independent school teachers. The committees write and review items, and reach consensus regarding the appropriateness of the questions. Questions judged to be acceptable after the committee review are then pretested and analyzed. Questions that are statistically sound are selected and assembled into test forms.

The SSAT Is Reliable

The SSAT is a highly reliable test. A test is said to have a high reliability if it produces similar results under consistent conditions. Reliability coefficients range between 0.00 (no reliability) and 1.00 (perfect reliability). On the SSAT, the scaled-score reliability is higher than 0.90 for both the verbal and quantitative sections, and is approaching 0.90 for the reading section.

The SSAT Is a Norm-Referenced Test

A norm-referenced test interprets an individual tester's score relative to the distribution of scores for a comparison group, referred to as the *norm group.* The SSAT norm groups consist of all the test takers (same grade) who have taken the test for the first time on one of the Standard SSAT administrations in the United States and Canada typically within the past three years.

The SSAT reports percentile ranks, which are referenced to the performance of the norm group. For example, if you are in the sixth grade, and your percentile rank on the March 2019 verbal section is 90%, it means that verbal scores for 90% of all the other sixth-grade students (who have taken the test for one of the SSAT administrations in the United States and Canada, typically using the most recent three years of data) fall below your scaled score. The score report also provides this information for your grade. The same scaled score on the SSAT may have a slightly different percentile rank from year to year, and the SSAT percentile ranks should not be compared to those of other standardized tests because each test is taken by a different group of students.

In contrast, a criterion-referenced test interprets a test-taker's performance without reference to the performance of other test takers. For example, your percent correct from a classroom math test would be 90% if you answered 90% of the questions correctly. Your score is not referenced to the performance of anyone else in your class.

It is important to remember that the SSAT norm group is highly competitive. You are being compared to all the other students (same grade) who are taking this test for admission into private schools. Most important to remember is that the SSAT is just one piece of information considered by schools when making admission decisions, and for the vast majority of schools, students with a wide range of SSAT scores are admitted.

The SSAT Is a Standardized Test

The SSAT is scored in a consistent (or standard) manner. It adheres to standard administration processes and practices, based on the testing mode. The reported (or scaled) scores are comparable and can be used interchangeably, regardless of which test form was taken. A scaled score of 500 on the June 2018 Middle Level verbal section, for example, has the same meaning as the scaled score of 500 from the December 2016 Middle Level verbal section, although the forms are different. This score interchangeability is achieved through a statistical procedure referred to as *score equating*. Score equating is used to adjust for minor form difficulty differences, so that the resulting scores can be compared directly.

Standard also refers to the way in which tests are developed and administered. A standard process for writing, testing, and analyzing questions — before they ever appear on a live test — is used. Further, The Enrollment Management Association provides precise instructions to be followed by qualified and experienced test administrators from the moment students are admitted to the test center until the time of dismissal. Any deviations from the uniform testing conditions are reported in writing by the test administrator to The Enrollment Management Association. Of course, a student may apply for testing accommodations, but the processes and procedures for the test's administration remain the same.

Should I Guess on the SSAT?

The answer is: It depends. You must first understand how the test is scored.

When your test is scored, you will receive one point for each correct answer. One quarter of a point is deducted for each incorrect answer. You will not receive or lose points for questions that are not answered. If you guess, try guessing only when you can eliminate at least one (but optimally more than one) answer choice.

A few things to keep in mind:

Keep moving. Do not waste time on a question that is hard for you. If you cannot answer it, make a note of it, skip over it, and move on. If you have time left in the section, go back to it then.

Take care with each question. You receive one point for each correct answer, no matter how hard or easy the questions are. Approach all questions with equal consideration; don't risk losing points to careless errors on seemingly easy questions.

Check your answer sheet. If taking the test on paper, mark your answers in the correct row on the answer sheet. Be especially careful if you skip questions.

SSAT Practice Online

A perfect complement to this study guide, our online practice program is another official source for SSAT practice. SSAT Practice Online helps you prepare by providing practice questions similar to those appearing on the SSAT, and identification of exactly which topics you should focus on before you test. Other key features include: section tests that target quantitative, reading, or verbal practice; SSAT topic quizzes with tips on how to answer each question; and study tools. Visit ssat.org/practice or access the program via your SSAT account.

ssat.org/practice

Students who use a fee waiver for the SSAT registration are also provided free access to the online practice program for both the Middle and Upper Level SSAT, as well as free access to the Admission Academy, a resource to help families navigate the K-12 private school admission process.

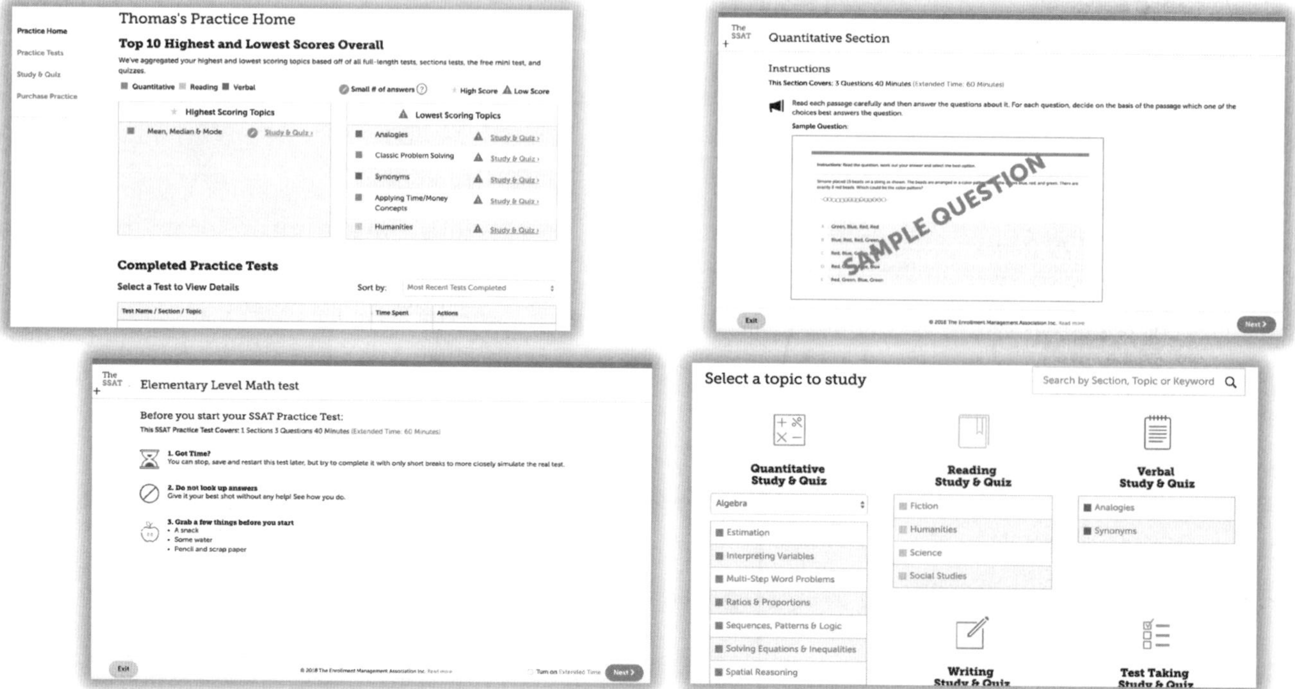

Chapter Two: About the Middle Level SSAT

The SSAT is a multiple-choice test that consists of verbal, quantitative (math), and reading comprehension sections. The Middle Level SSAT is for students in grades 5–7 and provides admission officers with an idea of your academic ability and "fit" in their schools. The best way to ensure that you perform as well as you possibly can on the SSAT is to familiarize yourself with the test. Understanding the format of the test and reviewing practice questions will make your test-taking experience easier. You'll feel more comfortable with the test and be able to anticipate the types of questions you'll encounter.

This chapter will introduce you to the kinds of questions you'll see on the Middle Level SSAT and the best ways to approach them. The sample questions that accompany each section will give you some practice before you tackle the practice tests that appear later in the book. In this chapter, we will also provide test-taking strategies that you should know when you take the Middle Level SSAT. The bonus of these test-taking strategies is that they may also help you perform better on the tests you take in school!

The Middle Level Test Consists of FIVE Sections:

1. Writing Sample

Number of questions: You will have a choice between two prompts.

What it measures: Your ability to think creatively, organize your ideas, and write clearly

Scored section: No, but it is provided to the schools you have selected to receive your score reports.

Time allotted: 25 minutes

Topics covered: Students are given a choice between two prompts: one prompt is a creative story-starter, and the other is a personal essay question. You choose one of them and write either a story or an essay.

The best way to make sure you perform as well as you can on the SSAT is to become familiar with the test.

2. Quantitative (Math) Section

Number of questions: 50, divided into two parts

What it measures: Your ability to solve quantitative problems

Scored section: Yes

Time allotted: 30 minutes for the first 25 problems, and 30 minutes for the final 25 problems

Topics covered: These problems test quantitative reasoning based on the following topics:

Number Concepts and Operations

- Decimals: Place Value and Computations
- Fractions: Concepts and Computations
- Integers: Computations and the Order of Operations
- Arithmetic Word Problems
- Number Sense/Number Theory
- Ratio, Rate, Proportions, and Converting Units
- Percent
- Estimation
- Sequences and Patterns

Continued on next page

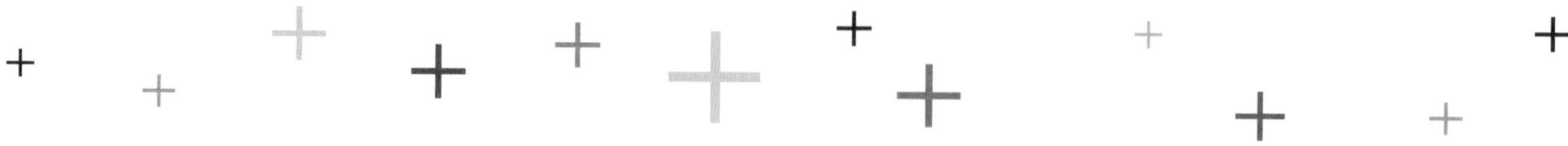

2. Quantitative (Math) Section *(continued)*

Geometry

- Length, Perimeter, Area
- Radius, Diameter, Circumference
- Surface Area and Volume
- Angle Relationships
- Visual/Spatial Reasoning

Algebra

- Simple Linear Equations and Inequalities
- Algebra Word Problems
- Simplification and Evaluation of Algebraic Expressions

Data Analysis

- Graphs and Tables
- Mean, Median, Mode, Range
- Probability
- Counting

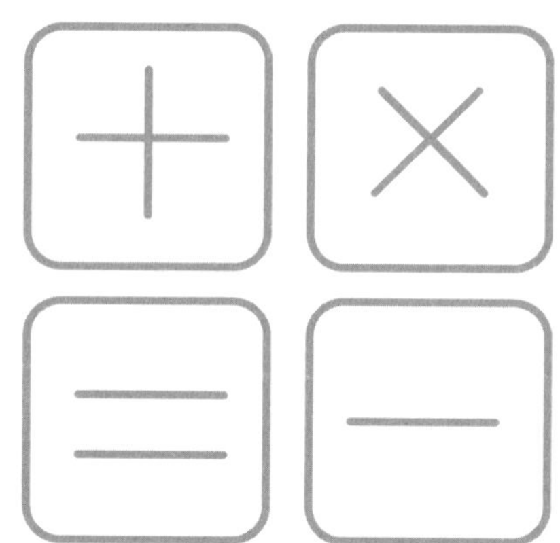

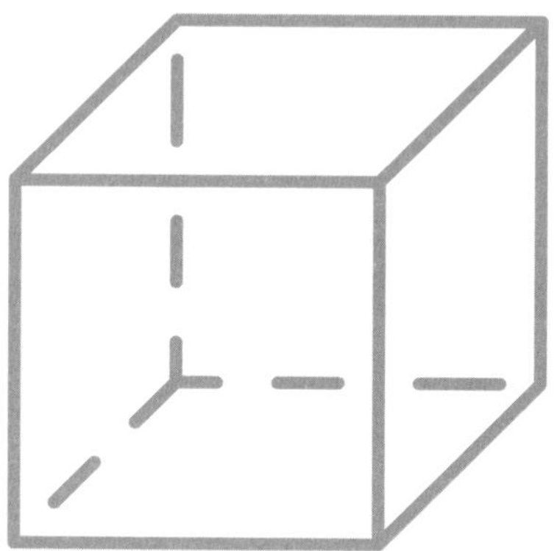

3. Reading Comprehension Section

Number of questions: 40

What it measures: Your ability to understand and interpret what you read

Scored section: Yes

Time allotted: 40 minutes

Topics covered: There are 7–8 reading passages, each 150–350 words in length. Passages are either literary or expository. Literary passages are drawn from works of fiction or poetry. Expository passages examine topics in the fields of science, social science, history, or the humanities.

Literary passages:

- Fiction
- Poetry

Expository passages:

- Science
- Social Science
- History
- Humanities (art, music, etc.)

4. Verbal Section

Number of questions: 60 (30 synonyms and 30 analogies)

What it measures: Your ability to understand the meanings of words and to recognize relationships between words with different meanings

Scored section: Yes

Time allotted: 30 minutes

Topics covered: These questions ask you to identify words that have similar meanings (synonyms) and identify word pairs that have similar relationships (analogies). The words tested are nouns, adjectives, or verbs.

5. Experimental Section

Number of questions: 16

What it measures: Verbal, reading comprehension, and quantitative skills

Scored section: No

Time allotted: 15 minutes

Topics covered: Six verbal, five reading, and five quantitative questions

Testing accommodation students requiring 1.5x time are not required to complete the experimental section.

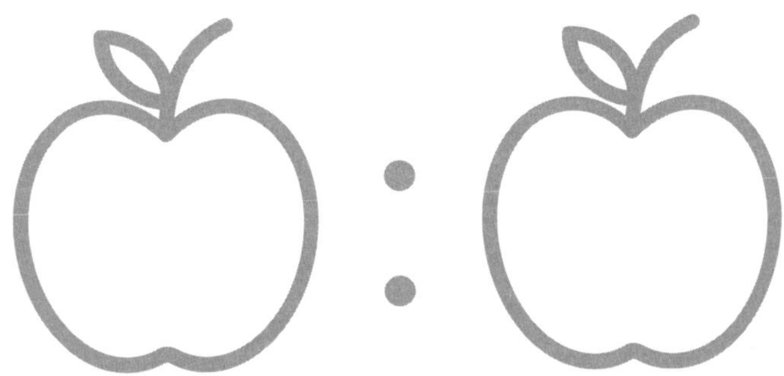

Test Overview

Section	Number of Questions	Time Allotted to Administer Each Section
Writing Sample	1	25 minutes
Break		10 minutes
Section 1 (Quantitative)	25	30 minutes
Section 2 (Reading)	40	40 minutes
Break		10 minutes
Section 3 (Verbal)	60	30 minutes
Section 4 (Quantitative)	25	30 minutes
Section 5 (Experimental)	16	15 minutes
Totals	**167[1]**	**3 hours, 10 minutes**

[1]*Of the 167 items including the writing sample, 150 questions are scored.*

1. The Writing Sample

At the beginning of the test, you will be asked to write a story or an essay in 25 minutes. You'll have a choice between two prompts. You may choose either (A) a creative story-starter or (B) a personal essay question.

What Are the Directions for the Writing Sample Section of the Test?

Schools would like to get to know you better through a story you tell or an essay you write. If you choose to write a story, use the sentence presented in A to begin. Make sure that your story has a beginning, middle, and end. If you choose to write a personal essay, base your essay on the topic presented in B. Please fill in the circle next to your choice.

How Are the Writing Prompts Presented?

EXAMPLE	(A) All I wanted was a glass of water. *or* (B) What is your favorite game to play? Describe the game and tell why you like it.

Just the Facts

The Writing Sample

Number of questions:
You will have a choice between a creative story-starter and a personal essay question.

What this measures:
Your ability to organize your ideas and write clearly.

Scored:
No, but it is delivered to the schools you have selected to receive your score reports.

Time allotted:
25 minutes

Tips for Getting Your Writing Sample Started

Read the prompts carefully. Take a few minutes to think about them and choose the one you prefer. Then, organize your thoughts before you begin writing (scrap paper for organizing your thoughts will be provided when you test). Be sure that you use a pencil, that your handwriting is legible, and that you stay within the lines and margins. Remember to be yourself and let your ideas flow or your imagination soar!

If you want to change what you have written, erase or neatly cross out the words you want to eliminate and add the new words so they are legible. Two line-ruled pages will be provided. Don't feel as if you have to fill both pages — just do your best to provide a well-written story or essay.

Remember: Your writing sample will not be scored. Schools use the sample to get to know you better through your writing.

Practice Writing Samples

This book includes practice writing sample prompts, which can be found at the beginning of the practice tests. Each sample includes directions, two prompts, and an answer sheet similar to the one you'll receive during the actual test.

Writing Sample Test-Taking Strategies

1. While creativity is encouraged, remember that the admission officers in the schools to which you are applying will be reading your writing sample. Be sure that your story or essay is one that you would not hesitate to turn in for a school assignment.
2. Read both prompts. Take a couple of minutes to think about what you're going to write. You can use your scrap paper to organize your thoughts.
3. Choose a working title for your story or essay. The Middle Level SSAT doesn't require a title, but a working title will help to keep you on track.
4. If you choose to write a story, make sure it has a beginning, a middle, and an end. Get involved in your story. Give details, describe emotions, and have fun.
5. If you choose to write a personal essay, be sure to provide interesting details to illustrate your thoughts and feelings.
6. If there's time, check your writing for spelling, punctuation, and grammatical errors.

2. The Quantitative Section

The quantitative (math) section of the Middle Level SSAT measures your knowledge of number concepts and operations, geometry, algebra, and data analysis. The words used in SSAT problems refer to mathematical operations with which you are already familiar.

> **Just the Facts**
> **The Quantitative Section**
> **Number of questions:** 50, divided into two parts
> **What it measures:** Your ability to solve problems involving number concepts and operations, geometry, algebra, and data analysis
> **Scored section:** Yes
> **Time allotted:** 30 minutes for the first 25 problems and 30 minutes for the final 25 problems

What Are the Directions for the Quantitative Section on the Test?

Following each problem in this section, there are five suggested answers. Work each problem in your head, in the blank space at the right of the page if taking the test on paper, or on scrap paper if taking the test on the computer. Then, look at the five suggested answers and decide which one is best.

How Are the Quantitative Problems Presented?

Many of the problems that appear in the quantitative section of the Middle Level SSAT are structured in mathematical terms that directly state the operation you need to perform to determine the best answer choice.

EXAMPLE:

13, 25, 37, ...

In the sequence above, 13 is the first number. Each number after the first is 12 more than the preceding number. What is the 10th number in the sequence?

(A) 35
(B) 49
(C) 72
(D) 121
(E) 133

The correct answer is (D).

Other questions are structured as word problems. A word problem often does not specifically state the mathematical operation or operations that you will need to perform in order to determine the answer. In these problems, your task is to carefully consider how the question is worded and the way the information is presented to determine what operations you will need to perform.

EXAMPLE:

Kathy and Donna ran a 3-mile race. Kathy ran the first 2 miles at a speed of 6 miles per hour and walked the last mile at a speed of 4 miles per hour. Donna ran the first mile at a speed of 10 miles per hour and walked the last 2 miles at a speed of 3 miles per hour. Which of the following statements is true about the timing of the race for Kathy and Donna?

(A) Kathy finished the race 3 minutes ahead of Donna.
(B) Kathy finished the race 4.5 minutes ahead of Donna.
(C) Kathy finished the race 11 minutes ahead of Donna.
(D) Donna and Kathy finished the race at the same time.
(E) Donna finished the race 4 minutes ahead of Kathy.

The correct answer is (C).

Quantitative Test-Taking Strategies

1. Read the problem carefully.
2. Pace yourself. Try not to spend too much time on one problem.
3. Be sure to use the "Use This Space for Figuring" area of your test book to do the scratch work. If taking the computer-based test at a Prometric test center, you will receive a white board. If taking the SSAT at Home, you may use scrap paper.
4. Always check to see if you have answered the question asked in the problem. Circling what's being asked can be helpful, so you don't mistakenly choose the wrong answer.
5. Watch for units of measure. Be sure you know and understand in which unit of measure the answer is supposed to be given.
6. Draw pictures. If you find that a problem is complicated, you can draw a graph, diagram — anything that will allow you to understand what the problem is asking.
7. Remember to mark your answers on the answer sheet if taking the test on paper! If your problem is solved in the test book but not marked on the answer sheet, it will not be counted.

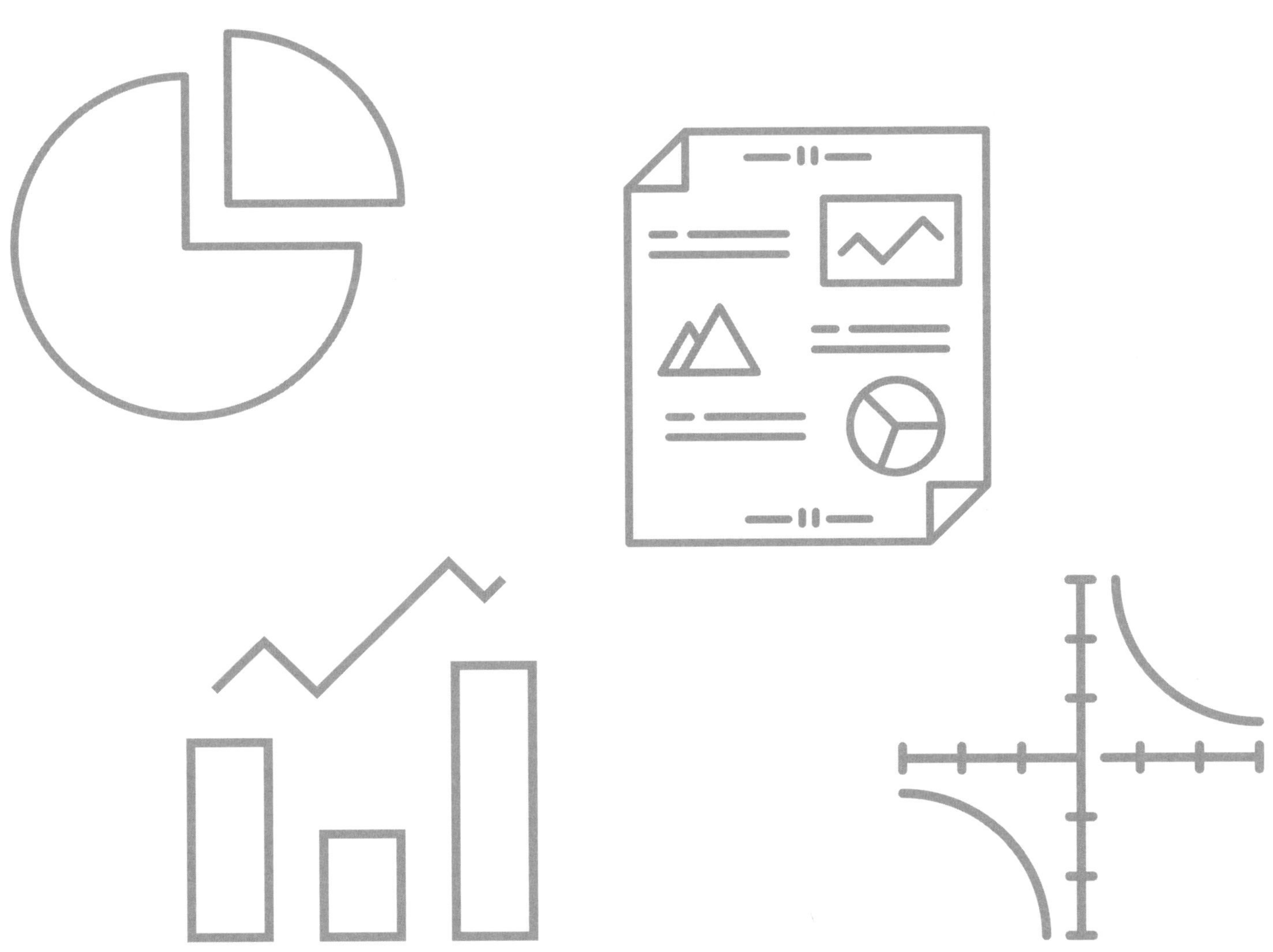

Sample Questions: Quantitative

On the following pages, you will find sample questions from these topics: Number Concepts and Operations, Geometry, Algebra, and Data Analysis. Each topic may also include a brief overview of related content.

Section I: Number Concepts and Operations

In this section, you will find 26 sample questions and related overviews of mathematics concepts in Number Concepts and Operations. The answers to these 26 questions are located at the end of this section.

Decimals: Place Value and Computations

A **decimal point**, which is placed after a whole number, separates the whole-number part of a number from its fractional part. Nonzero digits to the left of the decimal point indicate values greater than one. Digits to the right of the decimal point indicate values less than one.

For example:
Thirty-five and six-tenths is 35.6 written as a decimal number.
426.98 has 4 hundred<u>s</u>, 2 ten<u>s</u>, 6 ones, 9 ten<u>**ths**</u>, and 8 hundred<u>**ths**</u>.

$426.98 = 400 + 20 + 6 + \frac{9}{10} + \frac{8}{100}$

1. Which of the following decimals is greatest?
   (A) 1.065
   (B) 1.654
   (C) 1.645
   (D) 1.456
   (E) 1.045

---

2. Calculate: 1.1 + 20.3 + 4.97
   (A) 7.11
   (B) 8.10
   (C) 25.47
   (D) 26.37
   (E) 71.1

---

3. What is the value of 2.1 × 1.5 ?
   (A) 315
   (B) 31.5
   (C) 3.15
   (D) 0.315
   (E) 0.0315

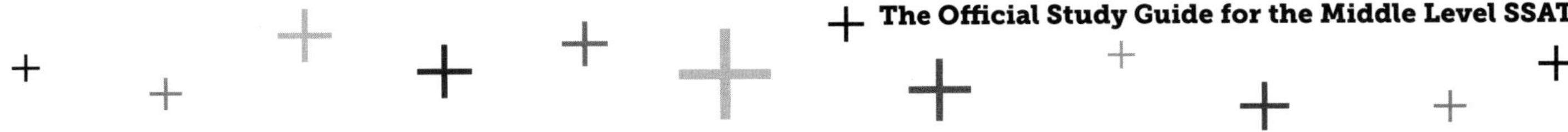

Fractions: Concepts and Computations

A **fraction** has a numerator and a denominator. The numerator is above the fraction bar, and the denominator is below the fraction bar. The numerator is divided by the denominator.

For example: $\frac{1}{2}$ 1 ↔ numerator, 2 ↔ denominator

When fractions have the same numerator but different denominators, the one with the larger denominator is smaller.

For example: $\frac{1}{8} < \frac{1}{4}$

4. The figure shown is divided into 6 triangles of equal size. The shaded region represents what fraction of the figure?

(A) $\frac{1}{4}$

(B) $\frac{1}{3}$

(C) $\frac{1}{2}$

(D) $\frac{2}{3}$

(E) $\frac{5}{6}$

---

5. Compute: $\frac{3}{2} + \frac{2}{5} - \frac{1}{4}$

(A) $\frac{1}{5}$

(B) $\frac{4}{11}$

(C) $\frac{27}{20}$

(D) $\frac{4}{3}$

(E) $\frac{33}{20}$

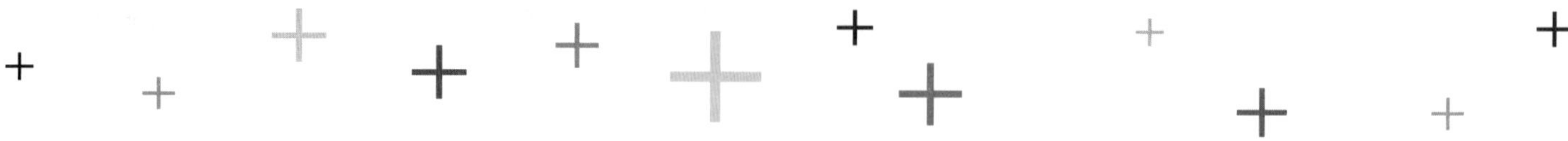

6. What is the value of $\frac{5}{3} \div \frac{3}{2}$?

   (A) $\frac{1}{10}$

   (B) $\frac{9}{10}$

   (C) $\frac{10}{9}$

   (D) $\frac{5}{2}$

   (E) 10

Integers: Computations and the Order of Operations

Integers are the whole numbers and their opposites: $\ldots, -2, -1, 0, 1, 2, \ldots$

The whole numbers are **positive** integers, and their opposites are **negative** integers. The number 0 is neither positive nor negative.

The **order of operations** is the method for simplifying an expression with multiple operations.
The order is as follows:

1) Perform operations inside grouping symbols.

2) From left to right, find the value of powers.

3) From left to right, multiply and divide.

4) From left to right, add and subtract.

7. Compute: $8 \times (-4) \times (-3)$
   (A) -32
   (B) -27
   (C) 27
   (D) 32
   (E) 96

---

8. Simplify: $6 + (-1)^2 \times (8 + 2)$
   (A) 15
   (B) 16
   (C) 50
   (D) 60
   (E) 70

Arithmetic Word Problems

Arithmetic word problems have real-life settings and can be solved using one or more steps. Some may require you to add, subtract, multiply, or divide the numbers in the problem. Others may require different problem-solving strategies like working backwards, drawing a picture, guessing and testing, or making a pattern.

9. Yesterday Jaaron ran 5.1 kilometers. Today he ran 2.01 kilometers. How many more kilometers did he run yesterday than today?
   (A) 3.11
   (B) 3.09
   (C) 2.09
   (D) 1.50
   (E) 1.40

---

10. Karen has $\frac{1}{3}$ of a pie and Mara has $\frac{1}{4}$ of the pie. What is the total fraction of the pie that Karen and Mara have?
   (A) $\frac{1}{6}$
   (B) $\frac{1}{2}$
   (C) $\frac{7}{12}$
   (D) $\frac{5}{6}$
   (E) $\frac{4}{3}$

---

11. A bookstore receives a shipment of 120 books. Of the books, $\frac{1}{3}$ are hardcover, and the rest are paperback. Of the paperback books, $\frac{3}{4}$ are fiction. How many paperback fiction books are in the shipment?
   (A) 20
   (B) 30
   (C) 60
   (D) 80
   (E) 90

12. An elevator in a building is currently on floor 21. After the elevator goes up 8 floors, down 5 floors, then up 4 floors, on which floor will the elevator be located?
    (A) 9
    (B) 14
    (C) 20
    (D) 28
    (E) 30

Number Sense / Number Theory

A **factor** of a number n is any integer that divides exactly into the number n. The number n is **divisible** by each of its factors. A **prime number** p is any integer with exactly <u>two</u> factors: 1 and p. An **even number** is an integer with the digit 0, 2, 4, 6, or 8 in the ones place. An **odd number** is an integer with the digit 1, 3, 5, 7, or 9 in the ones place.

13. Which of the following is divisible by 15 ?
    (A) 159
    (B) 225
    (C) 415
    (D) 560
    (E) 663

---

14. Which of the following is the least common multiple of 18, 24, and 60 ?
    (A) 6
    (B) 72
    (C) 120
    (D) 360
    (E) 720

---

15. How many prime numbers are between 30 and 60 ?
    (A) Seven
    (B) Eight
    (C) Nine
    (D) Ten
    (E) Eleven

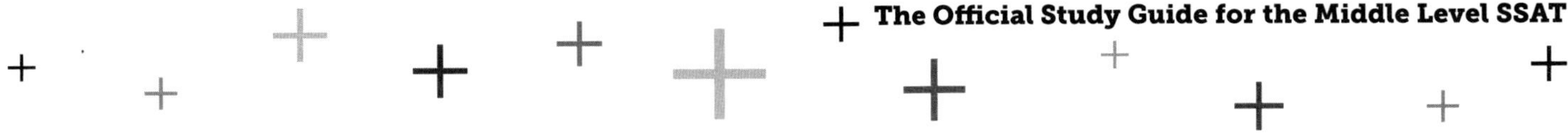

16. If k is an odd number, which of the following is an even number?
    (A) $k + 2$
    (B) $k - 10$
    (C) $3k + 1$
    (D) $4k - 1$
    (E) $k(k + 4)$

---

17. Which of the following is NOT a factor of 60×33 ?
    (A) 12
    (B) 20
    (C) 36
    (D) 40
    (E) 55

Ratio, Rate, Proportion, and Converting Units

A **ratio** compares one quantity with another quantity by division. When two ratios are equal, they form a **proportion**. A ratio that compares quantities with different units of measure (for example, miles per hour) is called a **rate**. A ratio can be expressed in several ways.

For example, the ratio 5 to 10 can also be expressed as $\frac{5}{10}$ or 5:10.

18. A school reports a student-to-teacher ratio of 6:1. How many students does the school have, if there are 45 teachers in the school?
    (A) 285
    (B) 270
    (C) 225
    (D) 151
    (E) 51

---

19. A train traveled 100 miles from City W to City X in 2 hours. The train then traveled 120 miles from City X to City Y in 80 minutes. What was the average speed, in miles per hour, at which the train traveled from City W to City Y?
    (A) 53
    (B) 66
    (C) 70
    (D) 73
    (E) 80

     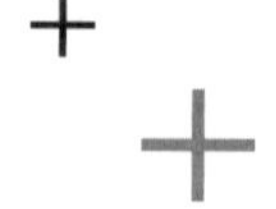  

20. A length of 100 meters is closest to which of the following lengths, in inches? (1 inch is approximately equal to 2.5 centimeters.)

(A) 40
(B) 250
(C) 400
(D) 2,500
(E) 4,000

Percent

Percent (%) is a ratio that compares a number to 100 by division.

For example, $\frac{40}{100}$ = 40%. The number 3 is 75% of 4 because $\frac{3}{4} = \frac{75}{100}$ = 75%.

21. Two friends went out to lunch and split the cost equally. The meal's cost was $20.40. Tax is an additional 5% on the meal's cost. The friends decide to leave 20% of the meal's cost (not including tax) for a tip. How much will each friend spend on the meal?

(A) $10.33
(B) $12.64
(C) $12.75
(D) $21.42
(E) $25.50

---

22. After changing the number 20 by a certain percent, the result is 50. Which of the following represents this percent change?

(A) A decrease of 40%
(B) An increase of 30%
(C) An increase of 60%
(D) An increase of 150%
(E) An increase of 250%

Estimation

Estimation problems can be presented in either a real-life or an abstract setting. When solving an estimation problem, round the numbers as close to the given number as possible. It may be to your advantage to look at the answer choices first before you begin to round numbers.

23. Of the following, which is closest to 110.2×39.998 ?
    (A) 8,000
    (B) 4,400
    (C) 4,000
    (D) 3,300
    (E) 3,000

---

24. Each morning from Monday through Friday, Mr. Ruiz travels 19.8 miles to work. After work, he travels 10.1 miles to a local gym. Then he travels home a distance of 9.9 miles. Of the following, which is closest to the total number of miles Mr. Ruiz travels Monday through Friday?
    (A) 100
    (B) 150
    (C) 200
    (D) 250
    (E) 300

Sequences and Patterns

For sequence problems, the pattern for generating the sequence will be stated. You may be asked to find a number or a figure in the patterns, or be given a number in the sequence and asked which term it is.

25. The first number in a sequence is 2, and the second number in the sequence is 5. Each number after the second is the product of the two preceding numbers. What is the sum of the first four numbers of the sequence?

    (A) 12
    (B) 50
    (C) 67
    (D) 500
    (E) 840

---

26. The first three figures in a geometric pattern are shown. The area of the first figure is 1. The area of each figure after the first is half the area of the preceding figure. What is the area of the 6th figure?

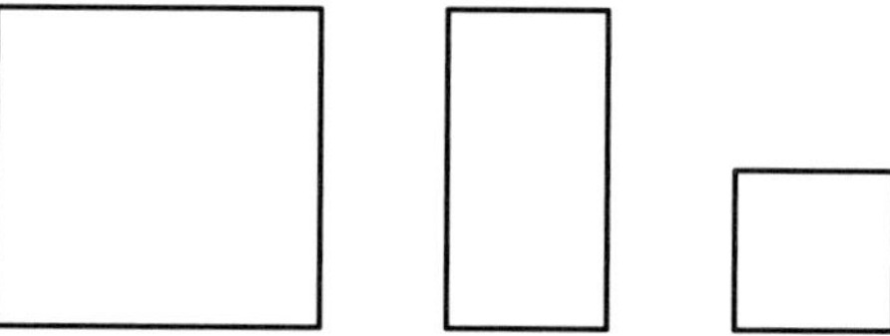

    (A) $\frac{1}{32}$
    (B) $\frac{1}{16}$
    (C) $\frac{1}{10}$
    (D) $\frac{1}{8}$
    (E) $\frac{1}{6}$

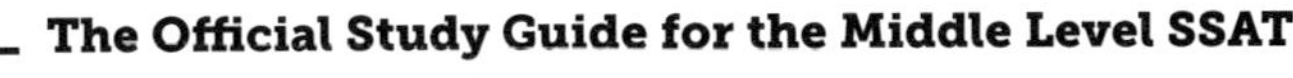

Answer Key
Section I: Number Concepts and Operations

1. **Answer (B) 1.654**

2. **Answer (D) 26.37**

$$\begin{array}{r} 1.1 \\ 20.3 \\ +\ 4.97 \\ \hline 26.37 \end{array}$$

3. **Answer (C) 3.15**
Multiply without decimals: $21 \times 15 = 315$
2.1 has 1 decimal place.
1.5 has 1 decimal place.
so, 2.1×1.5 has two decimal places:
$315 \rightarrow 3.15$

4. **Answer (D) $\frac{2}{3}$**

$\frac{4}{6} = \frac{2}{3}$

5. **Answer (E) $\frac{33}{20}$**
The least common multiple of 2, 4, and 5 is 20.
$\frac{3}{2} = \frac{30}{20}$; $\frac{2}{5} = \frac{8}{20}$; $\frac{1}{4} = \frac{5}{20}$
$\frac{30}{20} + \frac{8}{20} - \frac{5}{20} = \frac{33}{20}$

6. **Answer (C) $\frac{10}{9}$**

$\frac{5}{3} \div \frac{3}{2} = \frac{5}{3} \times \frac{2}{3} = \frac{10}{9}$

7. **Answer (E) 96**

$8 \times -4 = -32$; $-32 \times -3 = 96$

8. **Answer (B) 16**
$6 + (-1)^2 \times (8 + 2)$
$6 + 1 \times 10 = 6 + 10 = 16$

9. **Answer (B) 3.09**

$$\begin{array}{r} 5.10 \\ -\ 2.01 \\ \hline 3.09 \end{array}$$

10. **Answer (C) $\frac{7}{12}$**
The lowest common denominator is
$3 \times 4 = 12$
$\frac{1}{3} = \frac{4}{12}$; $\frac{1}{4} = \frac{3}{12}$
$\frac{4}{12} + \frac{3}{12} = \frac{7}{12}$

11. **Answer (C) 60**

There are $\frac{2}{3} \times 120 = 80$ paperback books.

Of those, $\frac{3}{4} \times 80 = 60$ are fiction.

12. **Answer (D) 28**
$21 + 8 - 5 + 4 = 29 - 5 + 4 = 24 + 4 = 28$

13. **Answer (B) 225**
Numbers that are divisible by 15 are divisible by 3 and by 5. Only 225, 415, and 560 are divisible by 5. Of these three numbers, only 225 is also divisible by 3. So 225 is divisible by 15.

14. **Answer (D) 360**
$18 = 2 \times 3 \times 3$
$24 = 2 \times 2 \times 2 \times 3$
$60 = 2 \times 2 \times 3 \times 5$
So, the LCM of 18, 24, and 60 is
$(2 \times 2 \times 2) \times (3 \times 3) \times 5 = 8 \times 9 \times 5 = 360.$

Answer Key

Section I: Number Concepts and Operations *(continued)*

15. Answer (A) Seven

There are seven prime numbers between 30 and 60. They are 31, 37, 41, 43, 47, 53, and 59.

16. Answer (C) $3k + 1$

Odd times odd gives an odd number, so $3k$ is odd. Odd plus odd gives an even number, so $3k + 1$ is even.

17. Answer (D) 40

$60 \times 33 = (2 \times 2 \times 3 \times 5) \times (3 \times 11)$

$= 2 \times 2 \times 3 \times 3 \times 5 \times 11$

Of the choices, $40 = 2 \times 2 \times 2 \times 5$, which has one more 2 in its prime factorization than 60×33, so 40 is not a factor of 60×33.

18. Answer (B) 270

$\frac{\text{students}}{\text{teachers}} = \frac{6}{1} = \frac{x}{45}$

$6(45) = 1(x)$

$270 = x$

19. Answer (B) 66

$\text{Average speed} = \frac{\text{total distance}}{\text{total time}}$

2 hours = 120 minutes

120 minutes + 80 minutes = 200 minutes

$200 \text{ minutes} = \frac{200}{60} \text{ hours} = \frac{10}{3} \text{ hours}$

$\frac{100 \text{ mi} + 120 \text{ mi}}{\frac{10}{3} \text{ hr}} = \frac{220 \text{ mi}}{\frac{10}{3} \text{ hr}}$

$= 220 \times \frac{3}{10}$

$= 66$ miles per hour

20. Answer (E) 4,000

1 meter = 100 centimeters

100 m = 10,000 cm

$\frac{10{,}000 \text{ cm}}{x \text{ in}} = \frac{2.5 \text{ cm}}{1 \text{ in}}$

$x = \frac{10{,}000}{2.5} = \frac{10{,}000}{25} = 4{,}000$

21. Answer (C) $12.75

Tip: 0.2 × $20.40 = $4.08

Tax: 0.05 × $20.40 = $1.02

Total: $20.40 + $5.10 = $25.50

Cost per friend: $25.50 ÷ 2 = $12.75

22. Answer (D) An increase of 150%

The number 20 <u>increases</u> 30 units to 50, which is represented by a percent increase of

$\frac{30}{20} = \frac{150}{100} = 150\%$

23. Answer (B) 4,400

110.2×39.998 is approximately $110 \times 40 = 4{,}400$.

24. Answer (C) 200

19.8 ≈ 20 miles; 10.1 miles ≈ 10 miles; 9.9 miles ≈ 10 miles; 20 + 10 + 10 = 40 and 40 × 5 = 200

25. Answer (C) 67

The first four numbers of the sequence are 2, 5, 10, 50. The sum is 2 + 5 + 10 + 50 = 67.

26. Answer (A) $\frac{1}{32}$

Following the pattern, the first 6 figures have areas $1, \frac{1}{2}, \frac{1}{4}, \frac{1}{8}, \frac{1}{16}, \frac{1}{32}$. So, the area of the 6th figure is $\frac{1}{32}$.

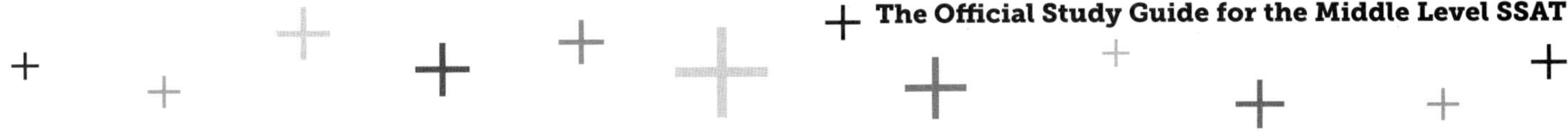

Section II: Geometry

For this section, you will find 10 sample questions and related overviews of mathematics concepts in Geometry. Geometric figures such as polygons, circles, or solids may appear in these questions. The answers to these 10 sample questions are located at the end of this section.

Length, Perimeter, and Area

Perimeter is the distance around a two-dimensional figure.
Area is the number of square units inside a two-dimensional figure.

For example:
In the square shown,
Perimeter = 4(5) = 20 units
Area = 5(5) = 25 square units

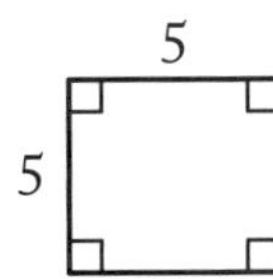

27. What is the perimeter of the triangle shown?
    - (A) 21.9 cm
    - (B) 19.4 cm
    - (C) 18.3 cm
    - (D) 15.8 cm
    - (E) 12.2 cm

6.1 cm
6.1 cm
9.7 cm

---

28. A diagram of a field is shown. What is the area of the field, in square feet?
    - (A) 37,000
    - (B) 30,000
    - (C) 15,000
    - (D) 700
    - (E) 500

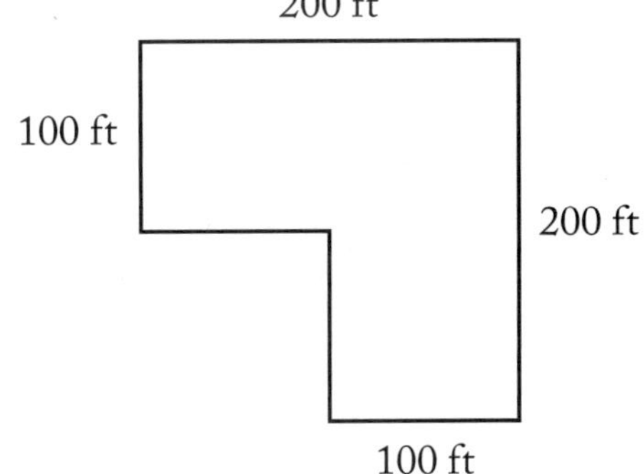

Radius, Diameter, and Circumference

The **radius** of a circle is a line segment with one endpoint at the center of the circle and the other endpoint on the circle. The **diameter** of a circle is a line segment that passes through the center of the circle and has endpoints on the circle. The **circumference** of a circle is the distance around the circle.

The radius r, diameter d, circumference C, and area A of a circle are all related by the formulas shown in the box.

$d = 2r$	$C = 2\pi r$
$A = \pi r^2$	$C = \pi d$
$\pi \approx 3.14$ units	

For example, in the circle shown with center C, line segments $\overline{AC}$, $\overline{BC}$, and $\overline{CD}$ are each a radius of the circle. Line segment $\overline{BD}$ is a diameter of the circle. If $BC = 10$, then $r = 10$, $d = 20$, $C = 20\pi$, and $A = 100\pi$.

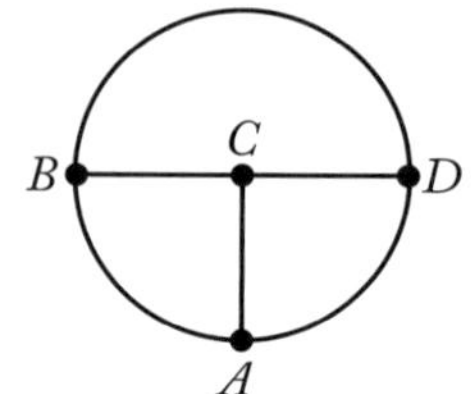

29. The figure shown represents the wheel on a model with center S. If the wheel has made 5 complete revolutions, and $RT = 11$cm, then, of the following, which is the best estimate for the distance traveled by the wheel?

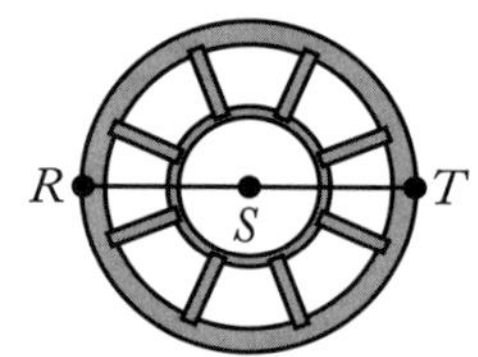

(A) 55 cm
(B) 110 cm
(C) 165 cm
(D) 220 cm
(E) 330 cm

---

30. For the circle shown with center Q, if $PQ = 4$ inches, which of the following is the area, in square inches, of the circle?

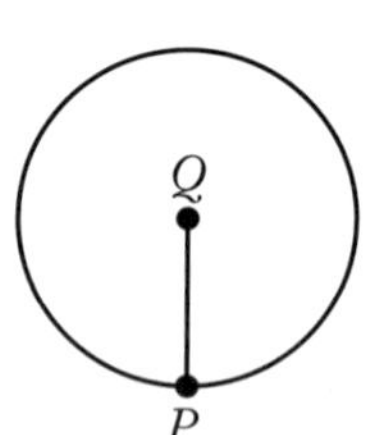

(A) 2π
(B) 4π
(C) 8π
(D) 10π
(E) 16π

Surface Area and Volume

Surface area is the total area of the surfaces of a three-dimensional figure.
Volume is the number of cubic units inside a three-dimensional figure.

For example:

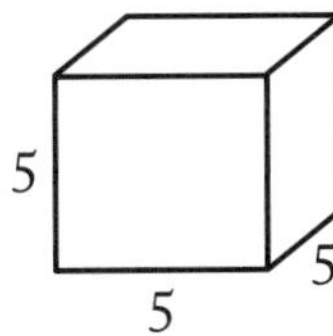

In the cube shown,

Surface area = 6(5)(5) = 150 square units

Volume = 5(5)(5) = 125 cubic units

31. For an art project, Tomas will paint the rectangular solid shown. He will paint the two shaded faces yellow and the remaining 4 faces blue. If $RU = 3$ meters, $UT = 2$ meters, and $ST = 1$ meter, what is the ratio of the areas, in square meters, of the faces painted yellow to the faces painted blue?

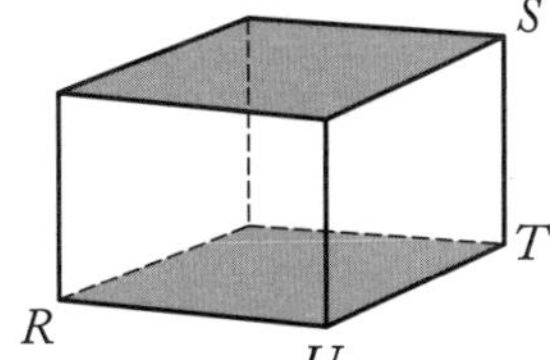

(A) 1 to 1
(B) 1 to 3
(C) 2 to 1
(D) 3 to 5
(E) 6 to 5

---

32. A case of 8 boxes is packed as shown. Each box is a cube with sides of 2 meters. What is the volume of the case, in cubic meters?

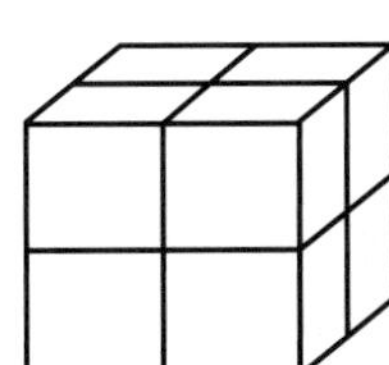

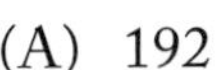

(A) 192
(B) 128
(C) 96
(D) 64
(E) 48

Angle Relationships

An **angle** consists of two segments, or two rays, that have the same endpoint. Angles are measured in degrees (°). The sum of the angles along a straight line is 180°. The sum of the internal angles of a triangle is also 180°. A square or rectangle has four 90° angles. The sum of the angles around the center of a circle is 360°.

33. In the figure, lines k and m intersect at a point with a line segment as shown. What is the value of y ?

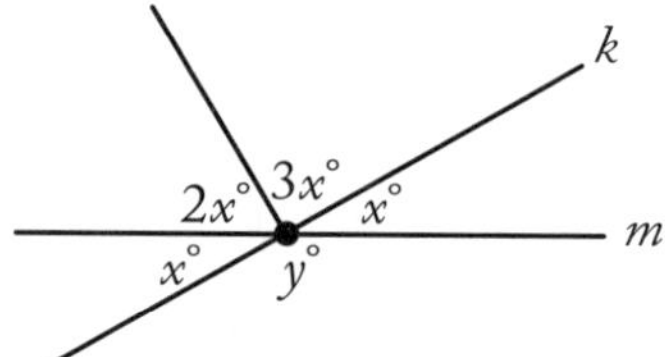

(A) 30
(B) 60
(C) 75
(D) 120
(E) 150

---

34. The figure shows an isosceles triangle with the base side extended. What is the value of $x + y$?

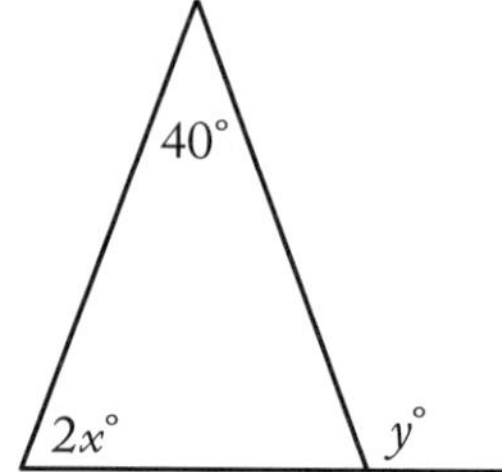

(A) 105
(B) 140
(C) 145
(D) 180
(E) 210

---

35. The figure shows two parallel lines intersected by a transversal line. What is the value of k ?

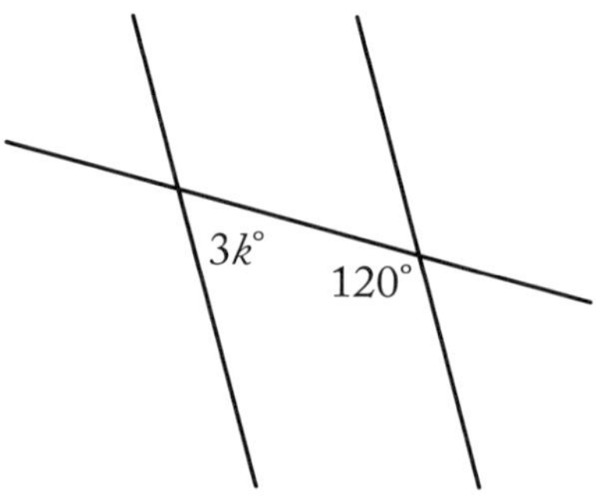

(A) 20
(B) 30
(C) 40
(D) 50
(E) 60

Visual/Spatial Reasoning

Problems that test Visual/Spatial Reasoning are all different. Examples of some types of problems that may be tested include visualizing different faces of a cube as the cube is turned, or rotating a figure about a point.

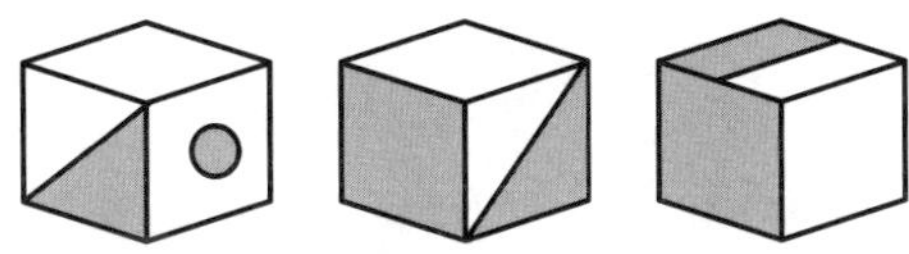

36. The figure above shows three views of a cube. Each face of the cube is different. Which of the following could be another view of the cube?

(A) 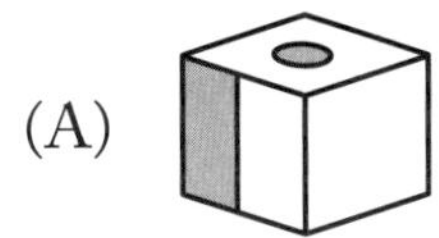

(B) 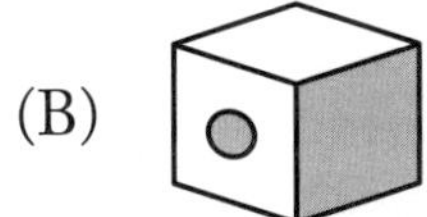

(C) 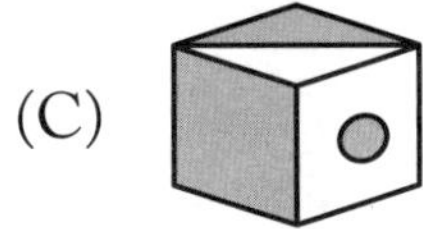

(D) 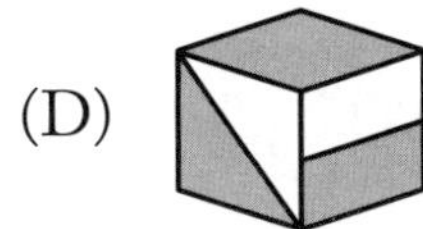

(E) 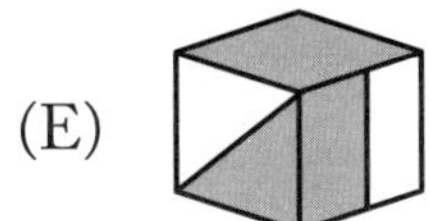

Answer Key
Section II: Geometry

27. Answer (A) 21.9 cm
6.1 cm + 6.1 cm + 9.7 cm = 21.9 cm

28. Answer (B) 30,000
The figure can be broken into 2 figures: one square with side lengths 100 feet by 100 feet, and one rectangle with side lengths 200 feet by 100 feet. $A = (100 \times 100) + (200 \times 100)$
$= 10{,}000 + 20{,}000 = 30{,}000$.

29. Answer (C) 165

$C = \pi d \approx 3 \times 11 = 33$ cm

So 5 revolutions is $5 \times 33 = 165$ cm.

30. Answer (E) 16π
$A = \pi r^2 \rightarrow A = \pi(4)^2 = 16\pi$

31. Answer (E) 6 to 5

Area of yellow is $6\text{m}^2 + 6\text{m}^2 = 12\text{m}^2$.

Area of blue is

$3\text{m}^2 + 2\text{m}^2 + 3\text{m}^2 + 2\text{m}^2 = 10\text{m}^2$.

So the ratio of the areas is 12 to 10 or 6 to 5.

32. Answer (D) 64
Each box has volume $2\text{m} \times 2\text{m} \times 2\text{m} = 8\text{ m}^3$. There are 8 boxes. So the volume is
$8 \times 8\text{ m}^3 = 64\text{ m}^3$.

33. Answer (E) 150
$3x + x + 2x = 180$
$6x = 180$
$x = 30$

$x + y = 180 \rightarrow 30 + y = 180 \rightarrow y = 150$

34. Answer (C) 145
Because the triangle is isosceles, $2x = 70$, so $x = 35$.

$y = 180 - 70 = 110$

so $x + y = 35 + 110 = 145$.

35. Answer (A) 20

The angles shown are supplementary angles, so

$120 + 3k = 180 \rightarrow 3k = 60 \rightarrow k = 20$.

36. Answer (A) 

Based on the given information, only choice A can be a view of the cube. The other four answer choices lead to contradictions in the three views that were given.

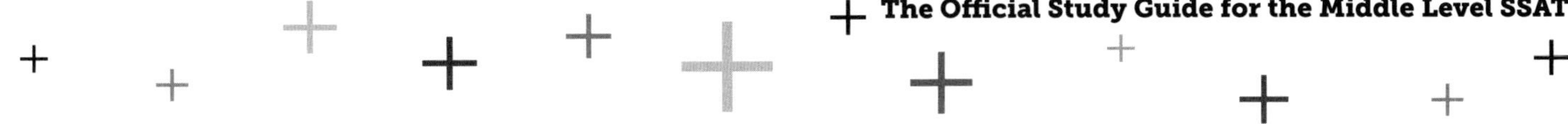

Section III: Algebra

For this section, you will find 6 sample questions and related overviews of mathematics concepts in Algebra. The answers to these 6 sample questions are located at the end of this section.

Simple Linear Equations and Inequalities

Algebra is a form of mathematics that uses variables, expressions, equations, and inequalities to represent situations and to solve problems. A **variable** is a letter, like x, which represents a number or quantity. The following are examples of expressions, equations, and inequalities.

Expressions : $2 + x$ and $3y^2$

Equations : $4b - 10 = 2$ and $2(a + 6) = 20$

Inequalities : $\frac{c}{3} \geq 6$ and $2r < 20$

$$10 + 2x = x + 1$$

37. What is the solution to the equation above?

(A) 10

(B) $\frac{11}{3}$

(C) 3

(D) $\frac{1}{3}$

(E) −9

$$2 + 4x > 30$$

38. For the inequality above, what is the least possible integer value of x ?

(A) 6
(B) 7
(C) 8
(D) 9
(E) 10

Algebra Word Problems

An algebra word problem can be presented in either a real-life or an abstract setting. Some word problems will require you to set up and solve an equation or inequality to arrive at the final answer. Other word problems will require you to translate words into an expression, equation, or inequality, which will be the final answer.

39. If 4 less than half a number n is 16, what is the value of n ?

(A) 12
(B) 20
(C) 24
(D) 32
(E) 40

---

40. Maria has x dollars and Alex has 5 dollars more than Maria. If Alex gives Maria 6 dollars, how many dollars will Alex have left?

(A) $x - 1$
(B) $x + 1$
(C) $5x + 1$
(D) $6x + 1$
(E) $6x - 1$

Simplification and Evaluation of Algebraic Expressions

Some algebra problems on the test may involve simplifying algebraic expressions by combining like terms, or by substituting values into expressions.

$$\begin{array}{r} 4a - 3b + c \\ -(8a + 3b + 2c) \\ \hline \end{array}$$

41. Which of the following is equivalent to the expression above?

(A) $-4a - c$
(B) $-4a + 3c$
(C) $4a - 6b - c$
(D) $-4a - 6b - c$
(E) $-4a - 6b + 3c$

---

42. If $x = 5$ and $y = -2$, what is the value of $2(x - y)^2$?

(A) 196
(B) 98
(C) 81
(D) 28
(E) 18

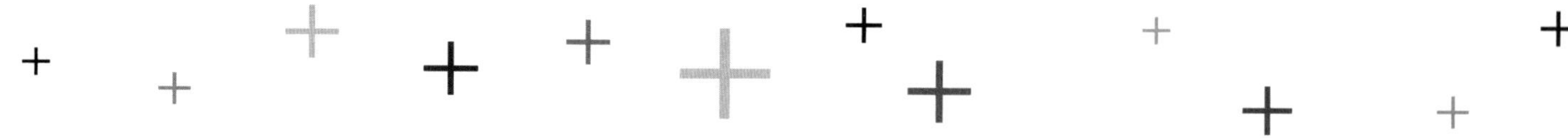

Answer Key
Section III: Algebra

37. Answer (E) -9

$10 + 2x = x + 1$
$10 + x = 1$
$x = -9$

38. Answer (C) 8

$2 + 4x > 30$
$4x > 28$
$x > 7$

So $x = 8$ is the least possible integer value of x.

39. Answer (E) 40

4 less than half n is 16 is the same as

$\frac{1}{2}n - 4 = 16$
$\frac{1}{2}n = 20$
$n = 40$

40. Answer (A) $x - 1$

$x + 5 - 6 \rightarrow x - 1$

41. Answer (D) $-4a - 6b - c$

$$\begin{array}{r} 4a - 3b + c \\ -\ (8a + 3b + 2c) \\ \hline \end{array}$$

$$\begin{array}{r} 4a - 3b + c \\ -\ 8a - 3b - 2c \\ \hline -4a - 6b - c \end{array}$$

42. Answer (B) 98

$2(x - y)^2 \rightarrow 2(5 - (-2))^2$
$= 2(7)^2 = 2(49) = 98$

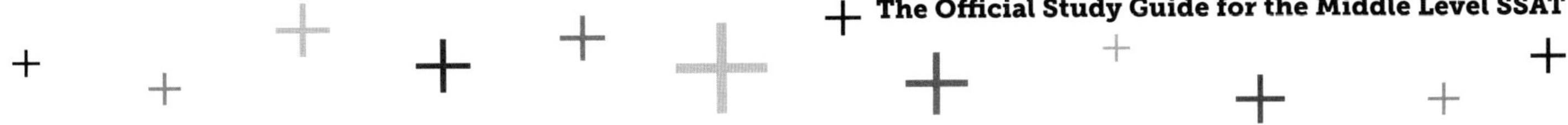

Section IV: Data Analysis

For this section, you will find 8 sample questions and related overviews of mathematics concepts in Data Analysis. The answers to these 8 sample questions are located at the end of this section.

Graphs and Tables

Graphs are used to present numerical information in visual form. A **bar graph** uses bars to make comparisons between parts of the data. A **line graph** uses line segments to show changes in the data over time. A **circle graph** uses a divided circle to compare parts of the data to the whole data set. A **dot plot** uses dots to display the number of each value in a data set. Examples of each are shown below.

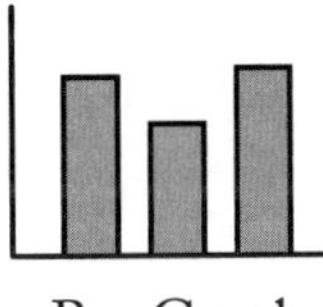
Bar Graph

Line Graph

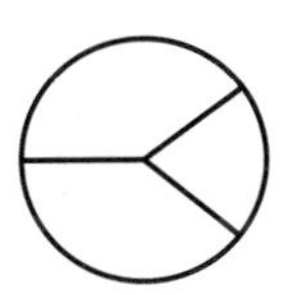
Circle Graph

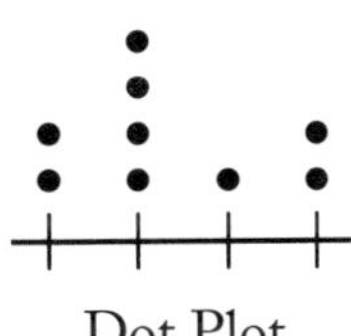
Dot Plot

43. The circle graph shows the percent of a day that Maurice spends on different activities on Wednesday. On Saturday, Maurice plans on spending twice as much time on chores and sports as he does on Wednesday. Which of the following is the best estimate of the number of hours he will spend on chores and sports on Saturday?

    (A) 4.3
    (B) 8.2
    (C) 12.5
    (D) 14.2
    (E) 15.8

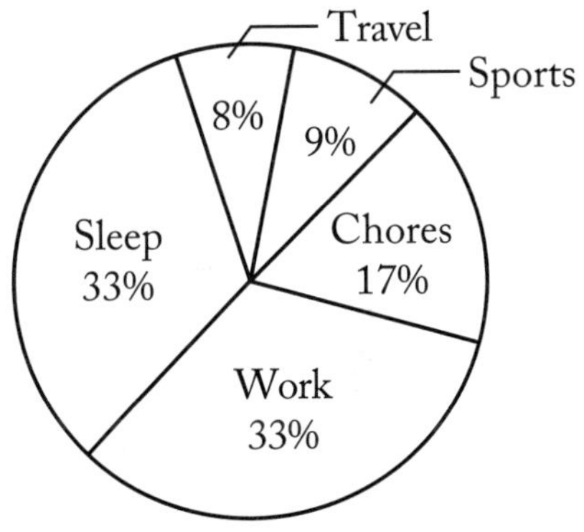

44. The bar graph shows the number of students in the Oldtown Middle School concert choir by grade. The music director predicts that next year the number of 8th graders in the concert choir will decrease by 10%. How many 8th graders will be in the concert choir next year?

    (A) 10
    (B) 18
    (C) 20
    (D) 25
    (E) 27

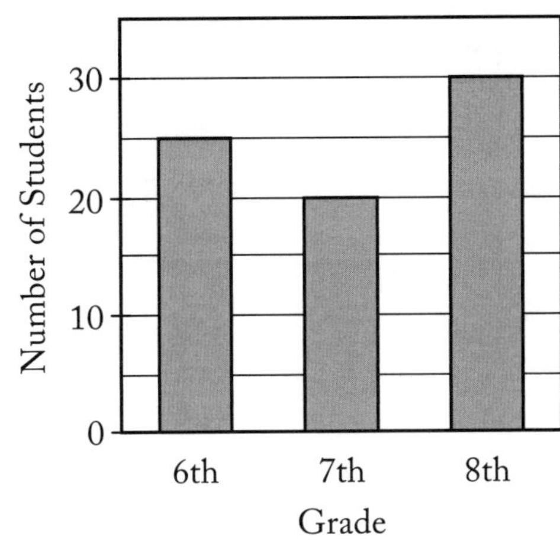

Mean, Median, Mode, Range

For a list of values:

- The **mean** is the sum of the values divided by the number of values;
- The **median** is the middle value, when the list is placed in either increasing or decreasing order;
- The **mode** is the value in the list that occurs the most; and
- The **range** results from subtracting the least value from the greatest value in the list.

$6, 15, 3, 15, 11, 0, 20$

45. What is the mean of the list above?

(A) 10
(B) 11
(C) 14
(D) 15
(E) 20

$44, m, 11, 78, 93, 29, 72$

46. If m is the median for the list of seven numbers above, what is the greatest possible value of m ?

(A) 71
(B) 72
(C) 78
(D) 82
(E) 93

$96°, 87°, 100°, 91°, 87°, 98°, 99°$

47. The daily high temperatures, in degrees Fahrenheit, for seven days in Cactus Town are shown above. What is the mode of the high temperatures, in degrees Fahrenheit?

(A) 96°
(B) 94°
(C) 91°
(D) 87°
(E) 13°

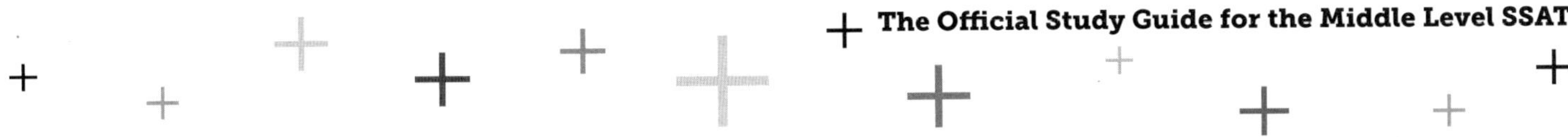

48. There are five integers in a list. The maximum value is 18 and the range is 11. The mode is half as large as the maximum value. If the list has one mode, what is the least possible sum of the numbers in the list?

(A) 51
(B) 53
(C) 56
(D) 58
(E) 60

Probability

Probability is the measure of the likelihood that an event will occur. The probability of an event is a number between 0 and 1. The closer a probability is to 0, the less likely an event will occur. The closer a probability is to 1, the more likely an event will occur. The probability of an event, *P*, is calculated by the ratio:

$$P = \frac{\text{number of specific outcomes}}{\text{total number of outcomes}}$$

49. In Jad's closet, he has 5 striped shirts, 2 white shirts, 6 blue shirts, and 7 yellow shirts. If he selects a shirt at random from the closet, what is the probability of selecting a striped shirt or a yellow shirt?

(A) $\frac{1}{4}$

(B) $\frac{7}{20}$

(C) $\frac{2}{5}$

(D) $\frac{3}{5}$

(E) $\frac{3}{4}$

Counting

Counting problems on the test may involve determining the number of paths to get from one point to another or determining the number of combinations that are possible in certain situations.

Red	Orange	Yellow	Green
Apple Grape Raspberry Strawberry	Cantaloupe Peach	Banana Mango	Apple Grape Kiwi Melon

50. A store makes centerpieces using different fruits. For each centerpiece, customers select one fruit from each of the columns in the table shown. How many different centerpieces are possible?

    (A) 6
    (B) 12
    (C) 32
    (D) 48
    (E) 64

Answer Key
Section IV: Data Analysis

43. Answer (C) 12.5

Twice as much time on chores and sports is $2 \times (9\% + 17\%)$ or 52%, so $(0.52)(24) = 12.48 \approx 12.5$.

44. Answer (E) 27

$30 \times 0.1 = 3$

$30 - 3 = 27$

45. Answer (A) 10

$$\frac{6 + 15 + 3 + 15 + 11 + 0 + 20}{7}$$

$$= \frac{70}{7} = 10$$

46. Answer (B) 72

The median m is the middle number of the ordered list. The six numbers in increasing order are 11, 29, 44, 72, 78, and 93, so $44 \le m \le 72$, and so the greatest value of m is 72.

47. Answer (D) 87°

The mode is the most common value in the list, or 87°.

48. Answer (A) 51

The maximum is 18, so the mode is 9, and the minimum is $18 - 11 = 7$.

So the list with the least possible sum is 7, 8, 9, 9, 18. So the sum is $7 + 8 + 9 + 9 + 18 = 51$.

49. Answer (D) $\frac{3}{5}$

$$P = \frac{\text{number of striped and yellow shirts}}{\text{total number of shirts}}$$

$$= \frac{5 + 7}{5 + 2 + 6 + 7} = \frac{12}{20} = \frac{3}{5}$$

50. Answer (E) 64

$4 \times 2 \times 2 \times 4 = 8 \times 8 = 64$

3. The Reading Comprehension Section

The reading comprehension section presents several reading passages, each followed by a series of questions designed to measure how well you understand what you have read. The questions ask not only about the ideas presented in the passage but also about the ways in which the author expresses those ideas. Passages are of two kinds: literary and expository. Literary passages are excerpts from works of fiction or poetry. They generally tell part of a story or develop a certain theme. Expository passages explore topics related to the humanities (art, music, etc.), history, science (biology, astronomy, technology, etc.), or social science (psychology, anthropology, etc.).

Just the Facts

Reading Comprehension

Number of questions:
40

What it measures:
Your ability to understand and interpret what you read

Scored section:
Yes

Time allotted:
40 minutes

What Are the Directions for the Reading Comprehension Section on the Test?

Read each passage carefully and then answer the questions about it. For each question, decide on the basis of the passage which one of the choices best answers the question.

What Types of Questions Are Presented in the Reading Comprehension Section?

There are five basic question types in the reading comprehension section. Examples of each question type are provided below:

1. Basic information

Understanding what is directly stated in the passage

Examples:

- According to the passage, the elephant's diet consists mainly of...
- In the second stanza, the poet indicates that she is...
- According to the passage, what accounts for the enduring popularity of Bach's music?
- What is the main idea of the passage?
- In the final paragraph, the author argues for...

2. Inference

Understanding what is implied but not directly stated in the passage

Examples:

- It can be inferred from the passage that the "old cabin" (line 8) was...
- The author's description of his childhood suggests that he...
- The author assumes that her readers are...
- The "grave concerns" mentioned in line 6 were most likely...
- The description of the "office" (line 10) implies that it was...

3. Language

Interpreting the author's use of specific words and phrases

Examples:

- As used in line 16, the word "fair" most nearly means...
- In line 7, the expression "safety net" refers to...
- In line 10, the pronoun "they" refers to...
- To describe the effects of the storm, the author makes use of which literary device?
- In the third stanza, the poet develops a metaphor drawn from the realm of...
- Throughout the poem, the "candle" serves as a symbol of...
- The rhyme scheme of the poem's last stanza is...

4. Purpose

Understanding the author's writing strategy: how the writing is structured and why it is structured that way

Examples:

- The main purpose of the final paragraph is to...
- The author mentions "fairy tales" (line 1) in order to...
- The narrator repeats the word "paper" (lines 6–7) in order to...
- Why is the detective's sentence left unfinished in line 17?
- The list in the third paragraph serves to...
- The examples cited in the second paragraph are intended to...
- How does the third paragraph relate to the second paragraph?

5. Tone

Recognizing the tone, mood, or style of the passage or the attitude of the author, speaker, or character

Examples:

- In the second paragraph, the author adopts a tone of...
- In the second stanza, the poet sounds a note of...
- In the first paragraph, the narrator creates an atmosphere of...
- The style of the passage is best described as...
- As indicated in the quotation (lines 9–10), Lawry's attitude toward modern art is one of...

How Are the Reading Comprehension Questions Presented?

The SSAT presents each passage (or poem) with a corresponding group of three to eight questions. The directions instruct you to read each passage and answer the questions about it.

> Little Jim was, for the time, Engine Number 36 and he was making the run between Syracuse and Rochester. He was fourteen minutes behind time, and the throttle was wide open. As a result, when he swung around the curve at the flower bed, a wheel of his cart destroyed a tulip. Number 36 slowed down at once and looked guiltily at his father, who was mowing the lawn. The doctor had his back to the accident, and he continued to pace slowly to and fro, pushing the mower.
>
> Jim dropped the handle of the cart. He looked at his father and at the broken flower. Finally, he went to the tulip and tried to stand it up, but it would only hang limply from his hand. Jim could not repair it. He looked again toward his father.

1. It can be inferred from the passage that the main cause of Jim's accident was

   (A) excessive speed
   (B) mechanical failure
   (C) lack of visibility
   (D) poor road conditions
   (E) miscommunication

   The correct answer is (A). The words "the throttle was wide open" (line 2) imply that Jim was traveling at top speed, and the words "As a result" (line 2) indicate that this was the reason that the wheel of his cart accidentally "destroyed a tulip" (line 3).

2. It can be inferred from the passage that Jim's father was a

   (A) farmer
   (B) doctor
   (C) gardener
   (D) train engineer
   (E) business executive

   The correct answer is (B). In line 4 the narrator indicates that Jim's father "was mowing the lawn" and in the next sentence (lines 4–5) refers to the person "pushing the mower" as "The doctor," so it may reasonably be inferred that Jim's father was a doctor.

3. After the accident, Jim was apparently most concerned about

   (A) getting to his destination
   (B) the damage to his cart
   (C) his father's reaction
   (D) preventing future collisions
   (E) the injuries he had sustained

   The correct answer is (C). The narrator indicates that immediately after the accident Jim "looked guiltily at his father" (lines 3–4) and then "looked at his father and at the broken flower" (line 6) and then "looked again toward his father" (line 8). The fact that Jim looked repeatedly at his father suggests that he was worried about what his father's reaction would be.

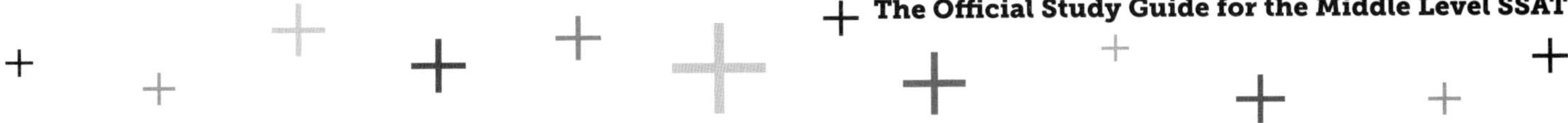

How Do You Answer the Reading Comprehension Questions?

As you read, determine the main idea. Identify the important details that move the narrative along or create a mood or tone. In expository passage, identify the details that support the writer's argument or illustrate the ideas being presented. The first sentence of each paragraph will give you a general sense of the topic. Identify the topic of each paragraph and underline or make note of key facts. Try to figure out the writer's intention, or purpose of the passage. Notice the writer's attitude, tone, and general style.

These habits can help you understand what you read, whether you are taking the SSAT, preparing for a history test, or getting ready to write an essay for your English class.

Reading Comprehension Test-Taking Strategies

1. Take time to read and understand the first sentence of each paragraph. This will provide you with a general sense of the topic.
2. Scan the answer choices, since they are generally short and provide excellent clues. If an answer choice refers you to a specific line in the passage, underline or make note of that line for reference.
3. Read each passage carefully. Follow the author's reasoning. Notice attitude, tone, and general style.
4. Pay attention to words such as always, never, every, and none. They may play an important role in the answer.
5. Identify the topic of each paragraph, key facts, and the author's purpose for writing. Underline or make note of the key facts for quick reference.
6. Read all answer choices carefully before you choose. When you find an answer choice that fails to satisfy the requirements of the question and statement, cross it out.

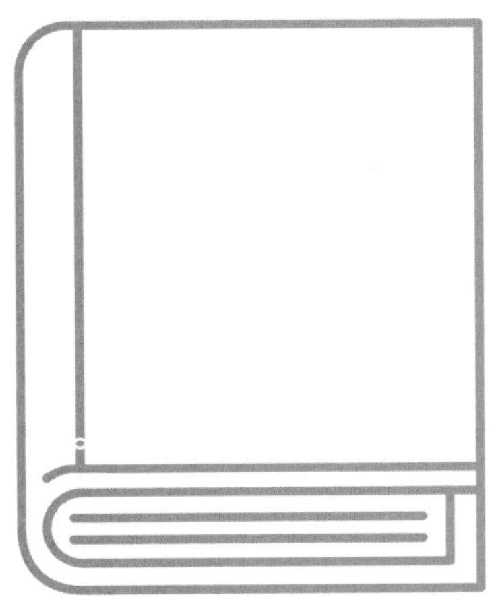

Sample Questions: Reading Comprehension

Directions: Read each passage carefully and then answer the questions about it. For each question, decide on the basis of the passage which one of the choices best answers the question.

It is often said that what separates man from beast is the ability to think logically. This is not true. A deer passing through the forest scents the ground and detects a certain odor. A sequence of ideas is generated in the mind of the deer. Nothing in the deer's experience has ever produced that odor except a wolf, and so the deer infers that wolves have passed that way. But it is a part of the deer's scientific knowledge, based on previous experience, that wolves are dangerous beasts. So, combining direct observation in the present with the application of a general principle based on past experience, the deer reaches the very logical conclusion that it would be wise to turn around and run in another direction. All this implies an understanding and use of scientific principles. And, strange as it may seem to speak of a deer possessing scientific knowledge, yet there is really no absurdity in the statement. The deer does possess scientific knowledge that differs in degree only, not in kind, from the knowledge of a physicist. Nor is the animal less scientific in the application of that knowledge than is the man. The animal that could not make accurate scientific observations of its surroundings and deduce accurate scientific conclusions from them would soon pay the penalty for its lack of logic.

1. The author's primary purpose in the passage is to
   (A) expose common errors of logic
   (B) compare two different methods
   (C) propose a new observational technique
   (D) challenge a widely held belief
   (E) differentiate two species of animal

2. The "direct observation" (line 6) made by the deer involved
   (A) seeing
   (B) hearing
   (C) smelling
   (D) tasting
   (E) touching

3. As it is used in line 9, the word "as" most nearly means
   (A) though
   (B) when
   (C) like
   (D) that
   (E) since

4. The "penalty" (line 14) that the deer would have to pay for a lack of logic would most likely be
   (A) getting lost in the forest
   (B) being attacked by wolves
   (C) failing to attract a mate
   (D) going without food
   (E) losing its habitat

Seven daughters had Lord Archibald,
All children of one mother.
I could not say in one short day
What love they bore each other.
A garland of seven lilies wrought—
Seven sisters that together dwell!
But he—bold knight as ever fought—
Their father—took of them no thought,
He loved the wars so well.

5. In lines 3–4, the speaker suggest that the sisters' love was
   (A) insincere
   (B) well hidden
   (C) indescribably strong
   (D) tragically short-lived
   (E) potentially destructive

6. As it is used in line 4, the word "bore" most nearly means
   (A) make weary
   (B) drill into
   (C) gave birth
   (D) felt toward
   (E) put up with

7. Line 5 provides an example of which literary device?
   (A) simile
   (B) metaphor
   (C) alliteration
   (D) onomatopoeia
   (E) hyperbole

8. The passage suggests that, as a father, Lord Archibald was
   (A) stern
   (B) proud
   (C) protective
   (D) considerate
   (E) neglectful

Answer Key: Reading Comprehension

1. **(D)** In the first sentence the author refers to a widely held ("often said") belief that animals do not think logically. In the second sentence the author challenges this belief, declaring it to be false. In the rest of the passage the author presents an extended argument showing why the belief is false.
2. **(C)** The author presents a scenario in which a deer "scents the ground and detects" the odor of a wolf (lines 2–3). This is the only direct observation that the deer makes, and it involves only the sense of smell.
3. **(A)** Of the five answer choices, "though" is the only word that makes sense when substituted for "as" in the passage: "And, strange though it may seem to speak of a deer possessing scientific knowledge, yet there is really no absurdity in the statement."
4. **(B)** The author is making the general point that animals would not be able to survive if they did not use logic. In the case of the deer, this means that if the deer did not logically conclude that the smell of the wolf implied danger, the deer would not take action to avoid the danger and would probably fall prey to the wolves, thus paying a penalty for its lack of logic.
5. **(C)** The words "I could not say in one short day" indicate that the sisters' love was so tremendous that the speaker would be unable to adequately describe it even if he had all day to do so.
6. **(D)** Of the five answer choices, "felt toward" is the only expression that makes sense when substituted for "bore" in the passage: "I could not say in one short day what love they felt toward each other."
7. **(B)** A metaphor is an expression that likens one thing to another by saying or implying that the one thing is the other. In line 5, the poet likens Lord Archibald's seven daughters to a flowery wreath by calling them "A garland of seven lilies wrought."
8. **(E)** The words "he…their father…took of them no thought" (lines 7–8) indicate that Lord Archibald did not think about and thus neglected his daughters.

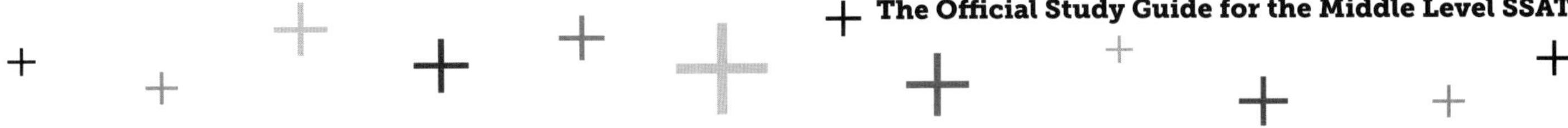

4. The Verbal Section

The verbal section of the Middle Level SSAT presents two types of questions: **synonyms** and **analogies**. The synonym questions primarily test the strength of your vocabulary. The analogy questions test not only your knowledge of individual words but also your ability to recognize logical relationships between pairs of words.

Just the Facts

The Verbal Section

Number of questions:
60 (30 synonyms and 30 analogies)

What it measures:
Your ability to understand the meanings of words and to recognize relationships between words with different meanings

Scored section:
Yes

Time allotted:
30 minutes

Synonyms

Synonyms are words that have the same or nearly the same meaning as another word. For example, *fortunate* is a synonym for *lucky; hoist* is a synonym for *raise*; and *melody* is a synonym for *tune*. Synonym questions on the SSAT ask you to choose a word that has a meaning similar to that of a given word.

What Are the Directions for the Synonym Section on the Test?

Each of the following questions consists of one word followed by five words or phrases. You are to select the one word or phrase whose meaning is closest to that of the word in capital letters.

How Are the Synonym Questions Presented?

Synonym questions present a single word in capital letters followed by five answer choices in lowercase letters.

EXAMPLE:	1. PREMONITION: (A) opening (B) firmness (C) discovery (D) conspiracy (E) forewarning **The correct answer is (E), forewarning.**

How Do You Answer Synonym Questions?

There is only one correct response, so make sure you consider all of the choices carefully. Don't just pick the first word that seems approximately right. If you're having difficulty deciding between two word choices, try making up a short sentence using the capitalized word and then ask yourself which choice would be the best substitute for the capitalized word in that sentence.

How Can You Build Your Vocabulary?

The best way to prepare is to read as much as you can to build your vocabulary. If you encounter an unfamiliar word in your reading, make sure you look it up in a dictionary (either online or in print). Keep track of the word and its meaning on an index card, notepad, or in notes on your smartphone. Keeping track of new words or words that are unfamiliar to you will help you build a tremendous vocabulary.

Another way to prepare is to learn the meaning of the word parts that make up many English words. These word parts consist of **prefixes, suffixes,** and **roots**. If you encounter an unfamiliar word, you could take apart the word and think about the parts.

The greater your vocabulary, the greater your chance of getting the correct answer.

Prefixes

Prefix	Meaning	Example
a-, an-	not, without	anonymous, amoral
ab-	from	abnormal
ad-	to, toward	advance, adhere
ante-	before	antebellum
anti-	against, opposite	antibacterial, antithesis
auto-	self	autobiography, automobile
bi-	two	bicycle, binary
circu(m)-	around	circumference, circulate
de-	away from	derail, defend
dia-	through, across	diagonal
dis-	away from, not	disappear, disloyal
en-	put in, into	encircle, enlist
ex-	out of	exit, exhale
extra-	outside of, beyond	extraordinary
hyper-	over, more	hyperactive, hyperbole
in-, ill-, im-	not	inanimate, illicit, impossible
in-, ill-, im-	in, into	insert, illuminate, impose
inter-	between	interact
intra-	within	intrastate
macro-	large	macroeconomics
mal-	bad, wrong	malady, malpractice
micro-	small	microscope
mono-	one	monopoly, monotonous
multi-	many	multicolor, multiply
non-	without, not	nonsense
peri-	around	perimeter, periscope
post-	after	postscript
pre-, pro-	before, forward	preview, prologue
semi- (also hemi-)	half	semicircle, hemisphere
sub-	under	subway, submarine
syn-, sym-	same	synonym, sympathy
trans-	across	transport, transit
tri-	three	triangle, triple
un-	not	unkind
uni-	one, together	unity, unique

Suffixes

Suffix	Meaning	Example
-able (-ible)	able to be	habitable, edible
-acy	state or quality	privacy, literacy
-al	relating to, belonging to	theatrical
-an (-ian)	relating to, belonging to	equestrian
-ance, -ence	state or quality	brilliance, patience
-ant	a person	informant, participant
-arian	a person	librarian, vegetarian
-cide	act of killing	genocide
-cracy	rule, government, power	aristocracy
-dom	state or quality	wisdom, freedom
-dox	belief	orthodox
-en	make a certain way	sharpen, sadden
-er, -or	person doing something	lover, actor
-ese	relating to a place	Japanese
-esque	in the style of/like	arabesque, grotesque
-fy	make a certain way	beautify, terrify, magnify
-ful	full of	graceful
-gam/-gamy	marriage, union	monogamous
-gon/-gonic	angle	decagon, trigonometry
-hood	state, condition, or quality	parenthood
-ile	relating to, capable of	juvenile, mobile
-ious, -ous	characterized by	contagious, studious
-ish	having the quality of	childish
-ism	doctrine, belief	socialism
-ist	person doing or advocating	dramatist, communist
-ity, -ty	quality of	ferocity
-ive	having a tendency	talkative, divisive
-ize	make a certain way	prioritize, advertize
-log(ue)	word, speech	analogy, dialogue
-ment	condition or action	ailment, assessment
-ness	state or quality	happiness, kindness
-phile	one who loves	bibliophile
-phobia	abnormal fear of	acrophobia
-ship	quality or position of	craftsmanship, dictatorship
-sion, -tion	action or condition	destruction, tension

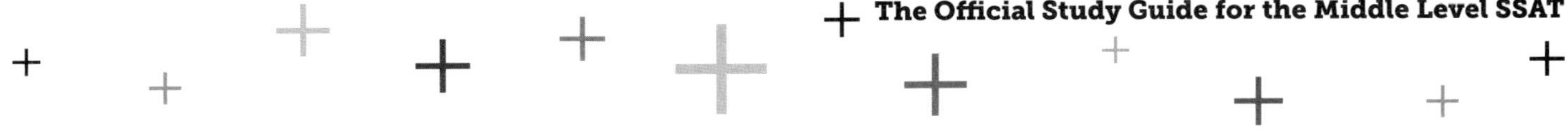

Word Roots G = Greek L = Latin

Root	Meaning	Example
ann, enn (L)	year	anniversary, perennial
anthrop (G)	man	anthropomorphism
ast(er) (G)	star	astrology, asterisk
audi (L)	hear	audible, audience
auto (G)	self	autobiography
bene (L)	good	beneficial
bio (G)	life	biography, biology
chron (G)	time	chronology, chronicle
civ (L)	citizen	civilization, civilian
cred (L)	believe	credential, incredible
dem(o) (G)	people	democracy, epidemic
dict (L)	say	predict, dictator
duc (L)	lead, make	conduct, reduce
gen (G & L)	give birth	genesis, generation
geo (G)	earth	geometry
graph (G)	write	autograph, graphic
jur, jus (L)	law	juror, justice, injure
log, logue (G)	thought, word	logical, prologue
luc (L)	light	lucid, translucent
man(u) (L)	hand	manual, manufacture
mand (L)	order	command, mandate
min (L)	small	minimal, diminish
mis, mit (L)	send	missile, transmit
nov (L)	new	novel, innovate
omni (L)	all	omnivore, omniscient
pan (G)	all	panorama, panacea
pater, patr (G & L)	father	paternal, patriarchy
path (G)	feel	sympathy
phil (G)	love	philosophy, philanthropist
phon (G)	sound	phonetic, telephone
photo (G)	light	photosynthesis
poli (G)	city	political, metropolis
port (L)	carry	deport, report
scrib, script (L)	write	prescribe, inscription
sens, sent (L)	feel	sentiment, resent
sol (L)	sun	solar, parasol

Word Roots G = Greek L = Latin

Root	Meaning	Example
tele (G)	far off	television
terr (L)	earth	terrestrial, inter
tract (L)	drag, draw	detract, traction
vac (L)	empty	evacuation, vacant
vid, vis (L)	see	invisible, video
vit (L)	life	vitality, vitamin
zo (G)	life	zoology

Sample Questions: Synonyms

Directions: Each of the following questions consists of a word followed by five words or phrases. You are to select the one word or phrase whose meaning is closest to the word in capital letters.

1. POISE:
   (A) creativity
   (B) respect
   (C) sympathy
   (D) composure
   (E) secrecy

2. BRANDISH:
   (A) shout
   (B) wave
   (C) emerge
   (D) struggle
   (E) label

3. RADIANT:
   (A) youthful
   (B) successful
   (C) impressive
   (D) glowing
   (E) peaceful

4. VERSATILE:
   (A) vigilant
   (B) adaptable
   (C) friendly
   (D) poetic
   (E) wise

5. WAFT:
   (A) jut
   (B) dive
   (C) drift
   (D) paddle
   (E) explore

6. SWAGGER:
   (A) fall
   (B) strut
   (C) guzzle
   (D) mumble
   (E) bet

7. SCURRY:
   (A) rush
   (B) bluff
   (C) topple
   (D) scribble
   (E) disperse

8. EGREGIOUS:
   (A) sociable
   (B) pitiful
   (C) flagrant
   (D) contemplative
   (E) communicable

Answer Key: Synonyms

1. (D) composure

2. (B) wave

3. (D) glowing

4. (B) adaptable

5. (C) drift

6. (B) strut

7. (A) rush

8. (C) flagrant

Verbal Analogies

An **analogy**, very generally, is a statement saying that one thing is similar to another thing. A simple example would be "Life is like a roller-coaster ride." The analogy questions in the verbal section of the SSAT ask you to compose a special kind of analogy, called a verbal analogy because it has to do with the meanings of words. A verbal analogy is a statement saying that the relationship between one pair of words is similar to the relationship between another pair of words. For example, the verbal analogy "Swim is to water as fly is to air" says that the verb "swim" is related to the noun "water" in the same way that the verb "fly" is related to the noun "air." To swim is to move through water, just as to fly is to move through the air.

The analogy portion of the SSAT asks you to identify the answer that best matches the relationship between two words.

What Are the Directions for the Verbal Analogies Section on the Test?

The following questions ask you to find relationships between words. For each question, select the answer choice that best completes the meaning of the sentence.

What Are the Things to Remember When Doing Analogies?

Parts of Speech

The parts of speech in the first word pair must match the parts of speech in the second word pair. If, for example, the words in the first pair are noun/adjective, then the words in the second pair must also be noun/adjective.

Word Order

If the first pair of words expresses a particular relationship, the second pair must express the same relationship in the same order.

Exactness

Sometimes two or more of the given choices would make sense. When this happens, choose the answer that most exactly fits the relationship between the words in the stem of the question.

How Are Verbal Analogies Presented?

The SSAT analogy questions present a **stem** followed by five **options**. The stem is an incomplete sentence, and each option offers a different way of finishing the sentence. The stem has the form **A is to B as**, (with **A** and **B** representing the first word pair), and the options have the form **C is to D** (with **C** and **D** representing the second word pair). When the stem and an option are put together, the result is a sentence of the form **A is to B as C is to D.**

EXAMPLE:	1. Loud is to hear as (A) sad is to cry (B) bright is to see (C) rude is to speak (D) angry is to feel (E) bland is to taste **The correct answer is (B).**

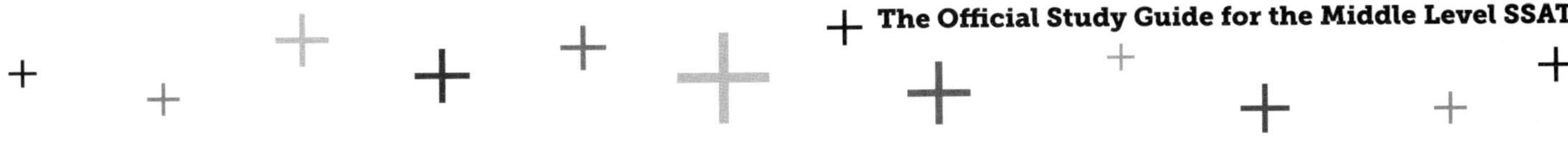

What Are Verbal Analogy Relationships?

Below are examples of some of the most common types of analogical relationships that you will find on the SSAT. This list is not complete; there are other types of verbal relationships not represented here.

1. **Antonyms**: X is the opposite of Y.
   EXAMPLE: Success is to failure as joy is to sadness.
2. **Degree:** To be X is to be extremely Y.
   EXAMPLE: Furious is to angry as enormous is to large.
3. **Type:** An X is a kind of Y.
   EXAMPLE: Sonnet is to poem as elm is to tree.
4. **Specific Type:** An X is a [gender] Y.
   EXAMPLE: Father is to parent as brother is to sibling.
5. **Specific Manner:** To X is to Y quickly.
   EXAMPLE: Glance is to look as jot is to write.
6. **Part:** An X is part of a Y.
   EXAMPLE: Chapter is to book as singer is to chorus.
7. **Specific Part:** An X is the outer part of a Y.
   EXAMPLE: Shell is to egg as rind is to orange.
8. **Specific Part:** An X is a unit of Y.
   EXAMPLE: Blade is to grass as grain is to sand.
9. **Associated Characteristic:** An X is Y.
   EXAMPLE: Liar is to dishonest as genius is to intelligent.
10. **Associated Characteristic:** Someone who Xes is Y.
    EXAMPLE: Attack is to aggressive as donate is to generous.
11. **Associated Characteristic:**
    Something X pertains to a Y.
    EXAMPLE: Solar is to sun as nautical is to ship.
12. **Associated Action:** An X Ys.
    EXAMPLE: Fugitive is to flee as arbiter is to decide.
13. **Associated Action:**
    Something that is X is easily Yed.
    EXAMPLE: Obvious is to see as weak is to overpower.
14. **Negative Association:**
    Someone who is X is NOT Ying.
    EXAMPLE: Awake is to sleep as silent is to talk.
15. **Negative Association:** Someone who is X lacks Y.
    EXAMPLE: Foolish is to wisdom as dauntless is to fear.
16. **Negative Association:**
    Something that is X cannot Y.
    EXAMPLE: Numb is to feel as immobile is to move.
17. **Associated Tool:** An X typically uses a Y.
    EXAMPLE: Farmer is to plow as navigator is to compass.
18. **Associated Material:** An X typically works with Y.
    EXAMPLE: Carpenter is to wood as tailor is to fabric.
19. **Associated Location:** An X is kept in a Y.
    EXAMPLE: Book is to library as artwork is to museum.
20. **Associated Location:** One Xes in a Y.
    EXAMPLE: Prosecute is to courtroom as compete is to arena.
21. **Purpose:** An X is used to Y.
    EXAMPLE: Pen is to write as shovel is to dig.
22. **Specific Purpose:** An X is used to measure Y.
    EXAMPLE: Yardstick is to length as scale is to weight.
23. **Purpose:** An X provides Y.
    EXAMPLE: Shield is to protection as blanket is to warmth.
24. **Specific Purpose:** An X protects a Y.
    EXAMPLE: Helmet is to head as glove is to hand.
25. **Product:** An X produces Y.
    EXAMPLE: Cow is to milk as bee is to honey.
26. **Result:** Something that Xes increases in Y.
    EXAMPLE: Expand is to size as accelerate is to speed.
27. **Result:** One becomes an X by Ying.
    EXAMPLE: Student is to enroll as soldier is to enlist.
28. **Result:** What has Xed is Y.
    EXAMPLE: Perish is to dead as depart is to absent.
29. **Result:** Something X elicits Y.
    EXAMPLE: Humorous is to laughter as pathetic is to pity.
30. **Expression:** An X expresses Y.
    EXAMPLE: Smile is to pleasure as sneer is to contempt.

How Do You Solve Verbal Analogy Questions?

A useful strategy for solving analogies is to use a **bridge sentence**. A bridge sentence is a sentence that defines the relationship between two words using the letters **X** and **Y** in place of the words themselves. For instance, the bridge sentence **An X is not Y** defines the relationship between the words **coward** and **brave**.

Be careful of the order of the words when you're determining the corresponding relationships.

When those words are substituted for **X** and **Y**, the result is a true sentence: "A coward is not brave." Of course, there are other word pairs that fit the same bridge sentence—for example, **fool** and **wise**. What this tells you is that the relationship between **coward** and **brave** is the same as the relationship between **fool** and **wise**. The two word pairs are analogous.

When answering an analogy question, the first thing to do is figure out the relationship between the two main words in the stem and then try to represent that relationship in a bridge sentence. So, for instance, if the main words in the stem are **tulip** and **flower**, you'll probably recognize that a tulip is a kind of flower, and so you'll then formulate the bridge sentence **An X is a kind of Y**. Now that you have your bridge sentence, you can try out each of the word pairs in the options and see which pair fits the bridge sentence. For instance, if **stick** and **stone** are the words in one of the options, then you substitute these words for **X** and **Y** in the bridge sentence to produce the sentence "A stick is a kind of stone." But this sentence is obviously not true, and that tells you that the option with **stick** and **stone** is not the correct answer choice. If another option contains the words **apple** and **fruit**, then you substitute these words for **X** and **Y** to get the sentence "An apple is a kind of fruit." Since this sentence is true, the option that produced it must be the correct answer. You've solved the analogy!

Try this strategy out on the sample questions that follow.

+ + + + + Verbal Test-Taking Strategies + + + + +

1. The best way to improve your vocabulary is to read, read, and read some more.
2. Take note of unfamiliar words and look up their meanings.
3. Review the words you don't know.
4. Practice your vocabulary by taking the practice tests in this book. If you missed any of the verbal questions, read the questions and answers again, so you'll understand why you answered those questions incorrectly. Look them up and write them down.

Sample Questions: Analogies

Directions: The following questions ask you to find relationships between words. For each question, select the answer choice that best completes the meaning of the sentence.

1. Shore is to island as
   (A) arc is to circle
   (B) membrane is to cell
   (C) orbit is to satellite
   (D) element is to compound
   (E) scale is to note

2. Tether is to restrain as
   (A) pen is to erase
   (B) freezer is to shiver
   (C) book is to write
   (D) bracket is to support
   (E) loaf is to slice

3. Knoll is to mountain as
   (A) leaf is to tree
   (B) grass is to meadow
   (C) pond is to lake
   (D) valley is to plateau
   (E) ocean is to wave

4. Grimace is to pain as
   (A) nod is to agreement
   (B) cheer is to victory
   (C) scowl is to frown
   (D) laugh is to joke
   (E) clench is to fist

5. Chaos is to orderly as
   (A) bravery is to confident
   (B) weather is to climatic
   (C) music is to soothing
   (D) danger is to safe
   (E) evidence is to persuasive

6. Clamorous is to quiet as
   (A) acrid is to bitter
   (B) dull is to smooth
   (C) savory is to delicious
   (D) tepid is to bland
   (E) brilliant is to dim

7. Zeal is to enthusiasm as
   (A) delight is to sorrow
   (B) patience is to irritation
   (C) terror is to speechlessness
   (D) curiosity is to openness
   (E) bliss is to happiness

8. Chassis is to car as
   (A) frame is to house
   (B) trunk is to tire
   (C) address is to mailbox
   (D) intersection is to traffic
   (E) furniture is to room

9. Bewilder is to confusion as
   (A) surprise is to boredom
   (B) befriend is to discord
   (C) reprimand is to pride
   (D) threaten is to fear
   (E) accuse is to suspicion

10. Resist is to passive as
    (A) stretch is to flexible
    (B) hurry is to careless
    (C) grumble is to satisfied
    (D) investigate is to energetic
    (E) empathize is to tolerant

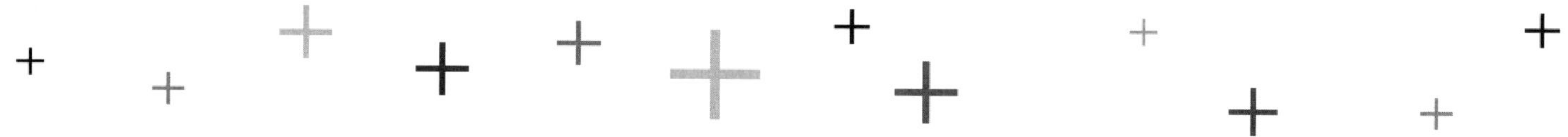

Answer Key: Analogies

1. **(B) membrane is to cell**
   An X forms the outer boundary of a Y.

2. **(D) bracket is to support**
   The purpose of an X is to Y something.

3. **(C) pond is to lake**
   X is a small geographic feature, and Y is a larger one.

4. **(A) nod is to agreement**
   To X is an indication of Y.

5. **(D) danger is to safe**
   X is a state in which things are not Y.

6. **(E) brilliant is to dim**
   Being X is the opposite of being Y.

7. **(E) bliss is to happiness**
   X is intense Y.

8. **(A) frame is to house**
   An X is the underlying structure of a Y.

9. **(D) threaten is to fear**
   To X someone causes that person to feel Y.

10. **(C) grumble is to satisfied**
    One who Xes is not Y.

Summing It Up

Here are a few things to keep in mind when you take the Middle Level SSAT:

- Make sure that you understand the directions before you start to work on any section. If there is anything that you do not understand, read the directions again.
- You don't need to answer every question on the test to score well. Some of the questions will be very easy and others will be difficult. Most students find that they do not know the answer to every question in every section. By working as quickly as you can without rushing, you should be able to read and think about every question.
- If you are not sure of an answer to a question, make note of it and move on. Make sure you also skip that question. If taking the test on paper, skip filling in that question's answer bubble on your answer sheet. If you have time remaining in that section, you can come back to questions you have not answered.
- If taking the test on paper, you may make as many marks on the test booklet as you need to. Just be sure to mark your answers on the answer sheet!
- Answers written in the test book will not count toward your score. Space is provided in the book for scratch work in the quantitative sections. Check often to make sure that you are marking your answer in the correct row on the answer sheet.
- If you decide to change an answer, be sure to erase your first mark on the answer sheet completely. If taking the SSAT at Home or computer-based SSAT, make sure you change your answer before completing the section.

THIS PAGE INTENTIONALLY LEFT BLANK.

Chapter Three: Scores

What Your Scores Mean

If you're like most people, you'll quickly scan the score report trying to find **the** magic number that will tell you whether the scores are "good." With an admission test like the SSAT, this is not an easy thing to do. First, remember that the purpose of an admission test is to offer a common measure of academic ability that can be used to compare all applicants. In the case of the SSAT, the testing population is a relatively homogeneous one — students applying to college-preparatory private schools. Given this, it is important to keep in mind that your scores are being compared only to students in this academically elite group.

As described in Chapter 1, admission tests differ from other tests such as classroom and achievement tests in significant ways. Achievement and classroom tests assess a specific body of knowledge that was covered. If all students perform well, the teacher and school system have fulfilled their objective. If all students performed well on an admission test, it would lose its value in helping differentiate between and among candidates.

Formula Scoring

The SSAT uses a method of scoring known in the testing industry as "formula scoring." Students earn one point for every correct answer, receive no points for omitted questions, and lose $\frac{1}{4}$ point for each incorrect answer. This is different from "right scoring," which computes the total score by counting the number of correct answers, with no penalty for incorrect answers. Formula scoring is used to eliminate the test taker's gain from random guessing.

This is why we suggest that you omit questions for which you cannot make an educated guess. Since most students have not encountered this kind of test before, it is an important concept to understand and experience prior to taking the SSAT. SSAT score reports provide detailed information by section on the number of questions right, wrong, and not answered to aid families and schools in understanding your test-taking strategies and scores.

The Score Report

It cannot be said often enough: *admission test scores are only one piece of the application.* The degree of emphasis placed on scores in a school's admission process depends on that school and on other information, such as transcripts, applicants' statements, and teacher recommendations.

The descriptions indicated by the letters below correspond to the lettered sections on the sample score report on page 63.

Ⓐ About You

Parents and students should review this section carefully. Is the student's name spelled correctly? Is the date of birth listed correctly? And — very important — when registering the student, was his/her current grade listed? The student's current grade is used to determine which test form he/she will take and dictates the comparison or norm groups. If the grade to which the student is applying is used for registration, he/she may get the wrong form and his/her SSAT scaled score will be compared with students a year (or grade) older. If any of this information is incorrect, contact The Enrollment Management Association immediately.

Ⓑ About the Test You Took

Again, parents and students should review this information for accuracy. For Test Level, the student will have taken the Middle Level SSAT since he/she is applying to grades 6–8. The Upper Level SSAT is for students in grades 8–11 who are applying to grades 9–12. There is a different score scale for each of these levels.

Ⓒ About Your Scores

SSAT scores are listed by section so you can understand the student's performance on each of the three scored sections: verbal, quantitative/math, and reading comprehension. A total score (a sum of the three sections) is also reported. For the Middle Level SSAT, the lowest number on the scale (440) is the lowest possible score a student can earn, and the highest number (710) is the highest possible score a student can earn.

Scores are first calculated by awarding one point for each correct answer and subtracting one quarter of one point for each incorrect answer. These scores are called raw scores. Raw scores can vary from one edition of the test to another due to differences in difficulty among different editions. A statistical procedure called *score equating* is used to adjust for these differences. After equating, the reported scores or scaled scores (e.g., the scores on the 440–710 scale for the Middle Level test) can be compared to each other across forms.

Score Range

Even after equating adjustments are made, no single test score provides a perfectly accurate estimate of proficiency. Many factors can affect a student's score. We provide a scaled-score range to suggest where a student's scores might fall if taking a different version of the test. Assuming the student's ability remains the same, there is a high likelihood that the scores would fall within the range indicated.

Continued on page 64

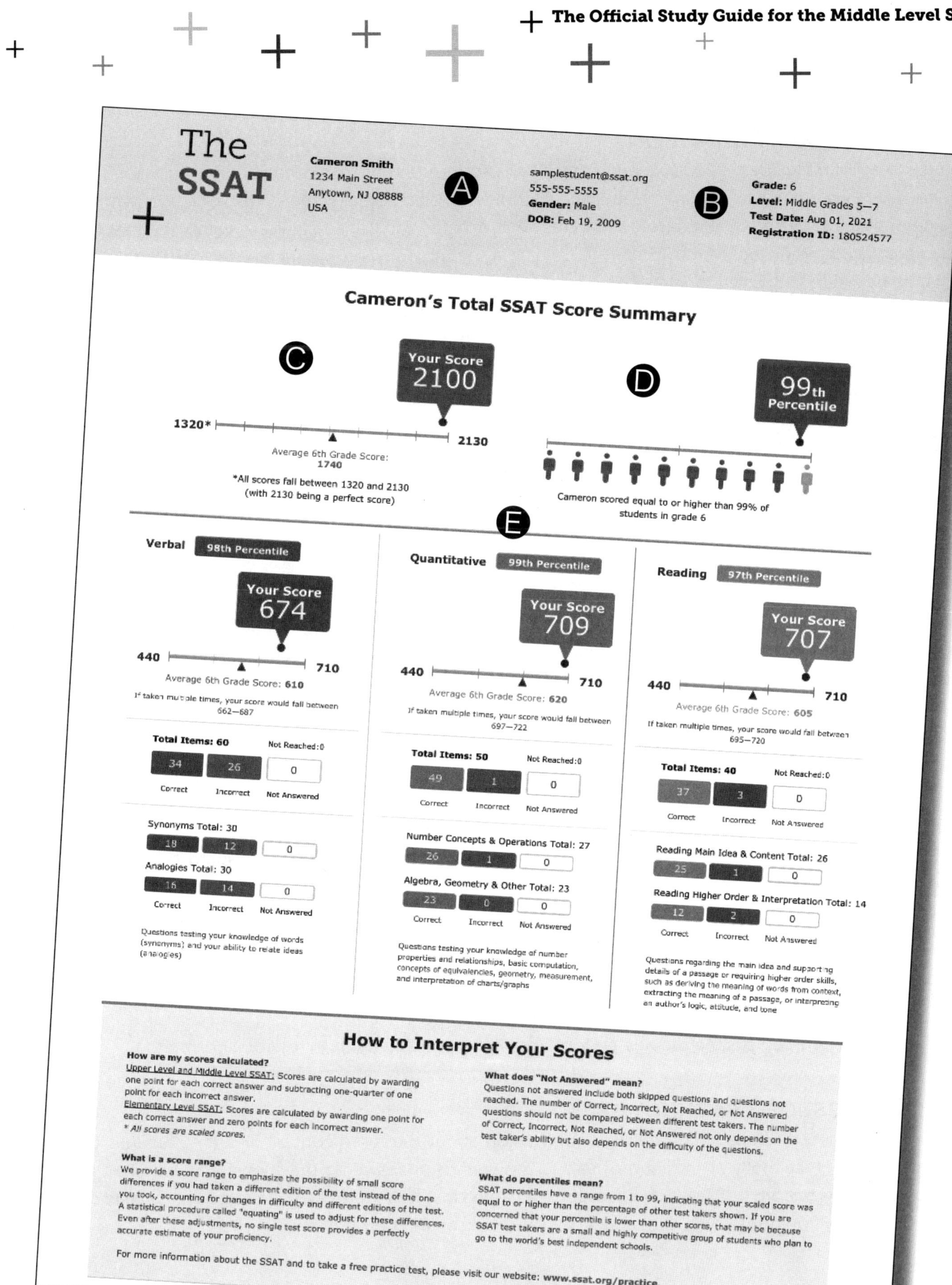

The SSAT

Cameron Smith
1234 Main Street
Anytown, NJ 08888
USA

A

samplestudent@ssat.org
555-555-5555
Gender: Male
DOB: Feb 19, 2009

B

Grade: 6
Level: Middle Grades 5–7
Test Date: Aug 01, 2021
Registration ID: 180524577

Cameron's Total SSAT Score Summary

C

Your Score 2100

1320* — 2130

Average 6th Grade Score: 1740

*All scores fall between 1320 and 2130 (with 2130 being a perfect score)

D

99th Percentile

Cameron scored equal to or higher than 99% of students in grade 6

E

Verbal 98th Percentile

Your Score 674

440 — 710

Average 6th Grade Score: **610**

If taken multiple times, your score would fall between 662—687

Total Items: 60 Not Reached: 0

Correct	Incorrect	Not Answered
34	26	0

Synonyms Total: 30

Correct	Incorrect	Not Answered
18	12	0

Analogies Total: 30

Correct	Incorrect	Not Answered
16	14	0

Questions testing your knowledge of words (synonyms) and your ability to relate ideas (analogies)

Quantitative 99th Percentile

Your Score 709

440 — 710

Average 6th Grade Score: **620**

If taken multiple times, your score would fall between 697—722

Total Items: 50 Not Reached: 0

Correct	Incorrect	Not Answered
49	1	0

Number Concepts & Operations Total: 27

Correct	Incorrect	Not Answered
26	1	0

Algebra, Geometry & Other Total: 23

Correct	Incorrect	Not Answered
23	0	0

Questions testing your knowledge of number properties and relationships, basic computation, concepts of equivalencies, geometry, measurement, and interpretation of charts/graphs

Reading 97th Percentile

Your Score 707

440 — 710

Average 6th Grade Score: **605**

If taken multiple times, your score would fall between 695—720

Total Items: 40 Not Reached: 0

Correct	Incorrect	Not Answered
37	3	0

Reading Main Idea & Content Total: 26

Correct	Incorrect	Not Answered
25	1	0

Reading Higher Order & Interpretation Total: 14

Correct	Incorrect	Not Answered
12	2	0

Questions regarding the main idea and supporting details of a passage or requiring higher order skills, such as deriving the meaning of words from context, extracting the meaning of a passage, or interpreting an author's logic, attitude, and tone

How to Interpret Your Scores

How are my scores calculated?
Upper Level and Middle Level SSAT: Scores are calculated by awarding one point for each correct answer and subtracting one-quarter of one point for each incorrect answer.
Elementary Level SSAT: Scores are calculated by awarding one point for each correct answer and zero points for each incorrect answer.
** All scores are scaled scores.*

What is a score range?
We provide a score range to emphasize the possibility of small score differences if you had taken a different edition of the test instead of the one you took, accounting for changes in difficulty and different editions of the test. A statistical procedure called "equating" is used to adjust for these differences. Even after these adjustments, no single test score provides a perfectly accurate estimate of your proficiency.

What does "Not Answered" mean?
Questions not answered include both skipped questions and questions not reached. The number of Correct, Incorrect, Not Reached, or Not Answered questions should not be compared between different test takers. The number of Correct, Incorrect, Not Reached, or Not Answered not only depends on the test taker's ability but also depends on the difficulty of the questions.

What do percentiles mean?
SSAT percentiles have a range from 1 to 99, indicating that your scaled score was equal to or higher than the percentage of other test takers shown. If you are concerned that your percentile is lower than other scores, that may be because SSAT test takers are a small and highly competitive group of students who plan to go to the world's best independent schools.

For more information about the SSAT and to take a free practice test, please visit our website: **www.ssat.org/practice**.

D SSAT Score Information

Beginning with the 2021–2022 academic year, SSAT provides reference information based on one norm group. The norm group, such as all students in grade 6, contains all test takers in the same grade level who have taken one of the Standard SSAT administrations in the United States and Canada typically within the past three years. If a test taker completed the SSAT in previous years, a second norm group, such as female students in grade 6, would have been displayed, indicating test takers of the same grade level and gender who have taken one of the Standard administrations in the United States and Canada within the past three years. The difference between the two norm groups is that the total norm group contains both male and female test takers, whereas the second norm group is gender specific. You will only see the grade-specific norm group going forward. You will also see the average scaled score attained by the group.

SSAT Percentile

The SSAT reports percentile ranks. The percentile rank is the percentage of students in the norm group whose scores fall below your scaled score. For example, if a seventh-grade student's verbal scaled score is 680 and the percentile rank is 72 on the verbal section in the total group, 72% of all seventh-grade students in the norm group had a verbal score lower than 680.

Many parents express concern that their student's SSAT percentiles are lower than those they have earned on other tests. Please remember that SSAT test takers are members of a small and highly competitive group of students who plan to attend some of the world's best schools. Do not be discouraged by what seems to be a lower score than the student usually attains on standardized testing.

It is important to remember that SSAT test takers are members of a small and highly competitive group of students who plan to attend some of the world's best private schools. Being in the middle of this group is still impressive!

International and Flex test scores are not included in the comparison norm group. However, international testers' scaled scores are compared to the domestic/Standard/first-time test-taker norm group described above.

SSAT Average Score

SSAT average scores provide additional context information for your SSAT scaled score on each of the three scored sections (verbal, quantitative/math, and reading). These average scores are based on the same norm group used to provide the SSAT percentiles.

The SSAT average score is the average performance of all other students in the total norm group.

E Test Question Breakdown

This section provides useful and detailed information about the test's content and the student's test-taking strategies. Look carefully at the ratio of wrong answers to unanswered questions. If the student had many wrong answers but omitted few or no questions, meaning that they were guessing quite a bit instead of skipping questions they couldn't answer, that could have an adverse effect on scores.

Supporting the Test Taker

Here are a few simple things you can do to help your student perform as well as possible on the SSAT.

Practice! Practice! Practice! Help your student structure time to take the practice tests in the next chapter. Act as the proctor — administer the timed practice tests while approximating testing conditions as closely as possible.

Review and encourage! Review any incorrect answers. Which sections or types of questions proved most difficult? Focus, encourage, and help your student sharpen those skills. Examine your student's guessing strategy. Try to determine the cause of the errors so that your student can develop a strategy for avoiding similar mistakes on the actual test.

Some common pitfalls:

- Accidentally marking the wrong circle on the answer sheet when the student knows the correct answer
- Making simple arithmetic mistakes

Double-checking answers and not rushing can help with this.

Extra help! If taking the practice tests reveals that your student lacks a particular skill that is necessary for success, seeking extra help for your student may be useful. If you would rather self-direct this process, consider signing up for SSAT Practice Online. With diagnostic tools, progress indicators, and study tools, it provides a full year of help and feedback.

Perspective is everything! Keep the importance of the SSAT in perspective and help your student do the same. The SSAT is an important and valuable part of the application package and students should prepare for it. But remember that the SSAT is just *one* part of the entire package. Schools will weigh your student's test scores along with other information.

Retaking the test? Scheduling options are available at ssat.org should your student want to retake the SSAT. In general, the lower the initial scores, the more likely the scores will increase the second time.

Rest up and eat well! Make sure your student gets enough sleep on the days leading up to the test and that he or she eats a healthy breakfast on the day it is administered.

Be prepared for the unexpected! If your student panics, freezes, or gets sick during the administration of the SSAT, she or he has the option to leave the test. It's important for you to know that if your child does leave the test, the results will be canceled. It's your responsibility, however, to alert The Enrollment Management Association immediately so that the scores are voided and not sent to schools. Please note that your fee for the canceled test will not be refunded, but for a service charge, you may reschedule for a new test date.

THIS PAGE INTENTIONALLY LEFT BLANK.

Chapter Four: The Character Skills Snapshot

What Is the Character Skills Snapshot?

The Character Skills Snapshot is an online assessment tool designed for students in grades 5 to 11 who are seeking entrance to private schools for grades 6 to 12. The purpose of the Snapshot is to measure essential character skills deemed important by private schools. The Snapshot is considered one new and important piece of the student admissions process, but it should not be used independently of other pieces of information to make admissions decisions.

What Is the Purpose of the Snapshot?

We know that schools care about students and how they grow — not just in cognitive skills such as writing and math, but also growing into good citizens with initiative, resilience, and social awareness — those skills that carry them forward into a successful adult life.

While character education is a hallmark of a private school education and is a salient piece of every school's mission, gaining insight into an applying student's current character skill development has been largely a matter of intuition and an investigative screening of the application. While many schools assess character in some way (e.g., via student interviews or teacher recommendations), reliance on unstandardized or inconsistent methods to assess character skills can introduce bias and subjectivity into the admissions process. This highlights the need for a standardized and empirically supported approach.

The Snapshot is meant to provide a snapshot in time of a student's character skills — it is not a fixed, absolute measure. It provides a way for schools to get to know a student better and an opportunity for them to enumerate the ways in which their communities can enrich and develop a student's developing skills.

How Was the Snapshot Designed?

The development of the Snapshot was research- and data-driven. Over the last six years, The Enrollment Management Association has put considerable time and resources towards developing the Snapshot. Spearheaded by the recommendation of the Think Tank on the Future of Assessment, EMA worked with 56 private schools and Educational Testing Service to conceptualize, build, pilot, and launch the Character Skills Snapshot. The Snapshot, a revolutionary new tool for the admissions process, enables member schools to include a standardized measure of character into their admissions process.

Prior to launching the Snapshot, multiple pretesting and field trials were conducted with more than 12,000 students completing the assessment. Additionally, user testing was conducted with parents to gain feedback on the design and content elements of the results reports, as well as the assessment itself.

What Does the Snapshot Measure?

The Snapshot measures seven character skills.

Character Skill	Definition	Example Preferences
Initiative	This skill describes the student's inclination to work on assignments in a timely manner and emphasizes the point at which a student chooses to start work rather than when the student finishes work.	Starts working on assignments early Does not do things at the last minute
Intellectual Engagement	This skill focuses on the student's enjoyment of and willingness to pursue learning opportunities, regardless of how much difficulty they might present.	Enjoys challenging assignments and tasks Likes to learn more about topics of interest
Open-Mindedness	This skill describes the student's willingness to try new things.	Is open to trying new and unfamiliar approaches Does not avoid trying new activities, experiences, music and/or food
Resilience	This skill highlights the student's ability to adjust to unexpected situations and changing circumstances.	Readily adapts when plans change Is comfortable in stressful situations
Self-Control	This skill focuses on the student's ability to monitor and control his or her thoughts and actions, and what he or she says to others.	Thinks carefully about what he or she says Thinks things through before making a decision
Social Awareness	This skill describes a student's ability to recognize the appropriate ways to interact with others.	Adapts behavior based on the particular context Attempts to resolve conflicts and act appropriately
Teamwork	This skill highlights the student's ability to engage in supportive behaviors and emphasizes empathetic qualities that enable productive collaboration with others.	Attempts to comfort friends when they are upset Tries to resolve conflicts between people in a group

The Character Skills Snapshot Consists of TWO Sections

The first section has 20–30 forced-choice questions, depending on the form. A forced-choice question presents three short statements and asks you to select the response that is MOST like you and the response that is LEAST like you. One option will always be left blank. (See Sample Questions at the end of this chapter.)

The second section has 10 situational judgment scenarios. You are asked to read each scenario then read the four corresponding responses. You are asked to rate the appropriateness of each response using a scale of 1 (not appropriate) to 4 (very appropriate). You can use the same ratings for each response. For example, if you think each response is very appropriate, you can use a rating of 4 for each option.

How Is the Snapshot Administered?

The Snapshot is administered online. After parents consent for their student(s) to take the Snapshot and respond to an integrity statement, the student can then log into their Student Access Portal and begin the Snapshot.

The tool is untimed, but usually takes about 30 minutes to complete.

Is the Snapshot Reliable?

Yes, the Snapshot is reliable. Reliability is a measure of consistency. Think of it this way: If you weigh yourself every day for a week and the scale registers the same weight, you can say that the scale is reliable. In statistics, reliability is measured on a scale from 0–1: "0" means no reliability at all and "1" means perfect reliability, which is rarely achieved in reality. Depending on the purpose of the test, the desired range of reliability can vary. For a noncognitive assessment like the Snapshot, a reliability of 0.7 or higher is preferable. The Snapshot has achieved this target reliability.

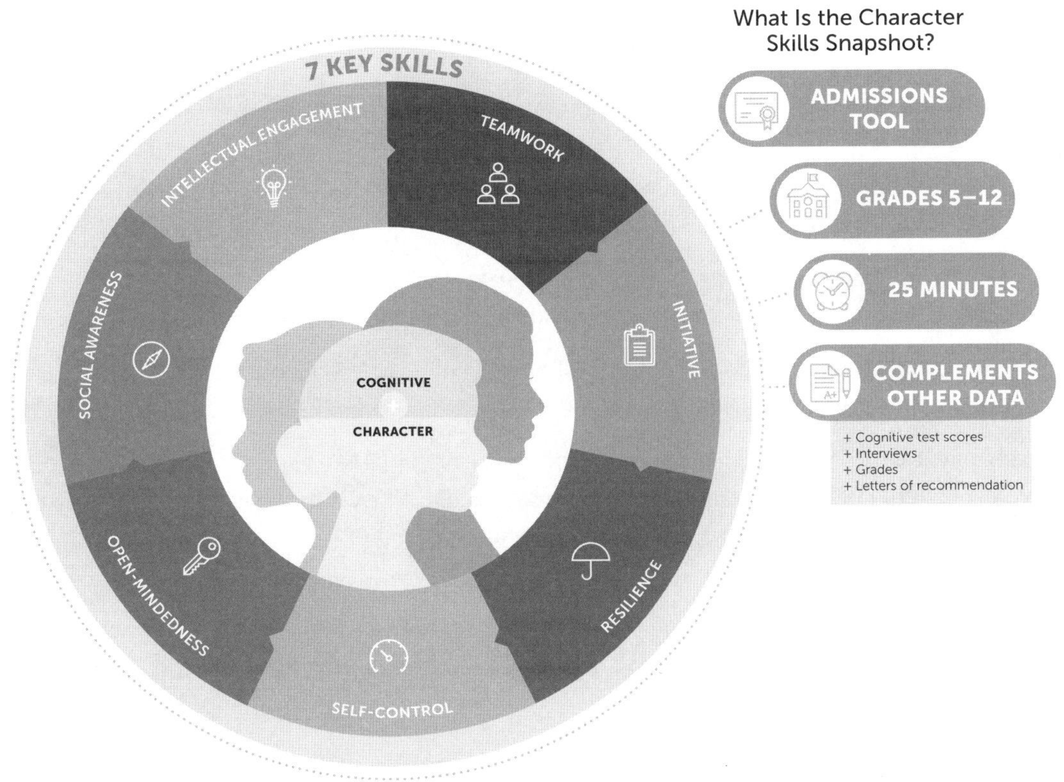

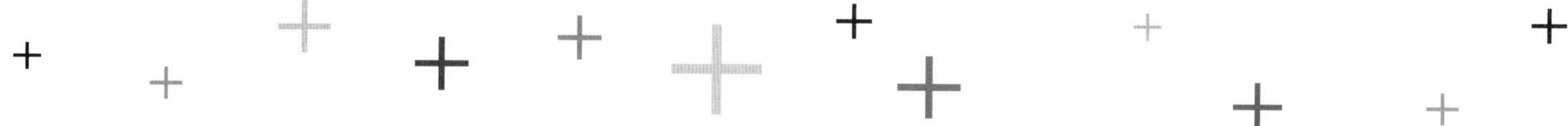

The Snapshot Is a Norm-Referenced Assessment

A norm-referenced assessment interprets an individual's results compared to the results distribution of a comparison group, referred to as the norm group. The Snapshot norm groups are based on a group of approximately 5,000 students who took the Snapshot during a given academic year. There are two norm groups for the Snapshot, determined by grade band. The middle-level norm group consists of all students in grades 5–7 applying to grades 6–8. The upper-level norm group consists of all students in grades 8–11 applying to grades 9–12.

The Snapshot reports results for each of the seven skills in three performance categories: Emerging, Developing, and Demonstrating.

Emerging	Developing	Demonstrating
The student's result fell into the lowest 25% (0–25th percentile) of scores in the comparison sample.	The student's result fell into the middle 50% (above 25th and below 75th percentile) of scores in the comparison sample.	The student's results fell in the upper 25% (at or above 75th percentile) of scores in the comparison sample.
The student is starting to show signs of this skill. Note that emerging does not imply a student does not have any of this skill.	The student displays the skill but is continuing to develop it.	The student displays a clear understanding and use of this skill. Note that demonstrating a skill does not imply that a student has mastered the skill. There is still room to grow.

Strategies for Taking the Snapshot

Relax. The Snapshot provides you with an opportunity to share more about yourself and your preferences as they relate to the seven character skills with schools. Remember, it is only one piece of the application.

Answer honestly. Remember this is the way you see yourself — not how your parents, your friends, your teacher, or your coach would describe you.

Select the choice that is MOST like you or the choice that is LEAST like you. You are sometimes going to have to make a difficult choice. You may see multiple options that are all like you or not like you at all.

Consider your answers carefully. The assessment will not allow you to go back and change your answers. Once a selection is made, it is final.

Do not misrepresent yourself. Trying to answer questions in such a way as to make yourself look good on any one skill may have an adverse effect on some of the other skills. Don't overthink your answers, just be yourself!

Sample Questions

Forced-Choice

Select the statement that describes you most accurately and the statement that describes you least accurately. There will always be one statement in each set of three that will not be dragged into the "most" and "least" boxes.

I say the first thing that comes to my mind.	I get bored when trying to solve difficult problems.	I avoid being emotionally involved in other people's problems.

Most like me

Least like me

I am open to trying new things.	I like to research topics that are interesting to me.	I am willing to help people whenever they ask for my help.

Most like me

Least like me

I do not like to change the way something is done if the current way still works.	Before doing something, I first think carefully about it.	It is easy for me to find something else to do if someone cancels at the last minute.

Most like me

Least like me

Situational Judgment

Please rate the appropriateness of each possible response from 1 (not appropriate at all) to 4 (very appropriate). You can apply the same rating to more than one response. If, for example, you believe that two of the possible responses would be 1 (not appropriate at all), you may mark them both with a 1.

After two weeks of late nights, Sarah feels overwhelmed by the demands of her Spanish class and the upcoming assessment. Sarah has been an attentive student, but Spanish does not come easy to her. She wants to meet with her Spanish teacher, but he has been ill during the week and will not return to school tomorrow. Unfortunately, this is the day before the test.

Possible Responses	**1** (not appropriate at all)	**2**	**3**	**4** (very appropriate)
Meet with the Spanish teacher and suggest that giving the test this week is not fair since he has been absent.				
Meet with the Spanish teacher and ask him if there is a way he can give her a few more days to prepare for the test.				
Speak to her parents and ask them to call the Spanish teacher to voice their concern about giving students a test immediately after the teacher was unavailable to students for so long.				
Meet with the Spanish teacher when he returns to discuss her recent progress and develop a long-term plan to improve.				

As a member of the student council, Caroline is on a committee that plans themes for school dances. While Caroline proposes a 1960's theme for the winter formal, the other members of the committee propose a "night at the movies" theme.

Possible Responses	**1** (not appropriate at all)	**2**	**3**	**4** (very appropriate)
Accept the proposal of the majority of committee members.				
Accept the proposal of the majority of committee members, but demand that she can choose the theme for the next dance.				
Resign from student council because she did not get her way.				
Accept the proposal of the majority of committee members, but quietly convince as many students as she can not to attend the dance.				

Middle Level Practice Tests

Trying Out the Middle Level SSAT

Now it's time to find out what it's actually like to take the Middle Level SSAT. Ask someone to help you set up a simulation — a re-creation of the experience that is as close as possible to actually taking the SSAT. Think of it as a dress rehearsal for the real thing. Simulating the SSAT experience can help you gain confidence and clarity about what to expect.

Remove (or photocopy) the answer sheet and use it to complete each practice test.

You can choose to do your simulation section by section or by taking an entire test from start to finish.

Here are the rules you'll need to follow to make your SSAT simulation as realistic as possible:

+ Ask your "test proctor" to keep time and tell you when to begin and end each section.
+ No talking or music is allowed during the SSAT; so, make sure the room in which you are taking the test is quiet and turn off anything that makes noise, such as your phone, iPod, or TV.
+ You will not be allowed to use any research material while taking the SSAT; so, put away your smartphone, laptop, books, dictionary, calculator, ruler, and notes.
+ Work only on one section during the time allotted. Do not go back to another section to finish unanswered questions.
+ Use sharpened #2 pencils and an eraser.
+ Fill in the answer sheet (located before each test in the book) just as you would during a regular test.

Simulating the Test: Section by Section

If your goal is to sharpen your test-taking techniques in a specific area, use the individual sections for the simulation. Review the exercises in Chapter 2 before beginning, and be sure to follow the instructions for each section carefully. Schedule the allotted time for each section, and ask the person supervising your simulation to time you, or set a timer for yourself.

As you will when you actually take the SSAT, mark your answer choices on the answer sheet.

Simulating the Test: Start to Finish

If your goal is to practice taking the entire SSAT (minus the experimental section), here's how to schedule your time blocks, including breaks:

Test Overview		
Section	**Number of Questions**	**Time Allotted to Administer Each Section**
Writing Sample	1	25 minutes
Break		10 minutes
Section 1 (Quantitative)	25	30 minutes
Section 2 (Reading)	40	40 minutes
Break		10 minutes
Section 3 (Verbal)	60	30 minutes
Section 4 (Quantitative)	25	30 minutes
Totals	**151**	**2 hours, 55 minutes**

You'll see that the total testing time is 2 hours and 35 minutes. When you add in the two breaks, the total time is 2 hours and 55 minutes (these practice tests do not include an experimental section). Be sure to use your breaks for stretching, getting a drink of water, and focusing your eyes on something other than a test paper. This will help clear your mind and get you ready for the next section.

A note about special timing: Some students are granted "time and a half" accommodations, and are given 1.5 times the minutes available for each test section, including the writing sample. Students who are granted 1.5x time do not take the experimental section.

THIS PAGE INTENTIONALLY LEFT BLANK.

Practice Test I: Middle Level Answer Sheet

Be sure each mark completely fills the answer space.
Start with number 1 for each new section of the test.

Section 1

1 ⒶⒷⒸⒹⒺ	6 ⒶⒷⒸⒹⒺ	11 ⒶⒷⒸⒹⒺ	16 ⒶⒷⒸⒹⒺ	21 ⒶⒷⒸⒹⒺ
2 ⒶⒷⒸⒹⒺ	7 ⒶⒷⒸⒹⒺ	12 ⒶⒷⒸⒹⒺ	17 ⒶⒷⒸⒹⒺ	22 ⒶⒷⒸⒹⒺ
3 ⒶⒷⒸⒹⒺ	8 ⒶⒷⒸⒹⒺ	13 ⒶⒷⒸⒹⒺ	18 ⒶⒷⒸⒹⒺ	23 ⒶⒷⒸⒹⒺ
4 ⒶⒷⒸⒹⒺ	9 ⒶⒷⒸⒹⒺ	14 ⒶⒷⒸⒹⒺ	19 ⒶⒷⒸⒹⒺ	24 ⒶⒷⒸⒹⒺ
5 ⒶⒷⒸⒹⒺ	10 ⒶⒷⒸⒹⒺ	15 ⒶⒷⒸⒹⒺ	20 ⒶⒷⒸⒹⒺ	25 ⒶⒷⒸⒹⒺ

Section 2

1 ⒶⒷⒸⒹⒺ	9 ⒶⒷⒸⒹⒺ	17 ⒶⒷⒸⒹⒺ	25 ⒶⒷⒸⒹⒺ	33 ⒶⒷⒸⒹⒺ
2 ⒶⒷⒸⒹⒺ	10 ⒶⒷⒸⒹⒺ	18 ⒶⒷⒸⒹⒺ	26 ⒶⒷⒸⒹⒺ	34 ⒶⒷⒸⒹⒺ
3 ⒶⒷⒸⒹⒺ	11 ⒶⒷⒸⒹⒺ	19 ⒶⒷⒸⒹⒺ	27 ⒶⒷⒸⒹⒺ	35 ⒶⒷⒸⒹⒺ
4 ⒶⒷⒸⒹⒺ	12 ⒶⒷⒸⒹⒺ	20 ⒶⒷⒸⒹⒺ	28 ⒶⒷⒸⒹⒺ	36 ⒶⒷⒸⒹⒺ
5 ⒶⒷⒸⒹⒺ	13 ⒶⒷⒸⒹⒺ	21 ⒶⒷⒸⒹⒺ	29 ⒶⒷⒸⒹⒺ	37 ⒶⒷⒸⒹⒺ
6 ⒶⒷⒸⒹⒺ	14 ⒶⒷⒸⒹⒺ	22 ⒶⒷⒸⒹⒺ	30 ⒶⒷⒸⒹⒺ	38 ⒶⒷⒸⒹⒺ
7 ⒶⒷⒸⒹⒺ	15 ⒶⒷⒸⒹⒺ	23 ⒶⒷⒸⒹⒺ	31 ⒶⒷⒸⒹⒺ	39 ⒶⒷⒸⒹⒺ
8 ⒶⒷⒸⒹⒺ	16 ⒶⒷⒸⒹⒺ	24 ⒶⒷⒸⒹⒺ	32 ⒶⒷⒸⒹⒺ	40 ⒶⒷⒸⒹⒺ

Section 3

1 ⒶⒷⒸⒹⒺ	13 ⒶⒷⒸⒹⒺ	25 ⒶⒷⒸⒹⒺ	37 ⒶⒷⒸⒹⒺ	49 ⒶⒷⒸⒹⒺ
2 ⒶⒷⒸⒹⒺ	14 ⒶⒷⒸⒹⒺ	26 ⒶⒷⒸⒹⒺ	38 ⒶⒷⒸⒹⒺ	50 ⒶⒷⒸⒹⒺ
3 ⒶⒷⒸⒹⒺ	15 ⒶⒷⒸⒹⒺ	27 ⒶⒷⒸⒹⒺ	39 ⒶⒷⒸⒹⒺ	51 ⒶⒷⒸⒹⒺ
4 ⒶⒷⒸⒹⒺ	16 ⒶⒷⒸⒹⒺ	28 ⒶⒷⒸⒹⒺ	40 ⒶⒷⒸⒹⒺ	52 ⒶⒷⒸⒹⒺ
5 ⒶⒷⒸⒹⒺ	17 ⒶⒷⒸⒹⒺ	29 ⒶⒷⒸⒹⒺ	41 ⒶⒷⒸⒹⒺ	53 ⒶⒷⒸⒹⒺ
6 ⒶⒷⒸⒹⒺ	18 ⒶⒷⒸⒹⒺ	30 ⒶⒷⒸⒹⒺ	42 ⒶⒷⒸⒹⒺ	54 ⒶⒷⒸⒹⒺ
7 ⒶⒷⒸⒹⒺ	19 ⒶⒷⒸⒹⒺ	31 ⒶⒷⒸⒹⒺ	43 ⒶⒷⒸⒹⒺ	55 ⒶⒷⒸⒹⒺ
8 ⒶⒷⒸⒹⒺ	20 ⒶⒷⒸⒹⒺ	32 ⒶⒷⒸⒹⒺ	44 ⒶⒷⒸⒹⒺ	56 ⒶⒷⒸⒹⒺ
9 ⒶⒷⒸⒹⒺ	21 ⒶⒷⒸⒹⒺ	33 ⒶⒷⒸⒹⒺ	45 ⒶⒷⒸⒹⒺ	57 ⒶⒷⒸⒹⒺ
10 ⒶⒷⒸⒹⒺ	22 ⒶⒷⒸⒹⒺ	34 ⒶⒷⒸⒹⒺ	46 ⒶⒷⒸⒹⒺ	58 ⒶⒷⒸⒹⒺ
11 ⒶⒷⒸⒹⒺ	23 ⒶⒷⒸⒹⒺ	35 ⒶⒷⒸⒹⒺ	47 ⒶⒷⒸⒹⒺ	59 ⒶⒷⒸⒹⒺ
12 ⒶⒷⒸⒹⒺ	24 ⒶⒷⒸⒹⒺ	36 ⒶⒷⒸⒹⒺ	48 ⒶⒷⒸⒹⒺ	60 ⒶⒷⒸⒹⒺ

Section 4

1 ⒶⒷⒸⒹⒺ	6 ⒶⒷⒸⒹⒺ	11 ⒶⒷⒸⒹⒺ	16 ⒶⒷⒸⒹⒺ	21 ⒶⒷⒸⒹⒺ
2 ⒶⒷⒸⒹⒺ	7 ⒶⒷⒸⒹⒺ	12 ⒶⒷⒸⒹⒺ	17 ⒶⒷⒸⒹⒺ	22 ⒶⒷⒸⒹⒺ
3 ⒶⒷⒸⒹⒺ	8 ⒶⒷⒸⒹⒺ	13 ⒶⒷⒸⒹⒺ	18 ⒶⒷⒸⒹⒺ	23 ⒶⒷⒸⒹⒺ
4 ⒶⒷⒸⒹⒺ	9 ⒶⒷⒸⒹⒺ	14 ⒶⒷⒸⒹⒺ	19 ⒶⒷⒸⒹⒺ	24 ⒶⒷⒸⒹⒺ
5 ⒶⒷⒸⒹⒺ	10 ⒶⒷⒸⒹⒺ	15 ⒶⒷⒸⒹⒺ	20 ⒶⒷⒸⒹⒺ	25 ⒶⒷⒸⒹⒺ

Section 5

1 ⒶⒷⒸⒹⒺ	5 ⒶⒷⒸⒹⒺ	9 ⒶⒷⒸⒹⒺ	13 ⒶⒷⒸⒹⒺ
2 ⒶⒷⒸⒹⒺ	6 ⒶⒷⒸⒹⒺ	10 ⒶⒷⒸⒹⒺ	14 ⒶⒷⒸⒹⒺ
3 ⒶⒷⒸ			
4 ⒶⒷⒸⒹⒺ	8 ⒶⒷⒸⒹⒺ	12 ⒶⒷⒸⒹⒺ	16 ⒶⒷⒸⒹⒺ

Experimental Section – See page 9 for details.

THIS PAGE INTENTIONALLY LEFT BLANK.

Writing Sample

Schools would like to get to know you better through a story you tell or an essay you write. If you choose to write a story, use the sentence presented in A to begin. Make sure that your story has a beginning, middle, and end. If you choose to write a personal essay, base your essay on the topic presented in B. Please fill in the circle next to your choice.

Ⓐ I had fifteen minutes to solve the puzzle.

Ⓑ What has been your favorite class in the past year or so? Describe the class and explain why it has been your favorite.

Use this page and the next page to complete your writing sample.

Continue on next page

THIS PAGE INTENTIONALLY LEFT BLANK.

SECTION 1
25 Questions

Following each problem in this section, there are five suggested answers. Work each problem in your head or in the blank space provided at the right of the page. Then look at the five suggested answers and decide which one is best.

Note: Figures that accompany problems in this section are drawn as accurately as possible EXCEPT when it is stated in a specific problem that its figure is not drawn to scale.

Sample Problem:

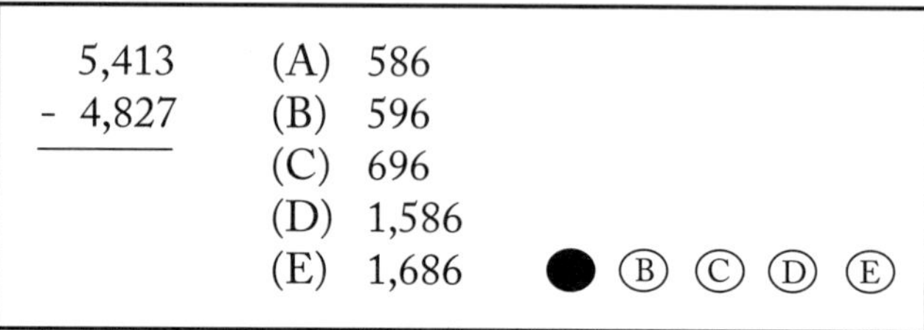

$$\begin{array}{r} 5{,}413 \\ -\ 4{,}827 \\ \hline \end{array}$$

(A) 586
(B) 596
(C) 696
(D) 1,586
(E) 1,686

● Ⓑ Ⓒ Ⓓ Ⓔ

USE THIS SPACE FOR FIGURING.

1. If $n + 5 = 5$, what is the value of n ?

(A) 0
(B) $\frac{1}{5}$
(C) 1
(D) 5
(E) 10

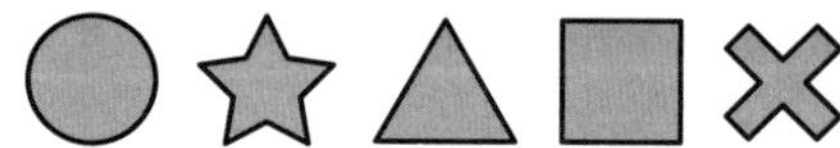

2. The sequence of shapes above repeats indefinitely as shown. Which shape is the 12th shape in the sequence?

(A)
(B) 
(C) 
(D)
(E)

GO ON TO THE NEXT PAGE.

USE THIS SPACE FOR FIGURING.

3. There were 20 illustrations in Julio's sketch pad. While at a museum, he drew x more illustrations in the sketch pad. Which expression represents the total number of illustrations in Julio's sketch pad after his museum visit?

(A) $\frac{x}{20}$

(B) $\frac{20}{x}$

(C) $20x$

(D) $20 - x$

(E) $20 + x$

4,■86

4. The ■ in the number above represents a digit from 0 through 9. If the number is less than 4,486, what is the greatest possible value for ■ ?

(A) 0
(B) 3
(C) 4
(D) 7
(E) 9

---

5. Which of the following is the sum of $\frac{3}{8}$ and $\frac{4}{7}$?

(A) $\frac{1}{8}$

(B) $\frac{3}{14}$

(C) $\frac{7}{15}$

(D) $\frac{33}{56}$

(E) $\frac{53}{56}$

GO ON TO THE NEXT PAGE.

USE THIS SPACE FOR FIGURING.

6. Ilona goes on a 4-hour hike from her campsite to a scenic lookout. The graph shows her altitude during the hike and the time it took her to reach each corresponding altitude. Based on the graph, the altitude of the scenic outlook is how many meters above the altitude of the campsite?

   (A) 100
   (B) 200
   (C) 300
   (D) 400
   (E) 500

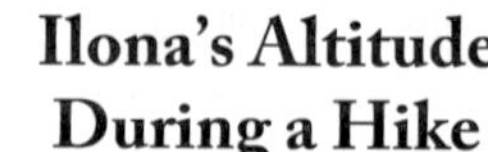

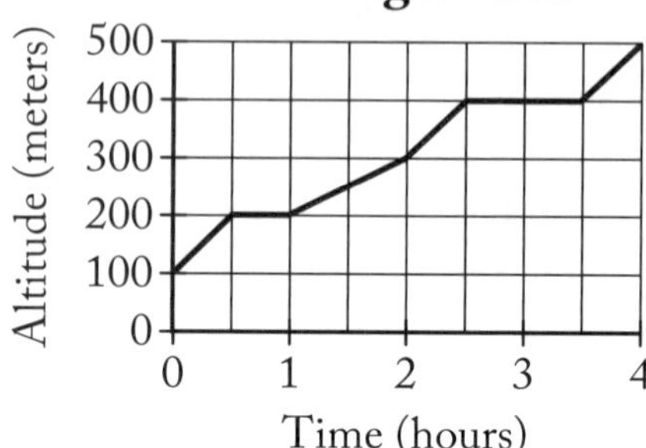

---

7. What is the value of $0.5 \times 23.5 \times 0.2$?

   (A) 0.0235
   (B) 0.235
   (C) 2.35
   (D) 23.5
   (E) 235

---

8. On a table, there are ten of each of the following types of coins: 1-cent, 5-cent, 10-cent, and 25-cent coins. If Edith needs exactly 36 cents, what is the least number of coins she must take from the table?

   (A) Two
   (B) Three
   (C) Four
   (D) Five
   (E) Six

---

9. What is the value of $\frac{1}{2}\left(\frac{3}{4} \times \frac{1}{3}\right)$?

   (A) $\frac{1}{8}$
   (B) $\frac{5}{24}$
   (C) $\frac{2}{9}$
   (D) $\frac{13}{24}$
   (E) $\frac{19}{12}$

GO ON TO THE NEXT PAGE.

USE THIS SPACE FOR FIGURING.

R S T V

10. In the figure above, segment $\overline{ST}$ has length 12, T is the midpoint of the segment $\overline{RV}$, and S is the midpoint of segment $\overline{RT}$. What is the length of the segment $\overline{SV}$?

(A) 12
(B) 18
(C) 24
(D) 36
(E) 48

---

11. Let ⓐ be defined by ⓐ $= a^2 + 1$, where a is a whole number.

What is the value of ③ ?

(A) 16
(B) 10
(C) 8
(D) 7
(E) 6

---

12. Each student at Central Middle School wears a uniform consisting of 1 shirt and 1 pair of pants. The table shows the colors available for each item of clothing. How many different uniforms are possible?

(A) Three
(B) Four
(C) Seven
(D) Ten
(E) Twelve

Uniform Choices	
Shirt Color	Pants Color
Tan Red White Yellow	Black Khaki Navy

---

13. If n is a positive odd integer, which of the following must be an even integer?

(A) $3n - 1$
(B) $2n + 3$
(C) $2n - 1$
(D) $n + 2$
(E) $\frac{3n}{2}$

GO ON TO THE NEXT PAGE.

USE THIS SPACE FOR FIGURING.

14. Joseph's car began the week with a full tank of gasoline. During the week, he drove his car 232 miles and paid \$32 for gasoline that week. At this rate, how many miles will he drive if he pays \$40 for gasoline next week?

(A) 240
(B) 288
(C) 290
(D) 320
(E) 332

---

15. Of the following fractions, which is closest to 37% ?

(A) $\frac{1}{3}$

(B) $\frac{1}{4}$

(C) $\frac{2}{5}$

(D) $\frac{3}{7}$

(E) $\frac{3}{8}$

---

16. At Banham School, there are 20 students in each class, and 5 classes wish to form 3 clubs. Each of the students must belong to only one club, and the membership of each club may not outnumber the membership of the other clubs by more than one student. What is the least possible number of students in one club?

(A) 15
(B) 20
(C) 21
(D) 33
(E) 34

GO ON TO THE NEXT PAGE.

USE THIS SPACE FOR FIGURING.

17. The rectangle shown is divided into 6 congruent squares. What fraction of the rectangle is shaded?

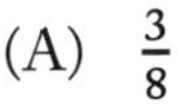

(A) $\frac{3}{8}$

(B) $\frac{5}{8}$

(C) $\frac{5}{9}$

(D) $\frac{7}{12}$

(E) $\frac{2}{3}$

---

18. In a game, 2 gold pieces may be exchanged for 6 silver pieces, and 7 silver pieces may be exchanged for 42 copper pieces. At this rate, how many copper pieces may be exchanged for 5 gold pieces?

(A) 10
(B) 18
(C) 36
(D) 72
(E) 90

---

19. The figure shown consists of three segments and two squares. Each square has side lengths of 2 centimeters, and AB = 6 centimeters, CD = 8 centimeters, and EF = 10 centimeters. Based on the figure, what is the length of n, in centimeters?

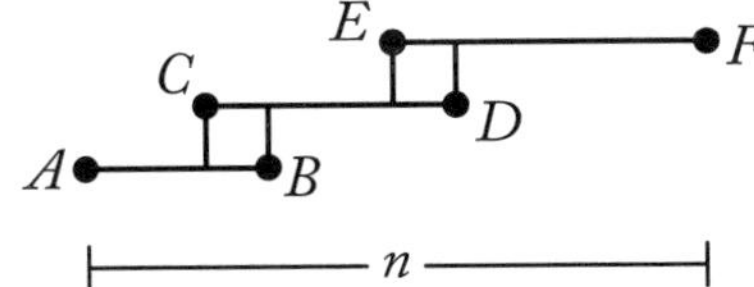

(A) 18
(B) 20
(C) 22
(D) 24
(E) 26

---

20. Calculate: $3 + 6 \times 2^3 \div 3 + 3^2$

(A) 21
(B) 24
(C) 27
(D) 28
(E) 33

GO ON TO THE NEXT PAGE.

USE THIS SPACE FOR FIGURING.

21. A square card that is blank on both sides is punched with 2 small holes. The top face of the card is shown in the figure. If the card is turned facedown, which of the following orientations of the card is NOT possible?

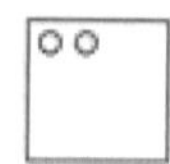

(A)

(B)

(C)

(D)

(E)

---

22. If a number n is even, which of the following expressions must be an integer?

(A) $\frac{3n}{2}$

(B) $\frac{3n}{4}$

(C) $\frac{n + 4}{4}$

(D) $\frac{n + 2}{3}$

(E) $\frac{3(n + 1)}{2}$

---

23. On Monday, Aidan reads $\frac{1}{3}$ of a book, and on Tuesday, Aidan reads $\frac{1}{4}$ of the remaining pages. To complete reading the book, he must read an additional 60 pages. How many pages are in the book?

(A) 720
(B) 360
(C) 144
(D) 120
(E) 72

GO ON TO THE NEXT PAGE.

USE THIS SPACE FOR FIGURING.

24. A square piece of paper has an area of 144 square inches. What is the circumference, in inches, of the largest circle that can be cut from the paper?
    (A) 12π
    (B) 24π
    (C) 36π
    (D) 72π
    (E) 144π

---

25. The number 120 is increased by 50%, and the result is then decreased by 30% to give the number x. What is the value of x ?
    (A) 174
    (B) 162
    (C) 144
    (D) 136
    (E) 126

STOP

IF YOU FINISH BEFORE TIME IS CALLED, YOU MAY CHECK YOUR WORK ON THIS SECTION ONLY. DO NOT TURN TO ANY OTHER SECTION IN THE TEST.

SECTION 2
40 Questions

Read each passage carefully and then answer the questions about it. For each question, decide on the basis of the passage which one of the choices best answers the question.

Matthew Cuthbert ought to have been sowing his turnip seed on the big red brook field away over by Green Gables. Mrs. Rachel knew that he ought because she had heard him tell Peter Morrison the evening before in William J. Blair's store over at Carmody that he meant to sow his turnip seed the next afternoon. Peter had asked him, of course, for Matthew Cuthbert had never been known to volunteer information about anything in his whole life. And yet here was Matthew Cuthbert, at half-past three on the afternoon of a busy day, placidly driving over the hollow and up the hill; moreover, he wore a white collar and his best suit of clothes, which was plain proof that he was going out of Avonlea; and he had the buggy and the sorrel mare, which betokened that he was going a considerable distance. Now, where was Matthew Cuthbert going and why was he going there? Had it been any other man in Avonlea, Mrs. Rachel, deftly putting this and that together, might have given a pretty good guess as to both questions. But Matthew so rarely went from home that it must be something pressing and unusual which was taking him; he was the shyest man alive and hated to have to go among strangers or to any place where he might have to talk. Matthew, dressed up with a white collar and driving in a buggy, was something that didn't happen often. Mrs. Rachel, ponder as she might, could make nothing of it, and her afternoon's enjoyment was spoiled.

1. Mrs. Rachel is portrayed in the passage as a
   (A) recluse
   (B) busybody
   (C) worrywart
   (D) matchmaker
   (E) rabble-rouser

2. As it is used in line 3, the word "meant" most nearly means
   (A) signified
   (B) destined
   (C) intended
   (D) implied
   (E) foretold

3. The author uses the expression "putting this and that together" (line 10) to describe a process of
   (A) combining resources
   (B) fabricating an excuse
   (C) building a consensus
   (D) formulating a conjecture
   (E) gathering suggestions

4. As he is depicted in the passage, Matthew Cuthbert has a reputation for being
   (A) gullible
   (B) conceited
   (C) ill-tempered
   (D) irresponsible
   (E) uncommunicative

5. The passage suggests that Mrs. Rachel's enjoyment of the afternoon "was spoiled" (line 15) because
   (A) she was unable to satisfy her curiosity
   (B) she had no one to work in her fields
   (C) she had no means of leaving Avonlea
   (D) she feared for her neighbor's safety
   (E) she was overcome with jealousy

GO ON TO THE NEXT PAGE.

In 1930 an astronomer at the Lowell Observatory made an exciting discovery. Telescopic photographs revealed a sizeable body, much larger than any known comet or asteroid, orbiting the Sun in the furthest reaches of the solar system. The newly discovered object was soon hailed as the ninth planet and given the name of Pluto.

However, toward the end of the twentieth century some astronomers began to raise doubts about Pluto's planetary status. Though substantial enough to have several moons of its own, Pluto was still much smaller than any other planet, and its eccentric orbit was tilted at a very different angle than those of its celestial siblings.

After carefully weighing the question of Pluto's planethood, the International Astronomical Union in 2006 ruled that in order to be classified as a planet, an object must meet three criteria. It must orbit the Sun; it must be nearly round in shape; and it must have cleared the neighborhood around its orbit. Pluto meets the first two criteria but not the third. Unlike the eight true planets, Pluto lacks the gravitational force to drive away the multitude of icy celestial objects that share its orbital zone. For that reason, the International Astronomical Union downgraded Pluto's status to that of a "dwarf planet."

6. The passage suggests that the general reaction to the discovery of Pluto was
   (A) fearful
   (B) hostile
   (C) enthusiastic
   (D) skeptical
   (E) puzzled

7. In line 6, the author uses the word "Though" to acknowledge that
   (A) Pluto had some claim to being considered a planet
   (B) there was strong popular support for Pluto's planetary status
   (C) the original classification of Pluto was made in haste
   (D) Astronomers were bitterly divided in their opinions about Pluto
   (E) Pluto did not fit the precise scientific definition of a planet

8. The author's use of metaphor in the last sentence of the second paragraph suggests that the solar system is like
   (A) an army
   (B) a family
   (C) a fleet
   (D) an atom
   (E) a machine

9. As it is used in line 10, the word "meet" most nearly means
   (A) gather
   (B) coincide
   (C) encounter
   (D) satisfy
   (E) confront

10. The words "For that reason" (line 14) refer to the fact that Pluto
   (A) is much smaller than any of the eight planets
   (B) has an eccentric and unusually tilted orbit
   (C) is located at the very edge of the solar system
   (D) allows other objects to occupy its neighborhood
   (E) is not sufficiently round in its shape

GO ON TO THE NEXT PAGE.

At 5 a.m. on an intensely hot summer day, President John Quincy Adams left the White House by stagecoach for Quincy, Massachusetts. It was July 9, 1826, just two days short of his fifty-ninth birthday. He had been up the night before "in anxiety and apprehension, until near midnight." The heat made him miserable. Candlelight attracted insects. There were no screens. The day before, he had gotten three letters from Quincy with the news that his ninety-one-year-old father, the second president of the United States, was on his deathbed. John Quincy had "flattered" himself that his father "would survive this summer, and even other years." A rider was on his way from Baltimore to tell him he was wrong.

11. As it is used in line 3, the word "up" most nearly means
    (A) aloft
    (B) prepared
    (C) successful
    (D) cheerful
    (E) awake

12. The author suggests that Adams' "anxiety" (line 3) was due to concern about
    (A) growing old
    (B) matters of state
    (C) the summer heat
    (D) a long stagecoach ride
    (E) his father's health

13. The author mentions that there were "no screens" (line 4) in order to emphasize that Adams was
    (A) living in poverty
    (B) exposed to the public
    (C) socially uninhibited
    (D) physically vulnerable
    (E) fully informed

14. The use of the word "flattered" (line 6) suggests that Adams was
    (A) exceedingly vain
    (B) engaged in wishful thinking
    (C) manipulative and insincere
    (D) generous in his praise of others
    (E) immensely popular

15. The final sentence of the passage implies that Adams would be told that
    (A) his father had passed away
    (B) it was unsafe to travel by stagecoach
    (C) the weather in Quincy was not as bad as he feared
    (D) he had misinterpreted the letters from Quincy
    (E) it was irresponsible of him to leave the White House

GO ON TO THE NEXT PAGE.

He rose at dawn, and, flushed with hope,
Shot o'er the seething harbour-bar,
And reached the ship, and caught the rope,
And whistled to the morning star.

And while on deck he whistled loud,
He heard a fierce mermaiden cry,
"Boy, though thou art young and proud,
I see the place where thou wilt lie.

The sands and yeasty surges mix
In caves about the dreary bay,
And on thy ribs the limpet sticks,
And on thy heart the scrawl shall play!"

"Fool!" he answered, "death is sure
To those that stay and those that roam;
But I will never more endure
To sit with empty hands at home.

My mother clings about my neck;
My sister clamours, 'Stay, for shame!'
My father raves of death and wreck, —
They are all to blame, they are all to blame.

God help me! save I take my part
Of danger on the roaring sea,
A devil rises in my heart,
Far worse than any death to me!"

16. The first stanza (lines 1-4) depicts a boy
    (A) recklessly destroying property
    (B) reluctantly performing a chore
    (C) eagerly beginning a new adventure
    (D) merrily cavorting with his friends
    (E) sadly leaving his family

17. The third stanza (lines 9-12) presents
    (A) a grim prophecy
    (B) a bitter accusation
    (C) a heartfelt prayer
    (D) an urgent request
    (E) a stern reprimand

18. In the fourth stanza (lines 13-16), the boy indicates that he
    (A) fears death
    (B) despises idleness
    (C) regrets his choice
    (D) desires fame and fortune
    (E) recognizes his foolishness

19. In the fifth stanza (lines 17-20), the boy's family are depicted as trying to
    (A) convince him that they are innocent
    (B) understand his point of view
    (C) discourage him from carrying out his plan
    (D) make amends for their misdeeds
    (E) reward him for his courage

20. In the final stanza (lines 21-24), the boy expresses the belief that
    (A) good always triumphs over evil
    (B) he will die if he does not go to sea
    (C) the dangers of the sea are greatly exaggerated
    (D) a life without hazard is not worth living
    (E) he will return safely from his journey

GO ON TO THE NEXT PAGE.

Passing through the woods in summer, we often find beautiful bits of a low form of plant growth called fungi, branching from the trees, covering old stumps, or poking their dainty heads up through the ground at our feet. How strikingly different are fungi from other plants! They have no leaves and none of that wonderful green coloring-matter, chlorophyll, which takes carbon from the air and hydrogen and oxygen from water and forms them into food for the plant, so making it an independent being. As the fungi lack this, they must get the food already made by some other plant or animal. That is the reason we find them attached to trees, logs, anything that will furnish them with the desired food.

21. As it is used in line 1, the word "Passing" most nearly means
    (A) transferring
    (B) extending
    (C) elapsing
    (D) undergoing
    (E) traveling

22. To describe how fungi appear "at our feet" (line 3), the author makes use of which literary device?
    (A) Onomatopoeia
    (B) Simile
    (C) Hyperbole
    (D) Personification
    (E) Alliteration

23. According to the passage, the lack of chlorophyll explains why fungi
    (A) have no leaves
    (B) grow where they do
    (C) are the color they are
    (D) are not classified as plants
    (E) are not eaten by forest animals

24. The author uses the word "independent" (line 6) to indicate that certain plants
    (A) are nutritionally self-sufficient
    (B) are unrelated to other species
    (C) are not considered part of the forest
    (D) grow freely without cultivation
    (E) thrive in isolation from other plants

25. The main purpose of the passage is to
    (A) illustrate the balance of nature
    (B) explain how plants synthesize food
    (C) distinguish fungi from other plants
    (D) identify which forest plants are edible
    (E) debunk a popular myth about fungus

GO ON TO THE NEXT PAGE.

The plan which I adopted, and the one by which I was most successful, was that of making friends of all the little white boys whom I met in the street. As many of these as I could, I converted into teachers. With their kindly aid, obtained at different times and in different places, I finally succeeded in learning to read. When I was sent on errands, I always took my book with me, and by going one part of my errand quickly, I found time to get a lesson before my return. I used also to carry bread with me, enough of which was always in the house, and to which I was always welcome; for I was much better off in this regard than many of the poor white children in our neighborhood. This bread I used to bestow upon the hungry little urchins, who, in return, would give me that more valuable bread of knowledge. I am strongly tempted to give the names of two or three of those little boys, as a testimonial of the gratitude and affection I bear them; but prudence forbids;—not that it would injure me, but it might embarrass them; for it is almost an unpardonable offence to teach slaves to read in this Christian country.

26. As revealed in the passage, the goal of the narrator's "plan" (line 1) was to
    - (A) exact revenge
    - (B) earn money
    - (C) attain freedom
    - (D) escape punishment
    - (E) acquire a skill

27. According to the passage, "the hungry little urchins" (line 8) were given bread in exchange for
    - (A) protection
    - (B) friendship
    - (C) instruction
    - (D) keeping quiet
    - (E) running errands

28. The narrator indicates that in regard to the "little boys" (lines 9-10) he felt
    - (A) envious
    - (B) superior
    - (C) guilty
    - (D) thankful
    - (E) ambivalent

29. In line 10, the narrator uses the word "not" in order to
    - (A) disprove a false allegation
    - (B) clarify a potentially misleading statement
    - (C) challenge a widely accepted assumption
    - (D) suggest an alternative hypothesis
    - (E) distinguish between two options

30. It can be inferred that at the time of the events described in the passage, the narrator was a
    - (A) slave
    - (B) fugitive
    - (C) schoolboy
    - (D) street urchin
    - (E) bread peddler

GO ON TO THE NEXT PAGE.

Never did a couple set forward on the flowery path of early and well-suited marriage with a fairer prospect of felicity. It was the misfortune of my friend, however, to have embarked his property in large speculations; and he had not been married many months, when, by a succession of sudden disasters, it was swept from him, and he found himself reduced almost to penury. For a time he kept his situation to himself, and went about with a haggard countenance, and a breaking heart. His life was but a protracted agony; and what rendered it more insupportable was the necessity of keeping up a smile in the presence of his wife; for he could not bring himself to overwhelm her with the news. She saw, however, with the quick eyes of affection, that all was not well with him. She marked his altered looks and stifled sighs, and was not to be deceived by his sickly and vapid attempts at cheerfulness. She tasked all her sprightly powers and tender blandishments to win him back to happiness; but she only drove the arrow deeper into his soul.

31. In line 2, "felicity" most likely refers to
   (A) worldly success
   (B) marital bliss
   (C) graceful speech
   (D) natural aptitude
   (E) good health

32. The author uses the word "speculations" (line 3) to describe
   (A) scientific theories
   (B) risky business ventures
   (C) jealous suspicions
   (D) unconfirmed rumors
   (E) philosophical reflections

33. Which of the following best describes the husband's "situation" (line 5) ?
   (A) He is being blackmailed.
   (B) His marriage is in jeopardy.
   (C) He is in trouble with the law.
   (D) He has a serious medical condition.
   (E) He is on the brink of financial ruin.

34. According to the passage, what made the husband's life "insupportable" (line 6) was the need to
   (A) curtail his lavish lifestyle
   (B) acknowledge his mistakes
   (C) maintain a false appearance
   (D) accept his wife's pity
   (E) ask friends for help

35. As it is used in line 9, the word "marked" most nearly means
   (A) noticed
   (B) graded
   (C) labeled
   (D) defaced
   (E) accentuated

GO ON TO THE NEXT PAGE.

But if you would see the purest, the sincerest, the most affecting piety of a parent's love, startle a young family of quails, and watch the conduct of the mother. She will not leave you. No, not she. But she will fall at your feet, uttering a noise which none but a distressed mother can make, and she will run, and flutter, and seem to try to be caught, and cheat your outstretched hand, and affect to be wing-broken and wounded, and yet have just strength to tumble along, until she has drawn you, fatigued, a safe distance from her threatened children and the young hopes of her heart; and then will she mount, whirring with glad strength, and away through the maze of trees you have not seen before, like a close-shot bullet, fly to her skulking infants.

36. The author uses the phrase "No, not she" (lines 2-3) to indicate that the mother quail
    (A) is too proud to move aside
    (B) shows no sign of distress
    (C) does not behave as expected
    (D) is unaware of any danger
    (E) neglects her maternal duties

37. The author uses the word "cheat" (line 4) to describe how the mother quail
    (A) feigns injury
    (B) eludes capture
    (C) flies through a maze
    (D) wearies her pursuer
    (E) disguises her voice

38. As it is used in line 6, the word "drawn" most nearly means
    (A) led
    (B) pulled
    (C) selected
    (D) stretched
    (E) portrayed

39. The simile in line 8 serves primarily to emphasize the mother quail's
    (A) ingenuity
    (B) speed
    (C) anguish
    (D) fear
    (E) elegance

40. The author describes the mother quail in a tone of
    (A) frustration
    (B) resentment
    (C) disbelief
    (D) admiration
    (E) triumph

STOP

IF YOU FINISH BEFORE TIME IS CALLED, YOU MAY CHECK YOUR WORK ON THIS SECTION ONLY. DO NOT TURN TO ANY OTHER SECTION IN THE TEST.

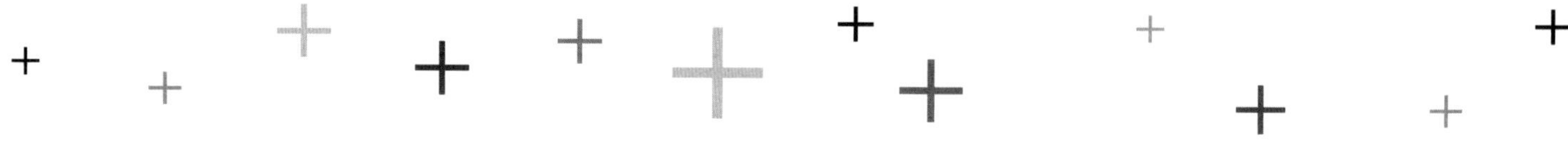

SECTION 3
60 Questions

This section consists of two different types of questions: synonyms and analogies. There are directions and a sample question for each type.

Synonyms
Each of the following questions consists of one word followed by five words or phrases. You are to select the one word or phrase whose meaning is closest to the word in capital letters.

Sample Question:

CHILLY:

(A) lazy
(B) nice
(C) dry
(D) cold
(E) sunny

Ⓐ Ⓑ Ⓒ ● Ⓔ

---

1. TRADE:
   (A) tax
   (B) rush
   (C) advise
   (D) flatten
   (E) exchange

2. CALM:
   (A) hide
   (B) soothe
   (C) drain
   (D) thicken
   (E) borrow

3. DONATE:
   (A) give
   (B) divide
   (C) confine
   (D) govern
   (E) copy

4. PRICELESS:
   (A) accurate
   (B) reckless
   (C) doubtful
   (D) invaluable
   (E) legal

5. SCARCE:
   (A) rare
   (B) evil
   (C) sudden
   (D) alarming
   (E) abandoned

6. THOROUGH:
   (A) actual
   (B) useful
   (C) careful
   (D) possible
   (E) novel

7. SYMPATHETIC:
   (A) compassionate
   (B) incompetent
   (C) straightforward
   (D) gullible
   (E) indifferent

8. AMBIANCE:
   (A) carousel
   (B) atmosphere
   (C) temperament
   (D) precaution
   (E) doubt

GO ON TO THE NEXT PAGE.

9. MEMENTO:
   (A) script
   (B) badge
   (C) speed
   (D) receipt
   (E) souvenir

10. HOAX:
   (A) maze
   (B) dream
   (C) riddle
   (D) prank
   (E) error

11. COLOSSAL:
   (A) sweet
   (B) smooth
   (C) huge
   (D) fierce
   (E) costly

12. AUTHENTIC:
   (A) written
   (B) ordinary
   (C) expert
   (D) real
   (E) ancient

13. CALAMITY:
   (A) rejection
   (B) slander
   (C) disaster
   (D) restriction
   (E) penalty

14. EMBELLISH:
   (A) adorn
   (B) boast
   (C) attack
   (D) obstruct
   (E) display

15. CONTRADICT:
   (A) destroy
   (B) exchange
   (C) reveal
   (D) impede
   (E) deny

16. EXPUNGE:
   (A) steal
   (B) uncover
   (C) erase
   (D) repel
   (E) release

17. ADHERE:
   (A) leave
   (B) climb
   (C) force
   (D) stick
   (E) hope

18. GLITCH:
   (A) error
   (B) denial
   (C) ejection
   (D) noise
   (E) lie

19. MEDLEY:
   (A) song
   (B) cure
   (C) average
   (D) mixture
   (E) reason

20. FAINT:
   (A) weak
   (B) harsh
   (C) false
   (D) blatant
   (E) insensitive

GO ON TO THE NEXT PAGE.

21. PROBABLE:
(A) visible
(B) restrictive
(C) accidental
(D) likely
(E) curious

22. ORATION:
(A) speech
(B) gesture
(C) applause
(D) request
(E) attitude

23. DWINDLE:
(A) delay
(B) rotate
(C) shrink
(D) steal
(E) fail

24. TRAILBLAZER:
(A) bodyguard
(B) pioneer
(C) scoundrel
(D) tycoon
(E) courier

25. ABSTAIN:
(A) taunt
(B) bother
(C) tarnish
(D) refrain
(E) wonder

26. FISSURE:
(A) disorder
(B) eruption
(C) entrance
(D) branch
(E) crack

27. RETORT:
(A) sharp answer
(B) naive question
(C) deafening shout
(D) arrogant demand
(E) convincing argument

28. ELATION:
(A) convenience
(B) appearance
(C) exclusion
(D) accuracy
(E) delight

29. CANDID:
(A) popular
(B) shallow
(C) frank
(D) literate
(E) ambitious

30. ANIMOSITY:
(A) monster
(B) hostility
(C) revenge
(D) keepsake
(E) excitement

GO ON TO THE NEXT PAGE.

Analogies

The following questions ask you to find relationships between words. For each question, select the answer choice that best completes the meaning of the sentence.

Sample Question:

Kitten is to cat as
(A) fawn is to colt
(B) puppy is to dog
(C) cow is to bull
(D) wolf is to bear
(E) hen is to rooster

Ⓐ ● Ⓒ Ⓓ Ⓔ

Choice (B) is the best answer because a kitten is a young cat just as a puppy is a young dog. Of all the answer choices, (B) states a relationship that is most like the relationship between kitten and cat.

---

31. Polish is to shiny as
    (A) caress is to soft
    (B) hone is to sharp
    (C) swelter is to hot
    (D) wash is to dirty
    (E) hoist is to heavy

32. Battery is to electricity as
    (A) oven is to temperature
    (B) closet is to door
    (C) bank is to money
    (D) kettle is to steam
    (E) orange is to juice

33. Composer is to score as
    (A) architect is to blueprint
    (B) customer is to receipt
    (C) traveler is to map
    (D) banker is to money
    (E) pilot is to aircraft

34. Seed is to sprout as
    (A) ball is to throw
    (B) garden is to tend
    (C) egg is to hatch
    (D) infant is to talk
    (E) rain is to trickle

35. Swarm is to bee as
    (A) ape is to monkey
    (B) herd is to buffalo
    (C) river is to fish
    (D) kennel is to dog
    (E) cocoon is to moth

36. Greedy is to wealth as
    (A) tranquil is to peace
    (B) concise is to brevity
    (C) irate is to malice
    (D) steadfast is to loyalty
    (E) vindictive is to revenge

37. Landscape is to painting as
    (A) wall is to mural
    (B) style is to clothing
    (C) tongue is to speech
    (D) car is to vehicle
    (E) blade is to grass

38. Toss is to throw as
    (A) stroll is to walk
    (B) gasp is to breathe
    (C) seek is to find
    (D) drop is to lift
    (E) dine is to eat

GO ON TO THE NEXT PAGE.

39. Glare is to light as
(A) mud is to dirt
(B) racket is to sound
(C) dike is to flood
(D) dream is to sleep
(E) sprint is to speed

40. Duck is to bird as
(A) iron is to metal
(B) daisy is to rose
(C) lake is to ocean
(D) peak is to mountain
(E) tree is to grove

41. Trivial is to importance as
(A) brazen is to courage
(B) stealthy is to thief
(C) genial is to enemy
(D) bland is to flavor
(E) jealous is to love

42. Praise is to condemn as
(A) endeavor is to fail
(B) observe is to notice
(C) increase is to diminish
(D) coax is to persuade
(E) immerse is to float

43. Comb is to hair as
(A) fork is to meat
(B) file is to nail
(C) glove is to hand
(D) glass is to water
(E) rake is to grass

44. Blanket is to warmth as
(A) bandage is to wound
(B) pillow is to head
(C) sail is to wind
(D) curtain is to privacy
(E) garment is to fashion

45. Incentive is to motivate as
(A) threat is to intimidate
(B) prohibition is to punish
(C) reminder is to remember
(D) feedback is to provide
(E) challenge is to accept

46. Employee is to hire as
(A) politician is to elect
(B) scholar is to study
(C) pedestrian is to walk
(D) athlete is to win
(E) benefactor is to donate

47. Eat is to devour as
(A) speak is to whisper
(B) lend is to borrow
(C) search is to find
(D) launch is to fly
(E) take is to seize

48. Hangar is to airplane as
(A) signal is to train
(B) runway is to landing
(C) ocean is to steamship
(D) turnpike is to hitchhiker
(E) garage is to automobile

49. Cold is to frigid as
(A) doubtful is to decisive
(B) tardy is to chronic
(C) rigid is to flexible
(D) happy is to ecstatic
(E) long is to distant

50. Cast is to actor as
(A) team is to player
(B) battle is to soldier
(C) party is to host
(D) movie is to director
(E) flock is to shepherd

GO ON TO THE NEXT PAGE.

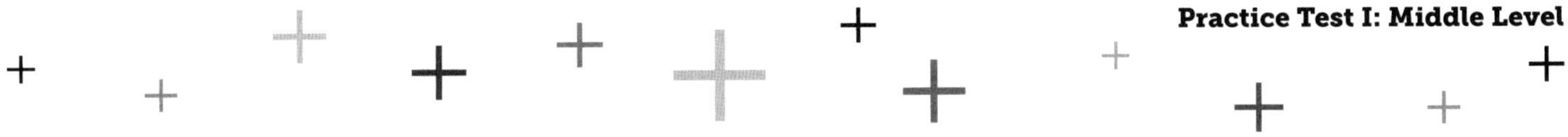

51. Hermit is to solitude as
    (A) hostage is to ransom
    (B) braggart is to modesty
    (C) prisoner is to punishment
    (D) refugee is to protection
    (E) scapegoat is to blame

52. Enticement is to lure as
    (A) debt is to borrow
    (B) approval is to condemn
    (C) obstacle is to block
    (D) bargain is to buy
    (E) clue is to investigate

53. Shovel is to dirt as
    (A) pen is to ink
    (B) spoon is to food
    (C) drill is to hole
    (D) wrench is to bolt
    (E) needle is to stitch

54. Generous is to stingy as
    (A) modest is to shy
    (B) large is to huge
    (C) ornate is to plain
    (D) plenty is to enough
    (E) patient is to late

55. Hurdle is to overcome as
    (A) victory is to celebrate
    (B) detour is to travel
    (C) penance is to atone
    (D) danger is to rescue
    (E) problem is to solve

56. Accidental is to chance as
    (A) incompetent is to skill
    (B) prosperous is to wealth
    (C) disastrous is to recovery
    (D) inevitable is to necessity
    (E) random is to prediction

57. Palace is to residence as
    (A) crown is to headpiece
    (B) trophy is to victory
    (C) ship is to fleet
    (D) temple is to religion
    (E) queen is to realm

58. Blood is to artery as
    (A) spout is to gutter
    (B) air is to balloon
    (C) water is to river
    (D) song is to voice
    (E) current is to wire

59. Compete is to rivalry as
    (A) dabble is to amateur
    (B) converse is to dialogue
    (C) condemn is to penalty
    (D) recover is to disaster
    (E) appease is to anger

60. Splinter is to wood as
    (A) grain is to rice
    (B) slate is to stone
    (C) pearl is to oyster
    (D) shard is to glass
    (E) lump is to sugar

STOP

IF YOU FINISH BEFORE TIME IS CALLED, YOU MAY CHECK YOUR WORK ON THIS SECTION ONLY. DO NOT TURN TO ANY OTHER SECTION IN THE TEST.

THIS PAGE INTENTIONALLY LEFT BLANK.

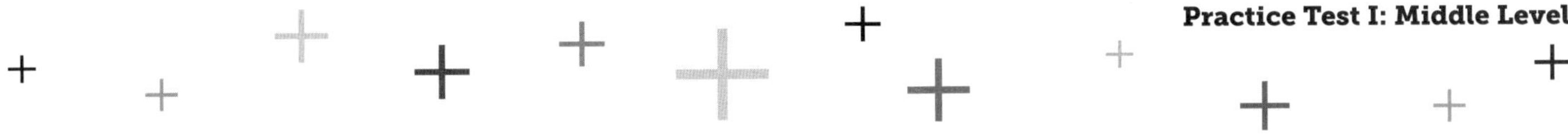

SECTION 4
25 Questions

Following each problem in this section, there are five suggested answers. Work each problem in your head or in the blank space provided at the right of the page. Then look at the five suggested answers and decide which one is best.

Note: Figures that accompany problems in this section are drawn as accurately as possible EXCEPT when it is stated in a specific problem that its figure is not drawn to scale.

Sample Problem:

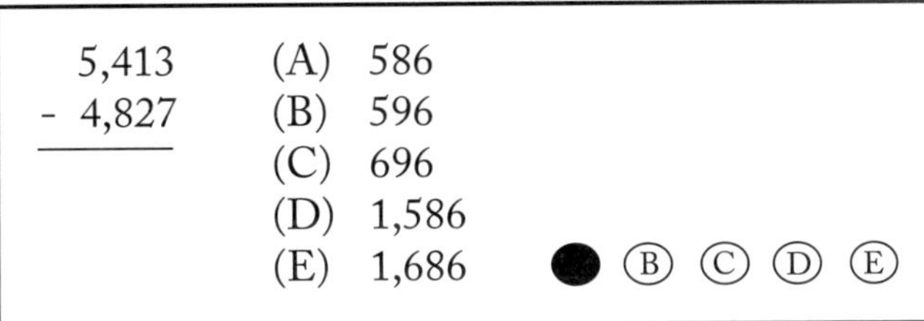

USE THIS SPACE FOR FIGURING.

1. If $x = 5$ and $y = 10$, what is the value of $2xy$?
   (A) 17
   (B) 30
   (C) 50
   (D) 60
   (E) 100

2. If 2 dozen toys are divided equally among 8 children, how many toys will each child receive? (1 dozen = 12)
   (A) 2
   (B) 3
   (C) 4
   (D) 5
   (E) 6

3. What is $\frac{3}{6} - \frac{1}{4}$?
   (A) $\frac{1}{12}$
   (B) $\frac{1}{6}$
   (C) $\frac{1}{4}$
   (D) $\frac{1}{2}$
   (E) 1

GO ON TO THE NEXT PAGE.

  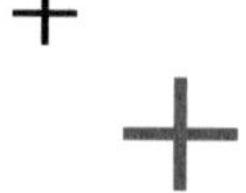 

USE THIS SPACE FOR FIGURING.

4. Javier lives 10.33 miles from school. His classmate, Gabriella, lives 6.8 miles from school. How much farther from school, in miles, does Javier live than Gabriella?

(A) 3.53
(B) 4.53
(C) 5.77
(D) 9.65
(E) 17.13

$$\frac{1}{3}, \frac{2}{4}, \frac{3}{5}, \frac{4}{6}, \frac{5}{7}, \ldots, \frac{10}{\square}$$

5. In the sequence above, $\frac{1}{3}$ is the first term. For each term after the first, the numerator and the denominator are each 1 more than the numerator and denominator in the preceding term. What is the value of $\square$?

(A) 12
(B) 13
(C) 14
(D) 18
(E) 30

---

6. In the map shown, Paul is located at the intersection of Broad Street and Main Street, and the side of each square represents one city block. Paul travels 2 city blocks east and 3 city blocks north. Which of the following points is his new location?

(A) *A*
(B) *B*
(C) *C*
(D) *D*
(E) *E*

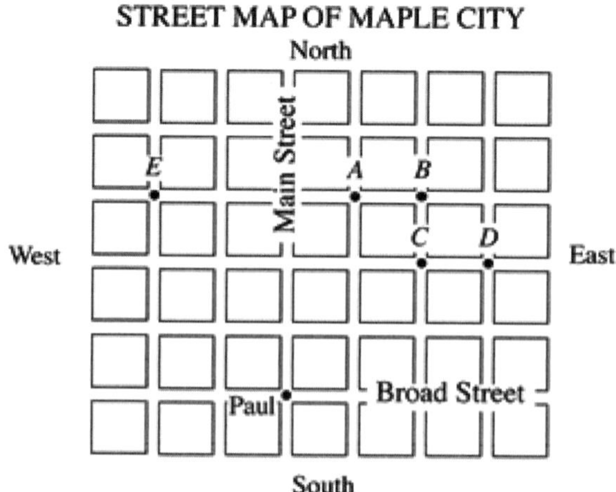

GO ON TO THE NEXT PAGE.

USE THIS SPACE FOR FIGURING.

7. If m is 4 more than k, then k must be

   (A) $\frac{1}{4}$ of m
   (B) 4 minus m
   (C) 4 times m
   (D) 4 less than m
   (E) 4 more than m

---

8. Janeene has a cellphone. She pays $50 per month for her plan, plus $2 for each call she makes that is outside of her area. Her total monthly bill in September was $70. How many calls did Janeene make outside of her area in September?

   (A) 40
   (B) 22
   (C) 20
   (D) 18
   (E) 10

---

9. What is 16% of 75 ?

   (A) 16
   (B) 12
   (C) 9
   (D) 8
   (E) 4

---

10. A certain machine can process 6,000 letters in 1 hour. At this rate, how many letters can the machine process in $\frac{1}{12}$ hour?

   (A) 5,000
   (B) 4,800
   (C) 720
   (D) 500
   (E) 480

---

11. Of the following, which is closest to the value of $\frac{998 \times 1{,}004}{48 \times 52}$?

   (A) 40
   (B) 200
   (C) 400
   (D) 2,000
   (E) 4,000

GO ON TO THE NEXT PAGE.

USE THIS SPACE FOR FIGURING.

12. The top view of a rectangular package of 6 tightly packed balls is shown. If each ball has a radius of 2 centimeters, which of the following are closest to the dimensions, in centimeters, of the rectangular package?

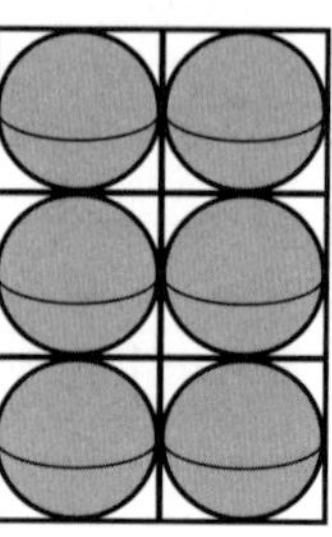

(A) $2 \times 3 \times 6$
(B) $4 \times 6 \times 6$
(C) $2 \times 4 \times 6$
(D) $4 \times 8 \times 12$
(E) $6 \times 8 \times 12$

---

13. Which of the following lists contains only prime numbers?
(A) 0, 1, 2, 3, 5
(B) 1, 2, 3, 4, 5
(C) 2, 3, 5, 7, 11
(D) 3, 7, 11, 13, 15
(E) 5, 9, 13 17, 23

---

14. Ann swims 6 laps every 5 minutes. At that rate, how many laps does she swim in one <u>hour</u>?
(A) 72
(B) 60
(C) 50
(D) 36
(E) 30

30, −15, 10, 35, −15, −30, 20

15. What is the median of the list above?
(A) −15
(B) 5
(C) 10
(D) 20
(E) 35

GO ON TO THE NEXT PAGE.

USE THIS SPACE FOR FIGURING.

16. In the figure, $ABEF$ is a rectangle, and $ABCD$ is a square. If $CE = 3$, and $EF = 5$, what is the area of rectangle $ABEF$?

(A) 15
(B) 24
(C) 26
(D) 31
(E) 40

B C E

A D F

---

17. The cost of using a parcel service is r dollars for the first 3 pounds and s dollars for each additional pound. Which of the following expressions represents the cost, in dollars, of sending a parcel that weighs 9 pounds?

(A) $r + 3s$
(B) $r + 6s$
(C) $3r + 6s$
(D) $3r + 9s$
(E) $9r + 9s$

---

18. Which of the following fractions has the least value?

(A) $\frac{3}{4}$

(B) $\frac{6}{11}$

(C) $\frac{7}{15}$

(D) $\frac{7}{16}$

(E) $\frac{9}{16}$

GO ON TO THE NEXT PAGE.

USE THIS SPACE FOR FIGURING.

19. The circle graph shows each part of a typical day that Marco spends on different activities. Based on the graph, how many hours does he spend per day on family time and on homework combined?

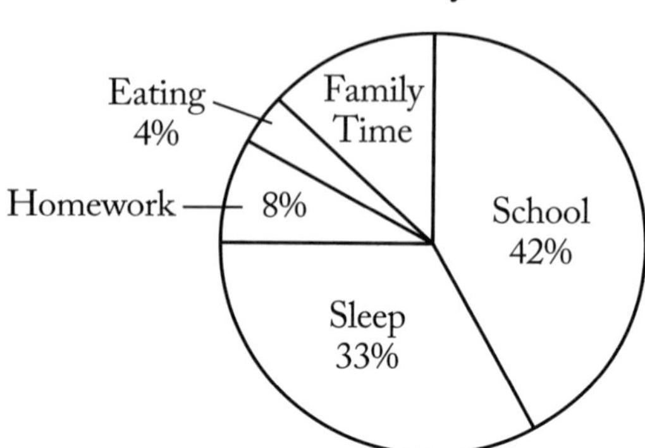

(A) 1.92
(B) 2.88
(C) 4.08
(D) 5.04
(E) 6.00

---

20. If $3 + 7 \times n = 6$, what is the value of n ?

(A) -4

(B) $\frac{3}{7}$

(C) $\frac{3}{5}$

(D) $\frac{9}{7}$

(E) 2

---

21. Which of the following is equivalent to $\frac{6}{12} \div 0.2$?

(A) 0.1
(B) 0.4
(C) 2.5
(D) 10
(E) 25

---

22. Sophie is making bows for packages and uses 1.25 meters of ribbon per bow. If she has 12 meters of ribbon and makes as many complete bows as possible, how much ribbon, in meters, will remain?

(A) 0.60
(B) 0.75
(C) 0.85
(D) 1.75
(E) 1.85

GO ON TO THE NEXT PAGE.

USE THIS SPACE FOR FIGURING.

23. In the figure shown, line t is parallel to line v, and lines r and s intersect lines t and v. What is the value of x ?

(A) 150
(B) 135
(C) 120
(D) 105
(E) 95

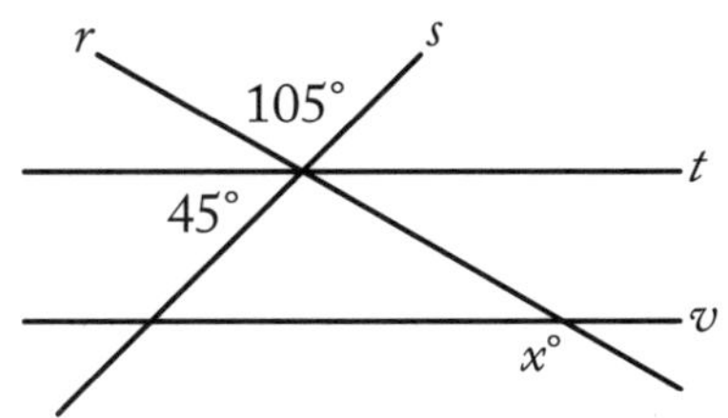

---

24. What is the value of $\frac{2}{3} \times \frac{1}{8} \div \frac{3}{4}$?

(A) $\frac{1}{18}$

(B) $\frac{1}{16}$

(C) $\frac{1}{12}$

(D) $\frac{1}{9}$

(E) $\frac{1}{6}$

---

25. If $40 < n^2 < 50$, of the following, which is a possible value of $2n$?

(A) 11
(B) 14
(C) 21
(D) 24
(E) 44

STOP

IF YOU FINISH BEFORE TIME IS CALLED, YOU MAY CHECK YOUR WORK ON THIS SECTION ONLY. DO NOT TURN TO ANY OTHER SECTION IN THE TEST.

THIS PAGE INTENTIONALLY LEFT BLANK.

Practice Test II: Middle Level Answer Sheet

Be sure each mark completely fills the answer space.
Start with number 1 for each new section of the test.

Section 1

1 ⒶⒷⒸⒹⒺ	6 ⒶⒷⒸⒹⒺ	11 ⒶⒷⒸⒹⒺ	16 ⒶⒷⒸⒹⒺ	21 ⒶⒷⒸⒹⒺ
2 ⒶⒷⒸⒹⒺ	7 ⒶⒷⒸⒹⒺ	12 ⒶⒷⒸⒹⒺ	17 ⒶⒷⒸⒹⒺ	22 ⒶⒷⒸⒹⒺ
3 ⒶⒷⒸⒹⒺ	8 ⒶⒷⒸⒹⒺ	13 ⒶⒷⒸⒹⒺ	18 ⒶⒷⒸⒹⒺ	23 ⒶⒷⒸⒹⒺ
4 ⒶⒷⒸⒹⒺ	9 ⒶⒷⒸⒹⒺ	14 ⒶⒷⒸⒹⒺ	19 ⒶⒷⒸⒹⒺ	24 ⒶⒷⒸⒹⒺ
5 ⒶⒷⒸⒹⒺ	10 ⒶⒷⒸⒹⒺ	15 ⒶⒷⒸⒹⒺ	20 ⒶⒷⒸⒹⒺ	25 ⒶⒷⒸⒹⒺ

Section 2

1 ⒶⒷⒸⒹⒺ	9 ⒶⒷⒸⒹⒺ	17 ⒶⒷⒸⒹⒺ	25 ⒶⒷⒸⒹⒺ	33 ⒶⒷⒸⒹⒺ
2 ⒶⒷⒸⒹⒺ	10 ⒶⒷⒸⒹⒺ	18 ⒶⒷⒸⒹⒺ	26 ⒶⒷⒸⒹⒺ	34 ⒶⒷⒸⒹⒺ
3 ⒶⒷⒸⒹⒺ	11 ⒶⒷⒸⒹⒺ	19 ⒶⒷⒸⒹⒺ	27 ⒶⒷⒸⒹⒺ	35 ⒶⒷⒸⒹⒺ
4 ⒶⒷⒸⒹⒺ	12 ⒶⒷⒸⒹⒺ	20 ⒶⒷⒸⒹⒺ	28 ⒶⒷⒸⒹⒺ	36 ⒶⒷⒸⒹⒺ
5 ⒶⒷⒸⒹⒺ	13 ⒶⒷⒸⒹⒺ	21 ⒶⒷⒸⒹⒺ	29 ⒶⒷⒸⒹⒺ	37 ⒶⒷⒸⒹⒺ
6 ⒶⒷⒸⒹⒺ	14 ⒶⒷⒸⒹⒺ	22 ⒶⒷⒸⒹⒺ	30 ⒶⒷⒸⒹⒺ	38 ⒶⒷⒸⒹⒺ
7 ⒶⒷⒸⒹⒺ	15 ⒶⒷⒸⒹⒺ	23 ⒶⒷⒸⒹⒺ	31 ⒶⒷⒸⒹⒺ	39 ⒶⒷⒸⒹⒺ
8 ⒶⒷⒸⒹⒺ	16 ⒶⒷⒸⒹⒺ	24 ⒶⒷⒸⒹⒺ	32 ⒶⒷⒸⒹⒺ	40 ⒶⒷⒸⒹⒺ

Section 3

1 ⒶⒷⒸⒹⒺ	13 ⒶⒷⒸⒹⒺ	25 ⒶⒷⒸⒹⒺ	37 ⒶⒷⒸⒹⒺ	49 ⒶⒷⒸⒹⒺ
2 ⒶⒷⒸⒹⒺ	14 ⒶⒷⒸⒹⒺ	26 ⒶⒷⒸⒹⒺ	38 ⒶⒷⒸⒹⒺ	50 ⒶⒷⒸⒹⒺ
3 ⒶⒷⒸⒹⒺ	15 ⒶⒷⒸⒹⒺ	27 ⒶⒷⒸⒹⒺ	39 ⒶⒷⒸⒹⒺ	51 ⒶⒷⒸⒹⒺ
4 ⒶⒷⒸⒹⒺ	16 ⒶⒷⒸⒹⒺ	28 ⒶⒷⒸⒹⒺ	40 ⒶⒷⒸⒹⒺ	52 ⒶⒷⒸⒹⒺ
5 ⒶⒷⒸⒹⒺ	17 ⒶⒷⒸⒹⒺ	29 ⒶⒷⒸⒹⒺ	41 ⒶⒷⒸⒹⒺ	53 ⒶⒷⒸⒹⒺ
6 ⒶⒷⒸⒹⒺ	18 ⒶⒷⒸⒹⒺ	30 ⒶⒷⒸⒹⒺ	42 ⒶⒷⒸⒹⒺ	54 ⒶⒷⒸⒹⒺ
7 ⒶⒷⒸⒹⒺ	19 ⒶⒷⒸⒹⒺ	31 ⒶⒷⒸⒹⒺ	43 ⒶⒷⒸⒹⒺ	55 ⒶⒷⒸⒹⒺ
8 ⒶⒷⒸⒹⒺ	20 ⒶⒷⒸⒹⒺ	32 ⒶⒷⒸⒹⒺ	44 ⒶⒷⒸⒹⒺ	56 ⒶⒷⒸⒹⒺ
9 ⒶⒷⒸⒹⒺ	21 ⒶⒷⒸⒹⒺ	33 ⒶⒷⒸⒹⒺ	45 ⒶⒷⒸⒹⒺ	57 ⒶⒷⒸⒹⒺ
10 ⒶⒷⒸⒹⒺ	22 ⒶⒷⒸⒹⒺ	34 ⒶⒷⒸⒹⒺ	46 ⒶⒷⒸⒹⒺ	58 ⒶⒷⒸⒹⒺ
11 ⒶⒷⒸⒹⒺ	23 ⒶⒷⒸⒹⒺ	35 ⒶⒷⒸⒹⒺ	47 ⒶⒷⒸⒹⒺ	59 ⒶⒷⒸⒹⒺ
12 ⒶⒷⒸⒹⒺ	24 ⒶⒷⒸⒹⒺ	36 ⒶⒷⒸⒹⒺ	48 ⒶⒷⒸⒹⒺ	60 ⒶⒷⒸⒹⒺ

Section 4

1 ⒶⒷⒸⒹⒺ	6 ⒶⒷⒸⒹⒺ	11 ⒶⒷⒸⒹⒺ	16 ⒶⒷⒸⒹⒺ	21 ⒶⒷⒸⒹⒺ
2 ⒶⒷⒸⒹⒺ	7 ⒶⒷⒸⒹⒺ	12 ⒶⒷⒸⒹⒺ	17 ⒶⒷⒸⒹⒺ	22 ⒶⒷⒸⒹⒺ
3 ⒶⒷⒸⒹⒺ	8 ⒶⒷⒸⒹⒺ	13 ⒶⒷⒸⒹⒺ	18 ⒶⒷⒸⒹⒺ	23 ⒶⒷⒸⒹⒺ
4 ⒶⒷⒸⒹⒺ	9 ⒶⒷⒸⒹⒺ	14 ⒶⒷⒸⒹⒺ	19 ⒶⒷⒸⒹⒺ	24 ⒶⒷⒸⒹⒺ
5 ⒶⒷⒸⒹⒺ	10 ⒶⒷⒸⒹⒺ	15 ⒶⒷⒸⒹⒺ	20 ⒶⒷⒸⒹⒺ	25 ⒶⒷⒸⒹⒺ

Section 5

1 ⒶⒷⒸⒹⒺ	5 ⒶⒷⒸⒹⒺ	9 ⒶⒷⒸⒹⒺ	13 ⒶⒷⒸⒹⒺ
2 ⒶⒷⒸⒹⒺ	6 ⒶⒷⒸⒹⒺ	10 ⒶⒷⒸⒹⒺ	14 ⒶⒷⒸⒹⒺ
3 ⒶⒷⒸ			
4 ⒶⒷⒸⒹⒺ	8 ⒶⒷⒸⒹⒺ	12 ⒶⒷⒸⒹⒺ	16 ⒶⒷⒸⒹⒺ

Experimental Section – See page 9 for details.

THIS PAGE INTENTIONALLY LEFT BLANK.

Writing Sample

Schools would like to get to know you better through a story you tell or an essay you write. If you choose to write a story, use the sentence presented in A to begin. Make sure that your story has a beginning, middle, and end. If you choose to write a personal essay, base your essay on the topic presented in B. Please fill in the circle next to your choice.

Ⓐ "Wow! That was amazing!" I said.

Ⓑ Describe one of your friends. What makes your relationship work?

Use this page and the next page to complete your writing sample.

Continue on next page

SECTION 1
25 Questions

Following each problem in this section, there are five suggested answers. Work each problem in your head or in the blank space provided at the right of the page. Then look at the five suggested answers and decide which one is best.

Note: Figures that accompany problems in this section are drawn as accurately as possible EXCEPT when it is stated in a specific problem that its figure is not drawn to scale.

Sample Problem:

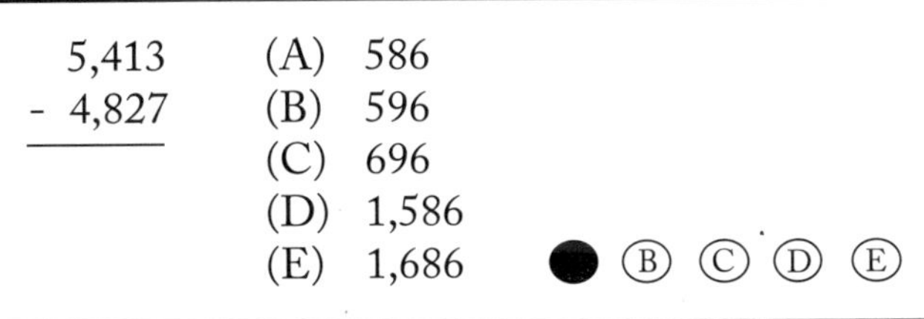

5,413
\- 4,827

(A) 586
(B) 596
(C) 696
(D) 1,586
(E) 1,686

● Ⓑ Ⓒ Ⓓ Ⓔ

USE THIS SPACE FOR FIGURING.

1. Calculate: 1.001 + 2.1 + 0.05

    (A) 1.027
    (B) 1.27
    (C) 3.151
    (D) 3.16
    (E) 3.60

2. One notepad costs \$0.79. Of the following, which is closest to the price of 3 of these notepads?

    (A) \$2.70
    (B) \$2.40
    (C) \$2.10
    (D) \$1.80
    (E) \$1.60

GO ON TO THE NEXT PAGE.

USE THIS SPACE FOR FIGURING.

3. In which of the following figures will a triangle be formed if points T and S are joined by a straight line?

(A) 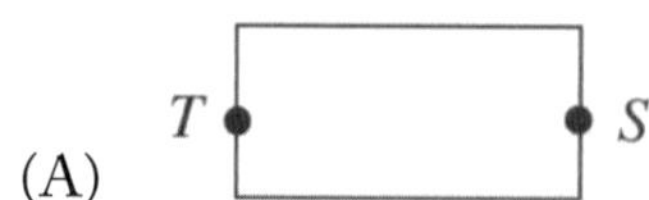

(B) 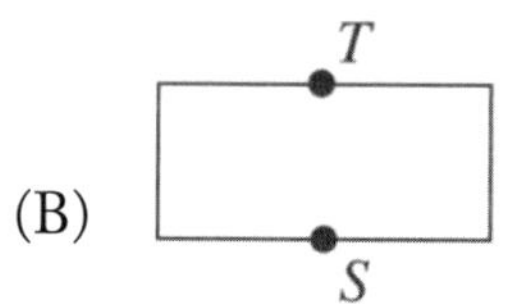

(C) 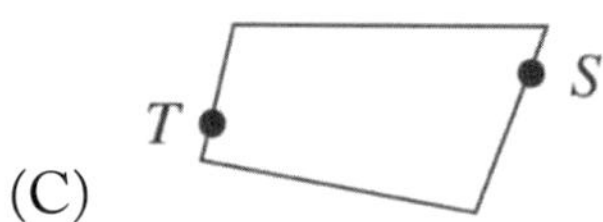

(D) 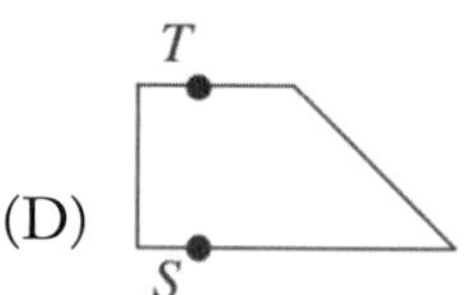

(E) 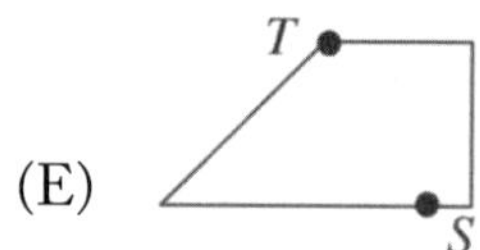

---

4. At a zoo, a baby rhinoceros weighs 120 pounds. A baby elephant weighs 80 pounds more than the baby rhinoceros. How much does the baby elephant weigh?

(A) 200 pounds
(B) 160 pounds
(C) 120 pounds
(D) 80 pounds
(E) 40 pounds

---

5. If $17 + 17 + 17 + 17 + 17 = 5 \times n$, what is the value of n ?

(A) 5
(B) 17
(C) 57
(D) 75
(E) 85

GO ON TO THE NEXT PAGE.

USE THIS SPACE FOR FIGURING.

6. Each team in a soccer league plays 16 games during the season. A certain team has won 8 games and lost 3 games. To date, what is the greatest number of games the team can lose during the remainder of the season and still win more than $\frac{1}{2}$ of the games in the season?
   (A) 1
   (B) 2
   (C) 3
   (D) 4
   (E) 5

---

7. If $x - \frac{1}{10} = \frac{2}{5}$, what is the value of x ?
   (A) $\frac{3}{5}$
   (B) $\frac{1}{2}$
   (C) $\frac{3}{10}$
   (D) $\frac{1}{5}$
   (E) $\frac{1}{10}$

---

8. Hilda polled 13 classmates on the number of hours of television watched in one week. Each response was recorded as a point in the dot plot. Which of the following is the median number of hours of television watched?
   (A) 16
   (B) 18
   (C) 20
   (D) 22
   (E) 24

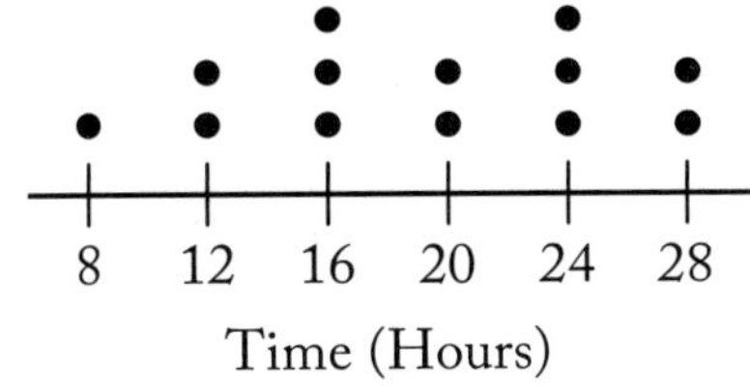

GO ON TO THE NEXT PAGE.

USE THIS SPACE FOR FIGURING.

9. What is $3 - \frac{1}{2} + \frac{7}{3}$?

    (A) $\frac{1}{6}$

    (B) $\frac{9}{5}$

    (C) $\frac{10}{3}$

    (D) $\frac{21}{5}$

    (E) $\frac{29}{6}$

Yellow, Red, Blue, Green, White

10. Mr. Valdez has shirts in each of the colors listed above. Each day he will select a shirt color by repeating the colors above in the order shown. If he wears a yellow shirt on the first day of the month, what will be the color of the shirt he will wear on the 30th day of the month?

    (A) Blue
    (B) Green
    (C) Red
    (D) White
    (E) Yellow

---

11. The figure shown contains three squares. The areas of the squares are 4, 9, and 16. What is the area of the figure?

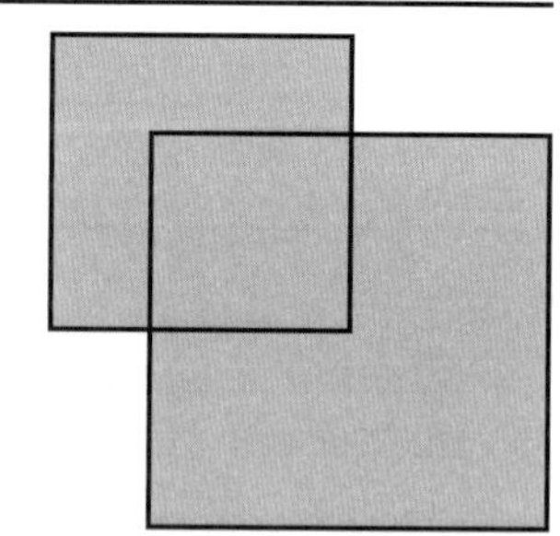

    (A) 11
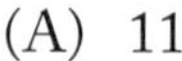
    (B) 17
    (C) 21
    (D) 25
    (E) 29

---

12. During a 3-mile walk, Rose walked the first mile in 10 minutes. If she continued to walk at the same rate, how long, in hours, did it take her to walk 3 miles?

    (A) $\frac{3}{4}$

    (B) $\frac{1}{2}$

    (C) $\frac{1}{3}$

    (D) $\frac{1}{4}$

    (E) $\frac{1}{6}$

GO ON TO THE NEXT PAGE.

USE THIS SPACE FOR FIGURING.

13. If 10% of a number is 40, what is 20% of the number?
   (A) 80
   (B) 50
   (C) 20
   (D) 12
   (E) 8

---

14. If each of the dimensions of a rectangular prism is doubled, how will the volume of the prism be affected?
   (A) It will be 2 times the original volume.
   (B) It will be 4 times the original volume.
   (C) It will be 6 times the original volume.
   (D) It will be 8 times the original volume.
   (E) It will be 9 times the original volume.

---

15. The □ in the number □.3 represents a digit from 0 through 9. Which of the following fractions is equivalent to □.3 ?
   (A) $\frac{\square + 3}{10}$
   (B) $\frac{\square + 3}{100}$
   (C) $\frac{10 \times (\square + 3)}{10}$
   (D) $\frac{(10 \times \square) + 3}{10}$
   (E) $\frac{(100 \times \square) + 3}{100}$

---

16. Which of the following lists will contain equal numbers when each number in the list is rounded to the nearest tenth?
   (A) 4.36, 4.41, 4.46, 4.409
   (B) 5.09, 5.14, 5.149, 5.17
   (C) 6.17, 6.08, 6.09, 6.14
   (D) 7.91, 7.98, 7.88, 7.85
   (E) 8.17, 8.23, 8.18, 8.209

---

17. Ellen has a fish tank with a volume of 40 liters. She went to the pet store and bought 16 tiny fish for the tank. If Ellen uses a water-to-fish ratio of 4 liters to 1 fish, how many of the fish she bought will need to go into a different tank?
   (A) 4
   (B) 6
   (C) 10
   (D) 12
   (E) 24

GO ON TO THE NEXT PAGE.

USE THIS SPACE FOR FIGURING.

18. Which of the following is Step 6 in the number trick shown?
    (A) Subtract 12.
    (B) Multiply by 3.
    (C) Add the number from step 1.
    (D) Subtract the number from step 1.
    (E) Subtract the number from step 1, twice.

Number Trick	
Step 1	Pick a number greater than 0.
Step 2	Multiply the number by 4.
Step 3	Then add 8.
Step 4	Take 50% of the sum.
Step 5	Then add 2.
Step 6	?
Result	The answer is 6.

$$76\%, 0.54, \frac{1}{2}, 35\%, \frac{3}{4}, 0.92$$

19. Which of the following expresses the list above in order from least to greatest?
    (A) $0.54, 0.92, \frac{1}{2}, \frac{3}{4}, 35\%, 76\%$
    (B) $\frac{1}{2}, \frac{3}{4}, 35\%, 0.54, 76\%, 0.92$
    (C) $\frac{1}{2}, 35\%, \frac{3}{4}, 0.54, 76\%, 0.92$
    (D) $35\%, 76\%, 0.54, \frac{1}{2}, \frac{3}{4}, 0.92$
    (E) $35\%, \frac{1}{2}, 0.54, \frac{3}{4}, 76\%, 0.92$

$$7x - 2(1 - x) - 3 + 4x$$

20. Which of the following is equivalent to the expression above?
    (A) $13x - 5$
    (B) $13x - 1$
    (C) $11x - 3$
    (D) $10x - 5$
    (E) $10x - 2$

---

21. On the first day of Luke's fitness plan, he completed 30 push-ups. On the second day, he completed 45 push-ups. What was the percent increase in the number of push-ups completed by Luke from the first to the second day?
    (A) 15%
    (B) 33%
    (C) 45%
    (D) 50%
    (E) 75%

GO ON TO THE NEXT PAGE.

USE THIS SPACE FOR FIGURING.

22. The sum of three consecutive even numbers is 258. Which of the following is the least number?

    (A) 82
    (B) 84
    (C) 85
    (D) 86
    (E) 88

---

23. For the circle with center C, the distance from the center to any point on the circle is 6. Which of the following CANNOT be the length of a line segment with endpoints on the circle?

    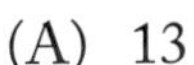

    (A) 13
    (B) 9
    (C) 8
    (D) 6
    (E) 4

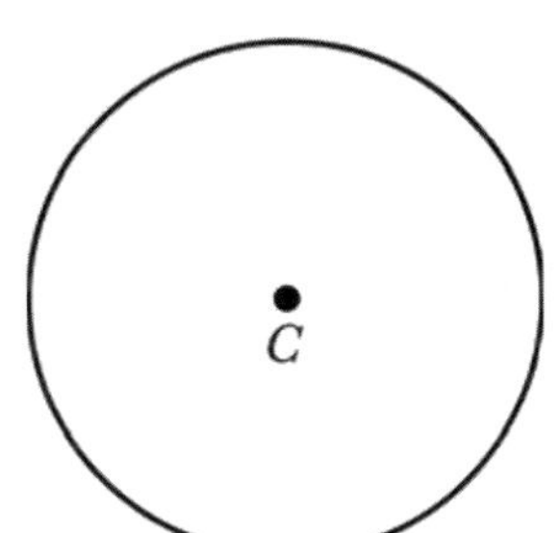

---

24. Solve for x: $-23 - (-2x) = -17$

    (A) -20
    (B) -3
    (C) 3
    (D) 6
    (E) 15

---

25. The floor dimensions of a rectangular living room are 20 feet by 18 feet. How many square yards of carpeting are needed to cover the floor? (1 yard = 3 feet)

    (A) 40
    (B) 45
    (C) 90
    (D) 240
    (E) 360

STOP

IF YOU FINISH BEFORE TIME IS CALLED, YOU MAY CHECK YOUR WORK ON THIS SECTION ONLY. DO NOT TURN TO ANY OTHER SECTION IN THE TEST.

SECTION 2
40 Questions

Read each passage carefully and then answer the questions about it. For each question, decide on the basis of the passage which one of the choices best answers the question.

In colonial New York and Boston, as well as in the smaller towns, women artisans and merchants made or sold everything from dry goods to china, furniture, and hardware. This was especially true after 1760, with the extension of the market for many items manufactured in the home. Women usually ran taverns and coffeehouses. Others were carpenters, cabinetmakers, braziers, soapmakers, cutlers, ropemakers, and even blacksmiths. The hardier of these occupations had generally been inherited from deceased husbands.

Women were also more active on the professional level, and for the same reasons: a short-handed country could not disdain womanpower, and in the Colonial era these occupations required little formal education. Women frequently taught in the common schools. Nurses and midwives had more patients than they could handle, and they and other women did a flourishing business by offering their services as doctors.

1. What is the primary reason the author gives for the involvement of women in the colonial economy?
   - (A) A desire for financial independence
   - (B) Advances in technology
   - (C) A labor shortage
   - (D) The growth of the population
   - (E) Men going off to war

2. As it is used in line 4, the word "ran" most nearly means
   - (A) sprinted
   - (B) extended
   - (C) campaigned
   - (D) managed
   - (E) fled

3. In line 5, the word "hardier" probably means
   - (A) weightier
   - (B) more strenuous
   - (C) more complex
   - (D) more time-consuming
   - (E) requiring more education

4. The author mentions all of the following occupations for women EXCEPT
   - (A) blacksmith
   - (B) doctor
   - (C) carpenter
   - (D) glassblower
   - (E) soapmaker

5. The author would most likely agree with which of the following statements about Colonial times?
   - (A) Some occupations, such as medicine and teaching, required extensive education.
   - (B) There were fewer women in the marketplace after 1760.
   - (C) It was essential that women made what they sold.
   - (D) The women of New York and Boston had better jobs than those of smaller towns.
   - (E) There was an increase in the number of professional women.

GO ON TO THE NEXT PAGE.

In the late 1970s, the Food and Drug Administration (FDA) approved the first vaccine that successfully prevented pneumococcal pneumonia. Researchers found that the rate that pneumonia occurs increases as we get older. In 2012, the FDA approved a new vaccine for adults 50 and older. This vaccine protects against thirteen strains of pneumococcal bacteria, which cause meningitis, pneumonia, and ear infections. The FDA said that 300,000 adults 50 years and older are hospitalized every year for pneumococcal pneumonia. Initial distribution was being aimed at persons over 65.

"Despite the wide use of antibiotics, pneumonia today is the sixth leading cause of death in the United States," an FDA representative said. "The type of pneumonia against which the vaccine protects accounts for a major portion of these deaths. The vaccine is effective in at least 80 percent of the people who receive it." Still, all these years later, the vaccine is a safe and effective way to prevent pneumonia.

6. The passage is primarily about
   (A) medical researchers
   (B) pneumococcal bacteria
   (C) a vaccine for pneumonia
   (D) illness in the United States
   (E) the Food and Drug Administration

7. The passage suggests that the vaccine approved in the late 1970s probably
   (A) reduced the number of deaths from pneumonia
   (B) made the use of antibiotics obsolete
   (C) increased the authority of the FDA
   (D) provided protection against illnesses other than pneumonia
   (E) increased health expenses for people in the United States

8. As it is used in line 4, the word "strains" most nearly means
   (A) pressures
   (B) exertions
   (C) melodies
   (D) injuries
   (E) types

9. The attitude of the "FDA representative" (line 9) toward use of the pneumococcal pneumonia vaccine is best described as
   (A) cautious
   (B) critical
   (C) fanatical
   (D) supportive
   (E) ambivalent

10. The style of the passage is most like that found in
    (A) a textbook
    (B) an almanac
    (C) a news article
    (D) an encyclopedia
    (E) an advertisement

GO ON TO THE NEXT PAGE.

With the invention of new diving equipment, scientists have been able to study animals such as the octopus in their ocean habitats. Investigators have given tests to octopuses and found that their intelligence is high compared to that of other mollusks.

In one interesting test, a live lobster was placed in a glass jar. In the mouth of the jar there was a cork stopper in which a small hole had been drilled. The jar was taken to sea and put in front of the entrance to the dwelling of an octopus. Octopuses like to eat lobsters, so in spite of the fact that it was surrounded by cameras, lights, and interested divers, the octopus came out and threw itself upon the lobster. When it discovered that it could not reach its prey, it turned red with anger and surprise, for the octopus shows its emotions by changing color.

Normally, the octopus would have been able to paralyze its victim with the poison from its salivary glands. But it could see the lobster was still moving around inside the jar. It became very impatient and began to explore the jar. The octopus then found the hole in the cork stopper and squeezed its arm inside. When the tip of the arm touched the lobster and the lobster moved, the octopus looked electrified. It seemed to realize that the stopper could be moved and in a few minutes it had pulled the stopper out of the jar with one arm and collected the lobster with two others.

11. The major purpose of the experiment described in the passage was to
   (A) test how the octopus solves problems
   (B) discover how the octopus poisons its victims
   (C) study the emotions displayed by an octopus
   (D) discover whether the octopus attacks lobsters
   (E) observe how the octopus behaves when surrounded by divers

12. According to the passage, what was the octopus' first reaction to the lobster in the jar?
   (A) Exploring the jar
   (B) Pulling out the cork
   (C) Eating the lobster
   (D) Throwing itself on the jar
   (E) Pushing its arm through the hole

13. According to the passage, the octopus shows its emotions by
   (A) changing color
   (B) waving its arms
   (C) hiding in caves
   (D) secreting poison
   (E) attacking its enemies

14. The passage implies that the octopus came out of its home because it
   (A) was attracted by the lights
   (B) wanted to eat the lobster
   (C) was frightened by the cameras
   (D) was interested in the scientists
   (E) had been coaxed by the divers

15. The main purpose of the passage is to
   (A) explain how scientists observe animals in inaccessible locations
   (B) demonstrate the workings of nature's food chain
   (C) compare the predatory habits of two different sea creatures
   (D) debunk a popular myth about the octopus
   (E) give an illustration of the octopus' superior intelligence

GO ON TO THE NEXT PAGE.

I wandered lonely as a cloud
That floats on high o'er vales and hills,
When all at once I saw a crowd,
A host, of golden daffodils,
Beside the lake, beneath the trees,
Fluttering and dancing in the breeze.

Continuous as the stars that shine
And twinkle on the Milky Way,
They stretched in never-ending line
Along the margin of a bay.
Ten thousand saw I at a glance,
Tossing their heads in sprightly dance.

The waves beside them danced, but they
Outdid the sparkling waves in glee.
A poet could not but be gay,
In such a jocund company.
I gazed—and gazed—but little thought
What wealth the show to me had brought.

For oft, when on my couch I lie
In vacant or in pensive mood,
They flash upon that inward eye
Which is the bliss of solitude,
And then my heart with pleasure fills,
And dances with the daffodils.

16. The figure of speech represented in line 12 is
  (A) simile
  (B) irony
  (C) hyperbole
  (D) alliteration
  (E) personification

17. The tone of the poem is best described as
  (A) humorous
  (B) mournful
  (C) chatty
  (D) joyful
  (E) detached

18. In line 16, "jocund" most nearly means
  (A) fancy
  (B) cheerful
  (C) sincere
  (D) imaginary
  (E) noisy

19. The poet uses the word "vacant" (line 20) to describe
  (A) a daydream
  (B) an illness
  (C) loneliness
  (D) his heart
  (E) his home

20. Which of the following best describes the main idea of the poem?
  (A) You should always be envious of the beauty of nature.
  (B) Flowers can often remind you of unpleasant past events.
  (C) Ocean waves can remind you of flowers moving with a breeze.
  (D) Gazing at the Milky Way can never replace the joy that flowers can bring.
  (E) Nature provides so much joy that even the memory of it can make you happy.

GO ON TO THE NEXT PAGE.

As Earth whirls along its endless journey through space, it has a companion that is always beside it—the moon. The moon is a small celestial body. It is only about one-fourth as big as Earth.

The moon is our nearest neighbor in space. The stars are billions of miles away. The sun is millions of miles away. But the moon is only about 239,000 miles away. That makes the moon truly a next-door neighbor.

In a way, the moon "belongs" to Earth. Just as Earth moves around the Sun, the moon moves around the Earth. It is held in place by the tug of Earth's stronger gravity. A celestial body that is held by another this way is called a satellite. The moon is Earth's satellite.

The moon is a ball of gray rock, some of which is covered with dust. It has no air or water—and, of course, no plants or animals. Its whole surface is nothing but mountains and plains of rock. When we look up at a full moon, we often see dark patches. These dark patches are the lowlands. They seem to form a shadowy face, which people have named "the man in the moon." The brighter parts of the moon are the highlands.

In ancient times, many people worshipped the moon. The Romans, who thought the moon was a goddess, named it Luna. Our word *lunar* means "of the moon."

21. Why does the author think that the moon "belongs" (line 6) to the Earth?
    - (A) The moon could not exist without the Earth.
    - (B) One can see the man in the moon from Earth.
    - (C) Ancient Romans considered it a goddess.
    - (D) It is a satellite of the Earth.
    - (E) It is Earth's nearest neighbor.

22. According to the passage, which of the following can be found on the moon?
    - (A) air
    - (B) water
    - (C) plants
    - (D) animals
    - (E) mountains

23. According to the passage, the face of the "man in the moon" (line 12) is formed by
    - (A) mountains
    - (B) lowlands
    - (C) craters
    - (D) forests
    - (E) seas

24. The author's main purpose for writing the passage is most likely to
    - (A) describe the origin of the word "lunar"
    - (B) dispel myths about the man in the moon
    - (C) inform the reader about the moon
    - (D) compare the moon and the Earth
    - (E) explain why the ancient Romans worshipped the moon

25. Which of the following statements is NOT asserted or implied in the passage?
    - (A) The moon is Earth's satellite.
    - (B) The moon is composed of the same materials as Earth.
    - (C) The moon's lowlands appear dark from the Earth.
    - (D) The moon is four times smaller than Earth.
    - (E) The moon is closer to the Earth than anything else in space.

GO ON TO THE NEXT PAGE.

One day the minister's wife rushed in where Spencervale people had feared to tread, went boldly to Old Lady Lloyd, and asked her if she wouldn't come to their Sewing Circle, which met fortnightly on Saturday afternoons.

"We are filling a box to send to our Trinidad missionary," said the minister's wife, "and we should be so pleased to have you come, Miss Lloyd."

The Old Lady was on the point of refusing rather haughtily. Not that she was opposed to missions—or sewing circles either—quite the contrary; but she knew that each member of the Circle was expected to pay ten cents a week for the purpose of procuring sewing materials; and the poor Old Lady really did not see how she could afford it. But a sudden thought checked her refusal before it reached her lips.

26. The first paragraph implies that the people of Spencervale find Old Lady Lloyd to be

(A) eccentric
(B) intimidating
(C) fascinating
(D) bothersome
(E) congenial

27. The passage implies that the main purpose of the Sewing Circle's project is

(A) charitable
(B) educational
(C) commercial
(D) political
(E) artistic

28. In the passage, Old Lady Lloyd is depicted as

(A) shy but cordial
(B) modest but accomplished
(C) impoverished but proud
(D) anxious and fretful
(E) curious and intrusive

29. In line 6, the narrator uses the expression "Not that . . ." to introduce

(A) a needed clarification
(B) a logical conclusion
(C) contradictory evidence
(D) an alternative viewpoint
(E) a dissenting opinion

30. As it is used in line 9, the word "checked" most nearly means

(A) inspected
(B) marked
(C) deposited
(D) verified
(E) stopped

GO ON TO THE NEXT PAGE.

Until the nineteenth century very little was known about the ancient history of Egypt. The brief statements of Hebrew writers in the Old Testament and some stories preserved by the Greeks were all that historians had to go on. There were also the writings that the ancient Egyptians themselves had carved in stone, but these were mysterious hieroglyphics written in a long forgotten language that no one could read.

But about 1800 A.D. some soldiers of Napoleon in Egypt, while laying foundations for a fort at the Rosetta mouth of the Nile, found a curious slab of black rock. This "Rosetta Stone" bore three inscriptions: one of these was in Greek, one in the ancient hieroglyphs of the pyramids, and the third in a later Egyptian writing, called demotic, which had likewise been forgotten. A French scholar, Champollion, shrewdly hypothesized that the three inscriptions all told the same story and therefore would each contain words similar in meaning to the words in the other two inscriptions. In 1822 he proved this to be true. Then, working from the Greek, he found the meanings of the hieroglyphics and so learned to read the long-forgotten language of old Egypt.

31. The passage is mainly about
   (A) how Hebrew and Greek writers viewed the ancient Egyptians
   (B) how the Rosetta Stone was discovered
   (C) how the Egyptians lived in ancient times
   (D) how the ancient Egyptian language was deciphered
   (E) how historians reacted to the discovery of the Rosetta Stone

32. As used in line 3, the expression "go on" most nearly means
   (A) continue
   (B) learn from
   (C) talk at length
   (D) move forward
   (E) happen

33. In the passage, Champollion is characterized as
   (A) temperamental
   (B) benevolent
   (C) ambitious
   (D) devious
   (E) clever

34. It can be inferred from the passage that Champollion
   (A) was a soldier in Napoleon's army
   (B) claimed possession of the Rosetta Stone for France
   (C) had studied the hieroglyphics of the pyramids
   (D) could read the ancient Greek language
   (E) published French translations of the inscriptions

35. The passage as a whole implies that Champollion's achievement resulted in
   (A) a revival of ancient Egyptian as a living language
   (B) enhanced prestige for French universities
   (C) a deeper understanding of the ancient history of Egypt
   (D) popular fascination with the culture of ancient Egypt
   (E) a new theory about the construction of the pyramids

GO ON TO THE NEXT PAGE.

On the 31st of August, 1846, I left Concord in Massachusetts for Bangor and the backwoods of Maine, by way of the railroad and steamboat. I was intending to accompany a relative of mine engaged in the lumber-trade in Bangor, as far as a dam on the west branch of the Penobscot, in which property he was interested. From this place, which is about one hundred miles by the river above Bangor, thirty miles from the Houlton military road, and five miles beyond the last log-hut, I proposed to make excursions to Mount Ktaadn, the second highest mountain in New England, about thirty miles distant, and to some of the lakes of the Penobscot, either alone or with such company as I might pick up there. It is unusual to find a camp so far in the woods at that season, when lumbering operations have ceased. I was glad to avail myself of the circumstance of a gang of men being employed there at that time repairing the injuries caused by the great freshet in the spring. The mountain may be approached more easily and directly on horseback and on foot from the northeast side, by the Aroostook road, and the Wassataquoik River, but in that case you see much less of the wilderness, none of the glorious river and lake scenery, and have no experience of the batteau and the boat man's life. I was fortunate also in the season of the year. In the summer myriads of black flies, mosquitoes, and midges make travelling in the woods almost impossible; but now their reign was nearly over.

36. According to the passage, which of the following occurred in the spring?
    (A) The author met his relative.
    (B) There were damaging floods.
    (C) The author travelled by train.
    (D) Insects interfered with travel.
    (E) Lumbering operations ceased.

37. As it is used in line 8, the phrase "pick up" most nearly means
    (A) lift
    (B) learn
    (C) detect
    (D) acquire
    (E) increase

38. The author indicates that when he encountered a "gang of men" (line 10) in the woods he was
    (A) justifiably annoyed
    (B) deeply puzzled
    (C) pleasantly surprised
    (D) mildly amused
    (E) somewhat fearful

39. The author indicates that he preferred to approach the "mountain" (line 11) by boat because
    (A) he disliked riding horses
    (B) he wanted to avoid insects
    (C) doing so made for an easier journey
    (D) doing so made for a shorter journey
    (E) doing so provided a more scenic route

40. To describe the period of time during which "black flies, mosquitoes, and midges" (line 15) dominate the woods, the author uses which of the following literary devices?
    (A) Metaphor
    (B) Onomatopoeia
    (C) Simile
    (D) Irony
    (E) Allusion

STOP

IF YOU FINISH BEFORE TIME IS CALLED, YOU MAY CHECK YOUR WORK ON THIS SECTION ONLY. DO NOT TURN TO ANY OTHER SECTION IN THE TEST.

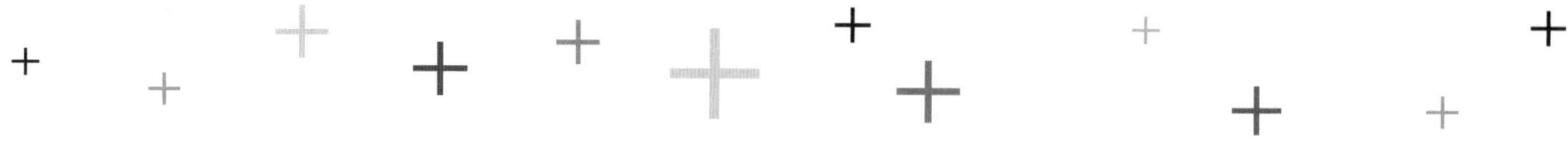

SECTION 3
60 Questions

This section consists of two different types of questions: synonyms and analogies. There are directions and a sample question for each type.

Synonyms
Each of the following questions consists of one word followed by five words or phrases. You are to select the one word or phrase whose meaning is closest to the word in capital letters.

Sample Question:

CHILLY:

(A) lazy
(B) nice
(C) dry
(D) cold
(E) sunny

Ⓐ Ⓑ Ⓒ ● Ⓔ

---

1. EMPHASIZE:
   (A) insert
   (B) stress
   (C) enlarge
   (D) force
   (E) create

2. COMMERCE:
   (A) trade
   (B) humor
   (C) advertisement
   (D) transportation
   (E) supply

3. LUMINOUS:
   (A) wealthy
   (B) beneficial
   (C) heavy
   (D) smooth
   (E) glowing

4. RESTRICT:
   (A) punish
   (B) interrupt
   (C) limit
   (D) capture
   (E) eliminate

5. EXCURSION:
   (A) reason
   (B) outing
   (C) delivery
   (D) upheaval
   (E) surplus

6. PROPHECY:
   (A) prayer
   (B) miracle
   (C) boast
   (D) prediction
   (E) command

7. HAZARD:
   (A) disaster
   (B) poison
   (C) danger
   (D) ambush
   (E) accident

8. EERIE:
   (A) silent
   (B) hesitant
   (C) spooky
   (D) exciting
   (E) suspect

GO ON TO THE NEXT PAGE.

9. DISCLOSE:
   (A) begin
   (B) erase
   (C) learn
   (D) expel
   (E) reveal

10. VALOR:
   (A) wealth
   (B) praise
   (C) pride
   (D) bravery
   (E) truth

11. CODDLE:
   (A) cheat
   (B) waver
   (C) confuse
   (D) pamper
   (E) delay

12. COARSE:
   (A) crude
   (B) stingy
   (C) bold
   (D) plain
   (E) angry

13. ROBUST:
   (A) dishonest
   (B) penniless
   (C) colossal
   (D) vigorous
   (E) significant

14. CONVERGE:
   (A) meet
   (B) spin
   (C) change
   (D) talk
   (E) fade

15. AMPLE:
   (A) timely
   (B) popular
   (C) worthy
   (D) expensive
   (E) abundant

16. PETITION:
   (A) roster
   (B) request
   (C) recurrence
   (D) protest
   (E) ballot

17. ALLURE:
   (A) refer
   (B) permit
   (C) trick
   (D) entice
   (E) invent

18. OBSOLETE:
   (A) stubborn
   (B) outdated
   (C) undeniable
   (D) nostalgic
   (E) impractical

19. WRITHE:
   (A) scribble
   (B) wash
   (C) complain
   (D) cringe
   (E) squirm

20. ADVERSE:
   (A) bizarre
   (B) sideways
   (C) infamous
   (D) unfavorable
   (E) straightforward

GO ON TO THE NEXT PAGE.

21. SPECTER:
(A) ghost
(B) display
(C) telescope
(D) guardian
(E) range

22. SUBTERRANEAN:
(A) frigid
(B) southern
(C) underground
(D) incompetent
(E) unobtainable

23. CONJECTURE:
(A) summon
(B) guess
(C) defame
(D) plead
(E) discard

24. WARY:
(A) fatigued
(B) hopeful
(C) cautious
(D) slender
(E) menacing

25. VANQUISH:
(A) disappear
(B) conquer
(C) neglect
(D) release
(E) deceive

26. PERPETUAL:
(A) rapid
(B) resistant
(C) everlasting
(D) enormous
(E) bothersome

27. ABATE:
(A) entrap
(B) inhabit
(C) embarrass
(D) diminish
(E) agree

28. INCENTIVE:
(A) decision
(B) reputation
(C) agreement
(D) observance
(E) motivation

29. PLACID:
(A) smug
(B) tranquil
(C) ordinary
(D) feeble
(E) wise

30. HOMAGE:
(A) honor
(B) debt
(C) habitat
(D) trait
(E) status

GO ON TO THE NEXT PAGE.

Analogies

The following questions ask you to find relationships between words. For each question, select the answer choice that best completes the meaning of the sentence.

Sample Question:

Kitten is to cat as
(A) fawn is to colt
(B) puppy is to dog
(C) cow is to bull
(D) wolf is to bear
(E) hen is to rooster

Ⓐ ● Ⓒ Ⓓ Ⓔ

Choice (B) is the best answer because a kitten is a young cat just as a puppy is a young dog. Of all the answer choices, (B) states a relationship that is most like the relationship between kitten and cat.

---

31. Closet is to clothing as
    (A) fireplace is to wood
    (B) window is to drapery
    (C) foyer is to entrance
    (D) basement is to house
    (E) cupboard is to food

32. Alarming is to concern as
    (A) hilarious is to amusement
    (B) marital is to wedding
    (C) unruly is to discipline
    (D) drowsy is to sleep
    (E) inept is to skill

33. Yawn is to boredom as
    (A) enrage is to anger
    (B) expect is to surprise
    (C) smile is to laughter
    (D) shrug is to shoulder
    (E) wince is to pain

34. Show is to see as
    (A) hide is to find
    (B) ask is to give
    (C) know is to learn
    (D) tell is to hear
    (E) earn is to take

35. Roof is to house as
    (A) icing is to cake
    (B) chair is to table
    (C) heel is to boot
    (D) page is to book
    (E) street is to city

36. Clarify is to clear as
    (A) change is to stable
    (B) liberate is to free
    (C) eat is to hungry
    (D) rejoice is to happy
    (E) offend is to rude

37. Enroll is to college as
    (A) graduate is to diploma
    (B) coach is to team
    (C) elect is to office
    (D) enlist is to army
    (E) teach is to class

38. Bone is to skeleton as
    (A) blood is to vein
    (B) girder is to steel
    (C) meter is to poem
    (D) painting is to sketch
    (E) word is to sentence

GO ON TO THE NEXT PAGE.

39. Sad is to sorrow as
(A) foolish is to laughter
(B) thirsty is to beverage
(C) uncertain is to doubt
(D) envious is to hatred
(E) lost is to location

40. Bead is to necklace as
(A) boxcar is to train
(B) square is to checkerboard
(C) wrist is to bracelet
(D) branch is to tree
(E) sand is to beach

41. Mural is to paint as
(A) statue is to stand
(B) lecture is to listen
(C) poem is to interpret
(D) graffiti is to write
(E) poster is to advertise

42. Ecstatic is to happy as
(A) miserly is to rich
(B) precious is to valuable
(C) punctual is to tardy
(D) notorious is to famous
(E) frail is to hardy

43. Shoe is to foot as
(A) nail is to finger
(B) shield is to armor
(C) tire is to wheel
(D) umbrella is to rain
(E) oar is to boat

44. Unsightly is to beauty as
(A) wicked is to virtue
(B) foolish is to humor
(C) audible is to sound
(D) sick is to remedy
(E) sour is to flavor

45. Inform is to knowledge as
(A) conceal is to truth
(B) accuse is to guilt
(C) embolden is to courage
(D) pacify is to anger
(E) appreciate is to value

46. Fragile is to break as
(A) stubborn is to yield
(B) crooked is to straighten
(C) sharp is to hone
(D) level is to slant
(E) portable is to carry

47. River is to stream as
(A) aisle is to church
(B) canyon is to cliff
(C) boulevard is to street
(D) mountain is to foot
(E) dock is to harbor

48. Err is to mistake as
(A) try is to effort
(B) ask is to answer
(C) lack is to supply
(D) weep is to pity
(E) owe is to payment

49. Echo is to sound as
(A) wave is to ocean
(B) gust is to wind
(C) reflection is to light
(D) circle is to shape
(E) period is to time

50. Culprit is to guilty as
(A) rival is to jealous
(B) dupe is to deceptive
(C) braggart is to humble
(D) celebrity is to famous
(E) fiend is to afraid

GO ON TO THE NEXT PAGE.

51. Tapestry is to wall as
    (A) pane is to window
    (B) threshold is to door
    (C) chandelier is to ceiling
    (D) clothing is to dresser
    (E) carpet is to floor

52. Aspire is to ambition as
    (A) dare is to courage
    (B) regret is to mistake
    (C) infer is to truth
    (D) doubt is to conviction
    (E) appease is to anger

53. Arena is to game as
    (A) sanctuary is to refuge
    (B) cafeteria is to menu
    (C) warehouse is to merchandise
    (D) studio is to artist
    (E) cinema is to movie

54. Lenient is to forgive as
    (A) anxious is to relax
    (B) content is to complain
    (C) meddlesome is to interfere
    (D) heroic is to admire
    (E) suspect is to accuse

55. Valiant is to cowardly as
    (A) cheery is to bleak
    (B) angry is to hostile
    (C) humid is to cold
    (D) unique is to obvious
    (E) open is to ajar

56. Doodle is to draw as
    (A) lurk is to wait
    (B) rest is to work
    (C) wander is to travel
    (D) whisper is to speak
    (E) stumble is to fall

57. Fence is to enclose as
    (A) gate is to enter
    (B) pillar is to support
    (C) roof is to slant
    (D) stair is to climb
    (E) road is to pave

58. Continuous is to interrupt as
    (A) illegible is to write
    (B) accidental is to intend
    (C) familiar is to accustom
    (D) patient is to await
    (E) reverent is to pray

59. Teach is to learn as
    (A) seize is to take
    (B) sow is to reap
    (C) remind is to forget
    (D) think is to believe
    (E) lend is to borrow

60. Mask is to face as
    (A) alibi is to crime
    (B) armor is to battle
    (C) alias is to name
    (D) mythology is to legend
    (E) hoax is to chicanery

STOP

IF YOU FINISH BEFORE TIME IS CALLED, YOU MAY CHECK YOUR WORK ON THIS SECTION ONLY. DO NOT TURN TO ANY OTHER SECTION IN THE TEST.

SECTION 4
25 Questions

Following each problem in this section, there are five suggested answers. Work each problem in your head or in the blank space provided at the right of the page. Then look at the five suggested answers and decide which one is best.

Note: Figures that accompany problems in this section are drawn as accurately as possible EXCEPT when it is stated in a specific problem that its figure is not drawn to scale.

Sample Problem:

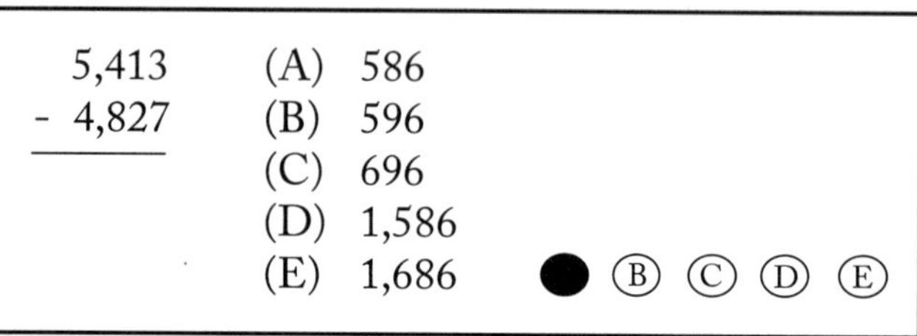
5,413
- 4,827

(A) 586
(B) 596
(C) 696
(D) 1,586
(E) 1,686

● Ⓑ Ⓒ Ⓓ Ⓔ

USE THIS SPACE FOR FIGURING.

1. There are 150 calories in a $\frac{1}{2}$-cup serving of a certain cereal.

   How many calories are in a 1-cup serving of the cereal?

   (A) 75
   (B) 225
   (C) 300
   (D) 450
   (E) 600

---

2. What is 5.01 – 3.22 ?

   (A) 1.79
   (B) 1.89
   (C) 2.21
   (D) 2.79
   (E) 2.89

---

3. Of the following sums, which has a value that is closest to 39 + 18 + 42 ?

   (A) 30 + 10 + 30
   (B) 30 + 10 + 40
   (C) 40 + 10 + 40
   (D) 40 + 20 + 40
   (E) 40 + 20 + 50

GO ON TO THE NEXT PAGE.

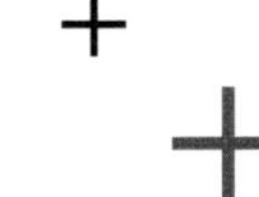

USE THIS SPACE FOR FIGURING.

4. The perimeter of a square is 2 feet. What is the length, in feet, of each side of the square?

(A) $\frac{1}{4}$

(B) $\frac{1}{2}$

(C) 1

(D) 4

(E) 8

---

5. If 500 + 100 + x + y = 668, what does $x + y$ equal?

(A) 8
(B) 60
(C) 68
(D) 600
(E) 1,268

---

6. A length of 2.5 meters is equivalent to a length of how many <u>millimeters</u>?

(A) 0.0025
(B) 0.25
(C) 25
(D) 250
(E) 2,500

---

7. If $x = 6$ and $y = 10$, what is the value of $\frac{2x}{y + 2}$?

(A) 2

(B) 1

(C) $\frac{5}{2}$

(D) $\frac{6}{7}$

(E) $\frac{3}{5}$

GO ON TO THE NEXT PAGE.

USE THIS SPACE FOR FIGURING.

8. Lisa is 16 years old, and Josh is half as old as Lisa. How old will Josh be when Lisa is 20 years old?

(A) 4
(B) 6
(C) 8
(D) 10
(E) 12

---

9. What is the value of $\frac{3}{7} \times \frac{21}{6}$?

(A) $\frac{1}{6}$

(B) $\frac{6}{49}$

(C) 1

(D) $\frac{3}{2}$

(E) $\frac{49}{6}$

---

10. The number 25 is 3 more than $\frac{1}{2}$ the number n. What is the value of n ?

(A) 11
(B) 22
(C) 44
(D) 47
(E) 56

---

11. Compute: $-3 + 2 \times 15 - 7$

(A) 20
(B) 13
(C) -8
(D) -22
(E) -40

GO ON TO THE NEXT PAGE.

USE THIS SPACE FOR FIGURING.

12. The ratio of the number of red pieces to the number of blue pieces in a game is 2:3. Which of the following could be the total number of red and blue pieces in the game?

(A) 6
(B) 8
(C) 9
(D) 10
(E) 12

---

13. Compute: $\frac{1}{3} \div \frac{1}{3}$

(A) 0

(B) $\frac{1}{9}$

(C) $\frac{1}{3}$

(D) 1

(E) 9

---

14. In the square shown, M is the midpoint of side $\overline{AB}$. What percent of the square is shaded?

(A) 25%
(B) 33%
(C) 50%
(D) 66%
(E) 75%

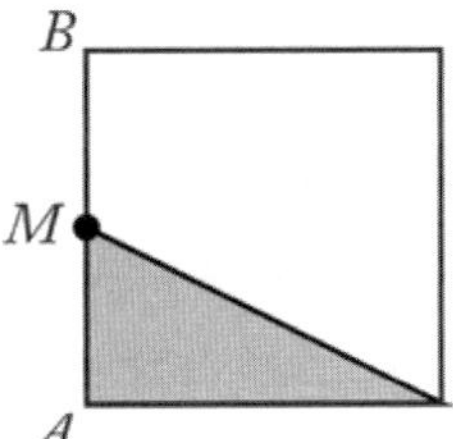

---

15. What is $\frac{1}{2}$ of $\frac{1}{6}$?

(A) 3

(B) $\frac{1}{3}$

(C) $\frac{1}{4}$

(D) $\frac{1}{8}$

(E) $\frac{1}{12}$

GO ON TO THE NEXT PAGE.

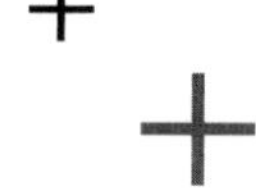

USE THIS SPACE FOR FIGURING.

16. A group of 4 people hire a taxi to take them to the airport. The company charges a fixed cost of \$40 for 2 people, and \$5 for each additional person. If the group chooses to split the cost equally, how much will each person pay?

(A) \$10.00
(B) \$11.25
(C) \$12.50
(D) \$21.25
(E) \$22.50

---

17. If $\frac{n}{3}$ is a whole number, which of the following could be the value of n?

(A) 343
(B) 353
(C) 403
(D) 473
(E) 483

---

18. The figure shows two parallel lines intersected by a transversal line. What is the value of x?

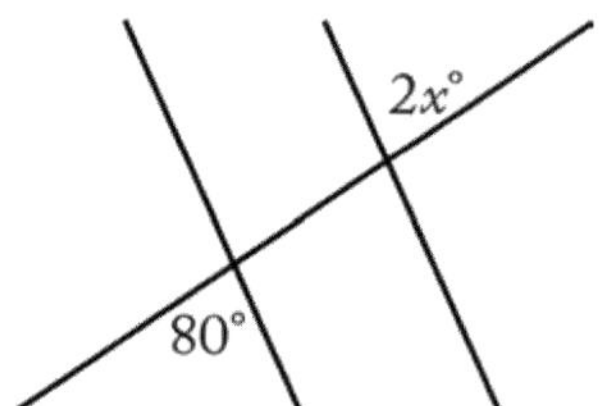

(A) 40
(B) 50
(C) 80
(D) 100
(E) 160

---

19. Last month, the mean weight of 3 dogs was 44 kilograms. By the end of this month, the weight for 2 of the dogs had increased by 3 kilograms, and the third dog's weight had stayed the same. What was the mean weight of the 3 dogs, in kilograms, at the end of this month?

(A) 45
(B) 46
(C) 47
(D) 50
(E) 53

GO ON TO THE NEXT PAGE.

USE THIS SPACE FOR FIGURING.

20. How many eighths are in 2.375 ?
    (A) 19
    (B) 13
    (C) 8
    (D) 5
    (E) 3

---

21. The temperature was $(x + 3)$ degrees Fahrenheit in the morning. By the evening, the temperature had doubled, and then decreased by 5 degrees Fahrenheit. Which of the following expressions represents the temperature, in degrees Fahrenheit, in the evening?
    (A) $2x - 4$
    (B) $2x - 2$
    (C) $2x - 1$
    (D) $2x + 1$
    (E) $2x + 2$

---

22. Which of the following figures can be formed by intersecting a plane and a cube?
    I. A point
    II. A triangle
    III. A rectangle

    (A) I only
    (B) II only
    (C) III only
    (D) II and III only
    (E) I, II, and III

GO ON TO THE NEXT PAGE.

USE THIS SPACE FOR FIGURING.

23. The table shows the original and current prices for five tablets. Based on the table, the original price of which tablet was reduced by 25% to give the current price?

(A) P
(B) Q
(C) R
(D) S
(E) T

Tablet	Original Price	Current Price
P	\$550	\$525
Q	\$500	\$400
R	\$600	\$150
S	\$300	\$275
T	\$400	\$300

---

24. If a positive whole number n is multiplied by a number less than 1, the answer MUST be

(A) greater than n
(B) less than n
(C) less than 1
(D) between 0 and 1
(E) 0

---

25. Donny and Travis are building a sand castle. While Donny works on the castle, Travis digs a moat around the castle in the shape of a circle, as shown. The inner circle has a diameter of 24 inches. The moat has a width of 4 inches. Based on the figure, what is the circumference, in inches, of the outer circle?

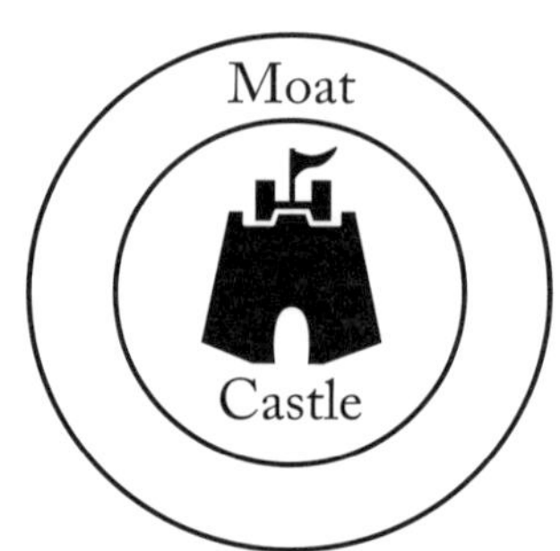

(A) 24π
(B) 28π
(C) 32π
(D) 56π
(E) 64π

STOP

IF YOU FINISH BEFORE TIME IS CALLED, YOU MAY CHECK YOUR WORK ON THIS SECTION ONLY. DO NOT TURN TO ANY OTHER SECTION IN THE TEST.

Practice Test III: Middle Level Answer Sheet

Be sure each mark completely fills the answer space.

Start with number 1 for each new section of the test.

Section 1

1 Ⓐ Ⓑ Ⓒ Ⓓ Ⓔ	6 Ⓐ Ⓑ Ⓒ Ⓓ Ⓔ	11 Ⓐ Ⓑ Ⓒ Ⓓ Ⓔ	16 Ⓐ Ⓑ Ⓒ Ⓓ Ⓔ	21 Ⓐ Ⓑ Ⓒ Ⓓ Ⓔ
2 Ⓐ Ⓑ Ⓒ Ⓓ Ⓔ	7 Ⓐ Ⓑ Ⓒ Ⓓ Ⓔ	12 Ⓐ Ⓑ Ⓒ Ⓓ Ⓔ	17 Ⓐ Ⓑ Ⓒ Ⓓ Ⓔ	22 Ⓐ Ⓑ Ⓒ Ⓓ Ⓔ
3 Ⓐ Ⓑ Ⓒ Ⓓ Ⓔ	8 Ⓐ Ⓑ Ⓒ Ⓓ Ⓔ	13 Ⓐ Ⓑ Ⓒ Ⓓ Ⓔ	18 Ⓐ Ⓑ Ⓒ Ⓓ Ⓔ	23 Ⓐ Ⓑ Ⓒ Ⓓ Ⓔ
4 Ⓐ Ⓑ Ⓒ Ⓓ Ⓔ	9 Ⓐ Ⓑ Ⓒ Ⓓ Ⓔ	14 Ⓐ Ⓑ Ⓒ Ⓓ Ⓔ	19 Ⓐ Ⓑ Ⓒ Ⓓ Ⓔ	24 Ⓐ Ⓑ Ⓒ Ⓓ Ⓔ
5 Ⓐ Ⓑ Ⓒ Ⓓ Ⓔ	10 Ⓐ Ⓑ Ⓒ Ⓓ Ⓔ	15 Ⓐ Ⓑ Ⓒ Ⓓ Ⓔ	20 Ⓐ Ⓑ Ⓒ Ⓓ Ⓔ	25 Ⓐ Ⓑ Ⓒ Ⓓ Ⓔ

Section 2

1 Ⓐ Ⓑ Ⓒ Ⓓ Ⓔ	9 Ⓐ Ⓑ Ⓒ Ⓓ Ⓔ	17 Ⓐ Ⓑ Ⓒ Ⓓ Ⓔ	25 Ⓐ Ⓑ Ⓒ Ⓓ Ⓔ	33 Ⓐ Ⓑ Ⓒ Ⓓ Ⓔ
2 Ⓐ Ⓑ Ⓒ Ⓓ Ⓔ	10 Ⓐ Ⓑ Ⓒ Ⓓ Ⓔ	18 Ⓐ Ⓑ Ⓒ Ⓓ Ⓔ	26 Ⓐ Ⓑ Ⓒ Ⓓ Ⓔ	34 Ⓐ Ⓑ Ⓒ Ⓓ Ⓔ
3 Ⓐ Ⓑ Ⓒ Ⓓ Ⓔ	11 Ⓐ Ⓑ Ⓒ Ⓓ Ⓔ	19 Ⓐ Ⓑ Ⓒ Ⓓ Ⓔ	27 Ⓐ Ⓑ Ⓒ Ⓓ Ⓔ	35 Ⓐ Ⓑ Ⓒ Ⓓ Ⓔ
4 Ⓐ Ⓑ Ⓒ Ⓓ Ⓔ	12 Ⓐ Ⓑ Ⓒ Ⓓ Ⓔ	20 Ⓐ Ⓑ Ⓒ Ⓓ Ⓔ	28 Ⓐ Ⓑ Ⓒ Ⓓ Ⓔ	36 Ⓐ Ⓑ Ⓒ Ⓓ Ⓔ
5 Ⓐ Ⓑ Ⓒ Ⓓ Ⓔ	13 Ⓐ Ⓑ Ⓒ Ⓓ Ⓔ	21 Ⓐ Ⓑ Ⓒ Ⓓ Ⓔ	29 Ⓐ Ⓑ Ⓒ Ⓓ Ⓔ	37 Ⓐ Ⓑ Ⓒ Ⓓ Ⓔ
6 Ⓐ Ⓑ Ⓒ Ⓓ Ⓔ	14 Ⓐ Ⓑ Ⓒ Ⓓ Ⓔ	22 Ⓐ Ⓑ Ⓒ Ⓓ Ⓔ	30 Ⓐ Ⓑ Ⓒ Ⓓ Ⓔ	38 Ⓐ Ⓑ Ⓒ Ⓓ Ⓔ
7 Ⓐ Ⓑ Ⓒ Ⓓ Ⓔ	15 Ⓐ Ⓑ Ⓒ Ⓓ Ⓔ	23 Ⓐ Ⓑ Ⓒ Ⓓ Ⓔ	31 Ⓐ Ⓑ Ⓒ Ⓓ Ⓔ	39 Ⓐ Ⓑ Ⓒ Ⓓ Ⓔ
8 Ⓐ Ⓑ Ⓒ Ⓓ Ⓔ	16 Ⓐ Ⓑ Ⓒ Ⓓ Ⓔ	24 Ⓐ Ⓑ Ⓒ Ⓓ Ⓔ	32 Ⓐ Ⓑ Ⓒ Ⓓ Ⓔ	40 Ⓐ Ⓑ Ⓒ Ⓓ Ⓔ

Section 3

1 Ⓐ Ⓑ Ⓒ Ⓓ Ⓔ	13 Ⓐ Ⓑ Ⓒ Ⓓ Ⓔ	25 Ⓐ Ⓑ Ⓒ Ⓓ Ⓔ	37 Ⓐ Ⓑ Ⓒ Ⓓ Ⓔ	49 Ⓐ Ⓑ Ⓒ Ⓓ Ⓔ
2 Ⓐ Ⓑ Ⓒ Ⓓ Ⓔ	14 Ⓐ Ⓑ Ⓒ Ⓓ Ⓔ	26 Ⓐ Ⓑ Ⓒ Ⓓ Ⓔ	38 Ⓐ Ⓑ Ⓒ Ⓓ Ⓔ	50 Ⓐ Ⓑ Ⓒ Ⓓ Ⓔ
3 Ⓐ Ⓑ Ⓒ Ⓓ Ⓔ	15 Ⓐ Ⓑ Ⓒ Ⓓ Ⓔ	27 Ⓐ Ⓑ Ⓒ Ⓓ Ⓔ	39 Ⓐ Ⓑ Ⓒ Ⓓ Ⓔ	51 Ⓐ Ⓑ Ⓒ Ⓓ Ⓔ
4 Ⓐ Ⓑ Ⓒ Ⓓ Ⓔ	16 Ⓐ Ⓑ Ⓒ Ⓓ Ⓔ	28 Ⓐ Ⓑ Ⓒ Ⓓ Ⓔ	40 Ⓐ Ⓑ Ⓒ Ⓓ Ⓔ	52 Ⓐ Ⓑ Ⓒ Ⓓ Ⓔ
5 Ⓐ Ⓑ Ⓒ Ⓓ Ⓔ	17 Ⓐ Ⓑ Ⓒ Ⓓ Ⓔ	29 Ⓐ Ⓑ Ⓒ Ⓓ Ⓔ	41 Ⓐ Ⓑ Ⓒ Ⓓ Ⓔ	53 Ⓐ Ⓑ Ⓒ Ⓓ Ⓔ
6 Ⓐ Ⓑ Ⓒ Ⓓ Ⓔ	18 Ⓐ Ⓑ Ⓒ Ⓓ Ⓔ	30 Ⓐ Ⓑ Ⓒ Ⓓ Ⓔ	42 Ⓐ Ⓑ Ⓒ Ⓓ Ⓔ	54 Ⓐ Ⓑ Ⓒ Ⓓ Ⓔ
7 Ⓐ Ⓑ Ⓒ Ⓓ Ⓔ	19 Ⓐ Ⓑ Ⓒ Ⓓ Ⓔ	31 Ⓐ Ⓑ Ⓒ Ⓓ Ⓔ	43 Ⓐ Ⓑ Ⓒ Ⓓ Ⓔ	55 Ⓐ Ⓑ Ⓒ Ⓓ Ⓔ
8 Ⓐ Ⓑ Ⓒ Ⓓ Ⓔ	20 Ⓐ Ⓑ Ⓒ Ⓓ Ⓔ	32 Ⓐ Ⓑ Ⓒ Ⓓ Ⓔ	44 Ⓐ Ⓑ Ⓒ Ⓓ Ⓔ	56 Ⓐ Ⓑ Ⓒ Ⓓ Ⓔ
9 Ⓐ Ⓑ Ⓒ Ⓓ Ⓔ	21 Ⓐ Ⓑ Ⓒ Ⓓ Ⓔ	33 Ⓐ Ⓑ Ⓒ Ⓓ Ⓔ	45 Ⓐ Ⓑ Ⓒ Ⓓ Ⓔ	57 Ⓐ Ⓑ Ⓒ Ⓓ Ⓔ
10 Ⓐ Ⓑ Ⓒ Ⓓ Ⓔ	22 Ⓐ Ⓑ Ⓒ Ⓓ Ⓔ	34 Ⓐ Ⓑ Ⓒ Ⓓ Ⓔ	46 Ⓐ Ⓑ Ⓒ Ⓓ Ⓔ	58 Ⓐ Ⓑ Ⓒ Ⓓ Ⓔ
11 Ⓐ Ⓑ Ⓒ Ⓓ Ⓔ	23 Ⓐ Ⓑ Ⓒ Ⓓ Ⓔ	35 Ⓐ Ⓑ Ⓒ Ⓓ Ⓔ	47 Ⓐ Ⓑ Ⓒ Ⓓ Ⓔ	59 Ⓐ Ⓑ Ⓒ Ⓓ Ⓔ
12 Ⓐ Ⓑ Ⓒ Ⓓ Ⓔ	24 Ⓐ Ⓑ Ⓒ Ⓓ Ⓔ	36 Ⓐ Ⓑ Ⓒ Ⓓ Ⓔ	48 Ⓐ Ⓑ Ⓒ Ⓓ Ⓔ	60 Ⓐ Ⓑ Ⓒ Ⓓ Ⓔ

Section 4

1 Ⓐ Ⓑ Ⓒ Ⓓ Ⓔ	6 Ⓐ Ⓑ Ⓒ Ⓓ Ⓔ	11 Ⓐ Ⓑ Ⓒ Ⓓ Ⓔ	16 Ⓐ Ⓑ Ⓒ Ⓓ Ⓔ	21 Ⓐ Ⓑ Ⓒ Ⓓ Ⓔ
2 Ⓐ Ⓑ Ⓒ Ⓓ Ⓔ	7 Ⓐ Ⓑ Ⓒ Ⓓ Ⓔ	12 Ⓐ Ⓑ Ⓒ Ⓓ Ⓔ	17 Ⓐ Ⓑ Ⓒ Ⓓ Ⓔ	22 Ⓐ Ⓑ Ⓒ Ⓓ Ⓔ
3 Ⓐ Ⓑ Ⓒ Ⓓ Ⓔ	8 Ⓐ Ⓑ Ⓒ Ⓓ Ⓔ	13 Ⓐ Ⓑ Ⓒ Ⓓ Ⓔ	18 Ⓐ Ⓑ Ⓒ Ⓓ Ⓔ	23 Ⓐ Ⓑ Ⓒ Ⓓ Ⓔ
4 Ⓐ Ⓑ Ⓒ Ⓓ Ⓔ	9 Ⓐ Ⓑ Ⓒ Ⓓ Ⓔ	14 Ⓐ Ⓑ Ⓒ Ⓓ Ⓔ	19 Ⓐ Ⓑ Ⓒ Ⓓ Ⓔ	24 Ⓐ Ⓑ Ⓒ Ⓓ Ⓔ
5 Ⓐ Ⓑ Ⓒ Ⓓ Ⓔ	10 Ⓐ Ⓑ Ⓒ Ⓓ Ⓔ	15 Ⓐ Ⓑ Ⓒ Ⓓ Ⓔ	20 Ⓐ Ⓑ Ⓒ Ⓓ Ⓔ	25 Ⓐ Ⓑ Ⓒ Ⓓ Ⓔ

Section 5

1 Ⓐ Ⓑ Ⓒ Ⓓ Ⓔ	5 Ⓐ Ⓑ Ⓒ Ⓓ Ⓔ	9 Ⓐ Ⓑ Ⓒ Ⓓ Ⓔ	13 Ⓐ Ⓑ Ⓒ Ⓓ Ⓔ
2 Ⓐ Ⓑ Ⓒ Ⓓ Ⓔ	6 Ⓐ Ⓑ Ⓒ Ⓓ Ⓔ	10 Ⓐ Ⓑ Ⓒ Ⓓ Ⓔ	14 Ⓐ Ⓑ Ⓒ Ⓓ Ⓔ
3 Ⓐ Ⓑ Ⓒ			
4 Ⓐ Ⓑ Ⓒ Ⓓ Ⓔ	8 Ⓐ Ⓑ Ⓒ Ⓓ Ⓔ	12 Ⓐ Ⓑ Ⓒ Ⓓ Ⓔ	16 Ⓐ Ⓑ Ⓒ Ⓓ Ⓔ

Experimental Section – See page 9 for details.

THIS PAGE INTENTIONALLY LEFT BLANK.

Writing Sample

Schools would like to get to know you better through a story you tell or an essay you write. If you choose to write a story, use the sentence presented in A to begin. Make sure that your story has a beginning, middle, and end. If you choose to write a personal essay, base your essay on the topic presented in B. Please fill in the circle next to your choice.

Ⓐ "How did you find it?" my friend asked.

Ⓑ Describe a time you failed at something and tell what you learned from it.

Use this page and the next page to complete your writing sample.

Continue on next page

SECTION 1
25 Questions

Following each problem in this section, there are five suggested answers. Work each problem in your head or in the blank space provided at the right of the page. Then look at the five suggested answers and decide which one is best.

Note: Figures that accompany problems in this section are drawn as accurately as possible EXCEPT when it is stated in a specific problem that its figure is not drawn to scale.

Sample Problem:

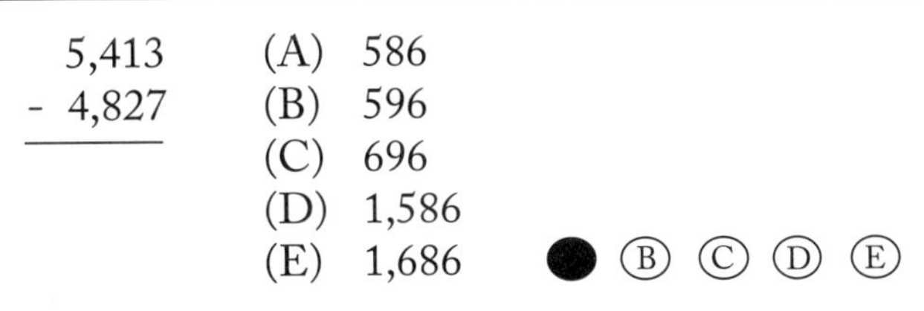

5,413
\- 4,827

(A) 586
(B) 596
(C) 696
(D) 1,586
(E) 1,686

USE THIS SPACE FOR FIGURING.

1. What number is halfway between 19 and 25 ?
   - (A) 19.5
   - (B) 20
   - (C) 21
   - (D) 22
   - (E) 23

---

2. Tony has 80 cents. If balloons cost 18 cents, what is the greatest number of balloons he can buy with this money?
   - (A) 4
   - (B) 5
   - (C) 6
   - (D) 8
   - (E) 10

---

3. If $\frac{2}{4} = \frac{4}{x}$, what is the value of x ?
   - (A) 6
   - (B) 8
   - (C) 10
   - (D) 12
   - (E) 16

GO ON TO THE NEXT PAGE.

USE THIS SPACE FOR FIGURING.

4. Segments $\overline{AE}$, $\overline{BF}$, $\overline{CF}$, and $\overline{DG}$ are shown on a grid with unit squares. Which of the following lists the segments in order from shortest to longest?

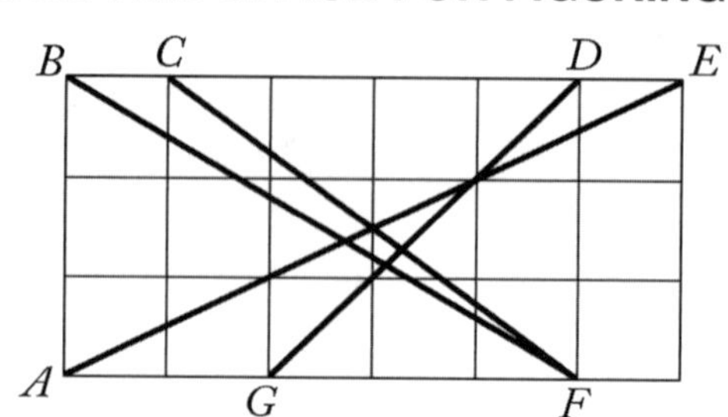

(A) $\overline{CF}$, $\overline{BF}$, $\overline{DG}$, $\overline{AE}$
(B) $\overline{CF}$, $\overline{DG}$, $\overline{BF}$, $\overline{AE}$
(C) $\overline{DG}$, $\overline{BF}$, $\overline{CF}$, $\overline{AE}$
(D) $\overline{DG}$, $\overline{CF}$, $\overline{BF}$, $\overline{AE}$
(E) $\overline{DG}$, $\overline{CF}$, $\overline{AE}$, $\overline{BF}$

---

5. When shipped from a certain publisher, magazines are packaged in bundles of 15. If a delivery van has bundles from the publisher only, which of the following could be the total number of magazines in the van?

(A) 402
(B) 403
(C) 410
(D) 415
(E) 420

---

6. What is the value of $6.4 - 1.8 + 2.4$?

(A) 2.2
(B) 5.8
(C) 7.0
(D) 7.8
(E) 10.6

---

7. A pitcher that is $\frac{2}{3}$ full contains 6 cups of juice. How many cups of juice does the pitcher hold when it is full?

(A) 4
(B) 8
(C) 9
(D) 12
(E) 18

GO ON TO THE NEXT PAGE.

USE THIS SPACE FOR FIGURING.

8. The first number in a sequence is 1, the second number is 2, and each number after the second is the sum of the two preceding numbers. What is the 6th number of the sequence?

   (A) 6
   (B) 8
   (C) 9
   (D) 13
   (E) 21

---

9. In which of the following figures could the area of the shaded region be less than $\frac{1}{2}$ of the total area of the figure?

   (A) 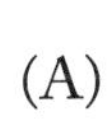 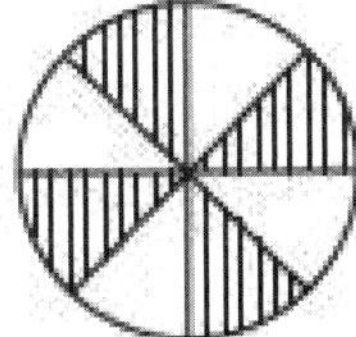

   (B) 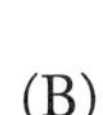 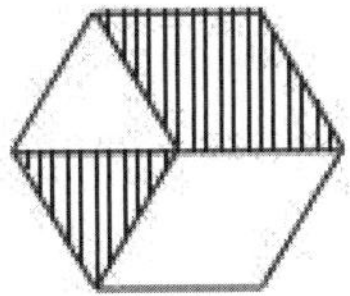

   (C) 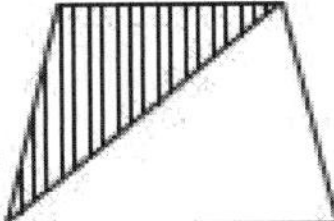

   (D) 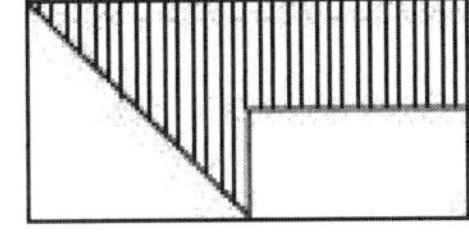

   (E) 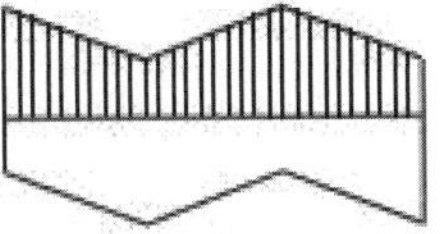

GO ON TO THE NEXT PAGE.

USE THIS SPACE FOR FIGURING.

10. At a social gathering, 3 large pizzas are ordered and each pizza is cut into 12 slices. If each person takes exactly 2 slices and there are 10 slices remaining, how many people are at the gathering?
    (A) 10
    (B) 13
    (C) 18
    (D) 26
    (E) 52

---

11. The ratio of 3 to 7 is the same as which of the following ratios?
    (A) 9 to 28
    (B) 9 to 14
    (C) 12 to 28
    (D) 12 to 21
    (E) 14 to 6

---

12. The sum of the ages of 3 children is 28. What will be the sum of their ages 4 years from now?
    (A) 40
    (B) 37
    (C) 35
    (D) 32
    (E) 31

---

13. All of the measures of the angles of a certain triangle are less than 90°. Which of the following could NOT be used to classify the triangle?
    (A) Acute
    (B) Obtuse
    (C) Scalene
    (D) Isosceles
    (E) Equilateral

GO ON TO THE NEXT PAGE.

USE THIS SPACE FOR FIGURING.

14. At a carnival, rides cost \$5 each and games cost \$2 each. Alicia brings \$35 with her to the carnival and goes on 4 rides. How many games can she play with the remaining money?

(A) 3
(B) 5
(C) 6
(D) 7
(E) 8

---

15. The number 12 is 20% of the number k. What is the value of k ?

(A) 6
(B) 24
(C) 48
(D) 50
(E) 60

---

16. If $3(x - 2) = 3$, what is the value of x ?

(A) −1
(B) 0
(C) 1
(D) 2
(E) 3

---

17. What is the value of $\frac{5}{8}$ divided by $\frac{2}{5}$?

(A) $\frac{1}{4}$

(B) $\frac{16}{25}$

(C) $\frac{25}{16}$

(D) 1

(E) 4

GO ON TO THE NEXT PAGE.

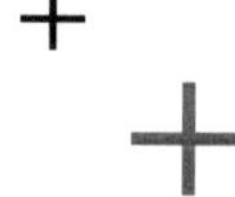

USE THIS SPACE FOR FIGURING.

18. In the triangle shown, what is the value of x ?
    (A) 23
    (B) 26
    (C) 28
    (D) 30
    (E) 32

$2x°$ $84°$ $x°$

---

19. The bar graph shows the monthly sales, in dollars, for a small online business. Of the following, which is closest to the percent by which sales increased from February to March?
    (A) 50%
    (B) 75%
    (C) 100%
    (D) 125%
    (E) 150%

Monthly Online Sales

Sales: \$4,000, \$3,000, \$2,000, \$1,000, \$0

January February March April

---

20. What is the value of $\frac{1}{3}\left(2+\frac{2}{5}\right)$?
    (A) $\frac{4}{15}$
    (B) $\frac{5}{8}$
    (C) $\frac{4}{5}$
    (D) $\frac{16}{15}$
    (E) $\frac{42}{15}$

---

21. How many yards are in 20 miles?
    (1 mile = 5,280 feet and 1 yard = 3 feet)
    (A) 316,800
    (B) 35,200
    (C) 3,520
    (D) 792
    (E) 88

GO ON TO THE NEXT PAGE.

USE THIS SPACE FOR FIGURING.

22. The figure shown consists of a rectangle and a right triangle. What is the area of the figure?

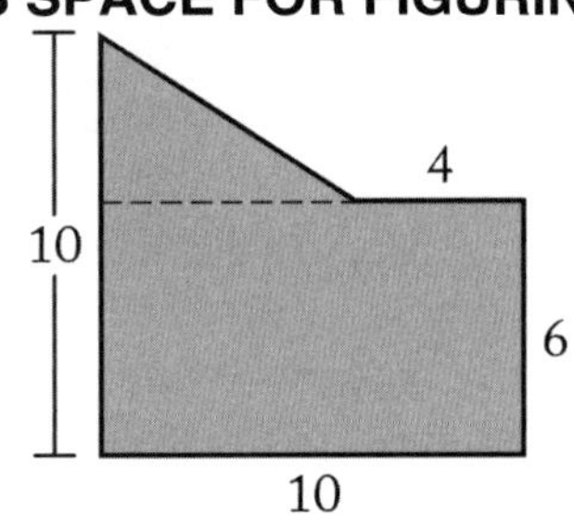

(A) 62
(B) 72
(C) 74
(D) 76
(E) 84

---

23. If 3 times a number x is less than 21, which of the following CANNOT be the value of x ?

(A) 8
(B) 6
(C) 4
(D) 2
(E) 0

---

24. The figure shows a large painting with a wooden frame. The width of the frame is 4 inches. What is the outer perimeter of the frame, in inches?

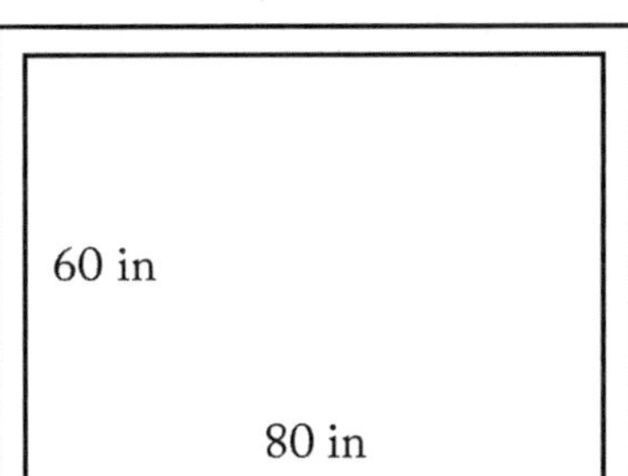

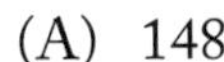

(A) 148
(B) 156
(C) 280
(D) 296
(E) 312

---

25. If $4x = x - 15$, what is the value of x ?

(A) −18
(B) −12
(C) −10
(D) −5
(E) −3

STOP

IF YOU FINISH BEFORE TIME IS CALLED, YOU MAY CHECK YOUR WORK ON THIS SECTION ONLY. DO NOT TURN TO ANY OTHER SECTION IN THE TEST.

SECTION 2
40 Questions

Read each passage carefully and then answer the questions about it. For each question, decide on the basis of the passage which one of the choices best answers the question.

The backbone of the single-humped camel is not curved upward in the middle, as many people suppose. It is as straight as the backbone of a horse. Humps on camels are composed mostly of fat, and they vary in size according to the physical condition of the animal. When camels are worked too hard and not fed enough, their humps shrivel up and become flabby. Much of their ability to travel long distances over the desert without food and water is due to reabsorption of the extra fat carried in the humps. Thus the hump serves as a sort of food supply department from which the camel receives nourishment in time of famine. Similarly, in certain breeds of sheep, extra fat is stored in the tail.

1. The author's primary purpose in the passage is to
   (A) compare camels to horses
   (B) give information about camels' humps
   (C) describe different kinds of camels
   (D) relate a myth about camels' humps
   (E) explain why traveling in the desert is hazardous

2. According to the author, many people suppose that
   (A) the backbones of most mammals are curved upward in the middle
   (B) a horse has a hump like that of a camel
   (C) the backbone of a single-humped camel is curved upward in the middle
   (D) a camel is a kind of horse
   (E) the backbone of a camel is surrounded by fat

3. The author states that the size of a camel's hump depends primarily on which of the following?
   (A) Where the camel lives
   (B) The physical condition of the camel
   (C) How much water the camel drinks
   (D) The age of the camel
   (E) How far the camel travels

4. The author states that the camel's hump serves the same function as what part of certain breeds of sheep?
   (A) The tail
   (B) The fat
   (C) The backbone
   (D) The wool
   (E) The stomach

5. According to the passage, the hump on a camel's back helps the camel
   (A) travel far in the desert without food and water
   (B) carry heavier burdens than other animals
   (C) keep warm on cold nights in the desert
   (D) move faster than a horse
   (E) protect itself when it is attacked by other animals

6. The author calls the camel's hump a "food supply department" (line 6) in order to show that the hump
   (A) is a good place for carrying extra feedbags
   (B) is the only edible part of a camel
   (C) helps a camel locate hidden food supplies
   (D) warns a camel when famine is approaching
   (E) stores fat which can be reabsorbed by the camel as food

GO ON TO THE NEXT PAGE.

(From a parent's letter to a child away at school)

You must study in order to be frank with the world; frankness is the child of honesty and courage. Say just what you mean to do on every occasion and take it for granted that what you mean to do is right. If a friend asks you a favor, you should grant it if it is reasonable; if not, tell your friend plainly why you cannot. You will wrong both your friend and yourself by equivocation of any kind. Never do a wrong thing to make a friend or keep one; friendship that requires you to do wrong is dearly purchased at a sacrifice. Deal kindly but firmly with all your classmates; you will find it the policy which wears best... If you have any fault to find with anyone, tell that person, not others, of what you complain; there is no more dangerous experiment than that of undertaking to be one thing before a person's face and another behind his or her back. We should live, act, and say nothing to the injury of anyone. It is not only best as a matter of principle, but it is the path of peace and honor.

7. What is the author probably trying to do?
   (A) Threaten
   (B) Condemn
   (C) Advise
   (D) Predict
   (E) Praise

8. The main topic of the passage is how to
   (A) interact with people
   (B) study efficiently
   (C) avoid danger
   (D) refuse requests
   (E) find fault with others

9. According to the passage, if a friend were to ask a favor, one should
   (A) agree to do it even if it is inconvenient
   (B) do it but ask for a favor in return
   (C) do it since a friend is asking
   (D) ask others whether one should do it
   (E) do it if what is being asked is not wrong

10. The author considers which of the following to be a dangerous experiment?
    (A) Studying at the expense of friendship
    (B) Hypocrisy toward others
    (C) Excessive kindness
    (D) Asking too many favors
    (E) Being overly honest with classmates

11. The author would most likely say that before one can be frank, it is important to
    (A) express sympathy whenever possible
    (B) discuss friends with others
    (C) overlook the faults of others
    (D) be firm in what one believes
    (E) do what friends want one to do

12. In line 1 the word "frank" most nearly means
    (A) outgoing
    (B) innocent
    (C) tactless
    (D) straightforward
    (E) abrupt

GO ON TO THE NEXT PAGE.

Boxwood was for many years the favorite wood for making flutes, recorders, oboes, and clarinets; it was the hardest, finest-grained wood readily available in Europe. Its disadvantage was a pronounced tendency to warp, and bent boxwood instruments can be seen in any large collection of old instruments. Boxwood is practically unobtainable in large enough dimensions for making instruments nowadays.

If the wooden instrument business had developed in North America, it seems likely that the commonly used wood might have been hard maple. That wood is also adversely affected by moisture and is not so dense as boxwood, but it has a fine grain and machines well. The suitability of maple, along with its availability in quite large dimensions, makes it almost the only wood that can be used for some instruments.

13. The passage is primarily about
    (A) the many uses of boxwood and maple
    (B) two woods suitable for making instruments
    (C) necessity of making instruments from hardwoods
    (D) collecting old wooden instruments
    (E) the development of the wooden instrument industry

14. The passage implies that boxwood
    (A) is not adversely affected by moisture
    (B) does not last as well as maple
    (C) is now readily obtainable in Europe
    (D) is the only wood used for some kinds of instruments
    (E) does not commonly grow in North America

15. The passage mentions all of the following properties of boxwood EXCEPT its
    (A) color
    (B) grain
    (C) scarcity
    (D) hardness
    (E) popularity

16. The author apparently considers the warping of boxwood instruments
    (A) a disgrace to their manufacturers
    (B) an indication of hard use
    (C) an unfortunate characteristic
    (D) a harmless phenomenon
    (E) an index of their quality

17. The passage was probably intended as
    (A) a tribute to the woodworkers of the past
    (B) an advertisement about wooden instruments
    (C) advice for collectors of old wooden instruments
    (D) a plea for conservation of endangered kinds of trees and woods
    (E) information about the manufacture of wooden instruments

GO ON TO THE NEXT PAGE.

Like many human endeavors, the Pony Express was born out of long-frustrated need. By 1860 almost half a million Americans lived west of the Rocky Mountains. Aside from the lures of land and gold, the primary concern was for news from home, those settled states east of the Missouri River.

Here he comes! . . . nearer and nearer . . . and man and horse rush past us and are gone in a flash!

Thus a famous writer, from a westbound stage, beheld a Pony Express rider, and thus the rider galloped into history.

In spite of the legendary full-tilt gallop, the fact is that the rider had to average only ten miles an hour, that in darkness or going uphill he slowed for safety or to spare the horse, as that he usually arrived on time.

The development of the Pony Express, like other episodes that have become epic, looms taller than truth, a buckaroo stew of fact and legend. And even facts have a legendary flavor.

18. According to the passage, people who were waiting for news from home lived
    (A) east of the Missouri River
    (B) in the Rocky Mountains
    (C) in the settled states
    (D) west of the Rocky Mountains
    (E) in the unsettled states of the East

19. The passage implies that the Pony Express rider rode
    (A) with great care
    (B) with great fear
    (C) to compete with other riders
    (D) only in the dark for safety
    (E) only through towns

20. From the information in the passage, we can be certain that the "famous writer" (line 7)
    (A) was once a Pony Express rider
    (B) wrote about the Pony Express rider
    (C) saw many Pony Express riders
    (D) wrote many stories about the West
    (E) thought historians misunderstood the role of the Pony Express

21. According to the passage, the original purpose of the Pony Express was to
    (A) provide a sporting event for competition and entertainment
    (B) help new settlers find home sites in the West
    (C) enable gold prospectors to communicate with one another
    (D) help people communicate with their families and friends
    (E) convey news of employment prospects to new settlers

22. In line 10 the word "spare" most nearly means
    (A) swap
    (B) reform
    (C) conserve
    (D) shortchange
    (E) cure

GO ON TO THE NEXT PAGE.

For their physical survival human beings require food and other organic materials that are provided by green plants using the energy of sunlight. Humans also require pure water and air as well as space for wholesome living. Like other animals, in order to maintain reasonable vigor, humans need exercise, recreation, and time to unwind. These needs, as well as all biological experience, suggest that humans will have to adjust their numbers to the capacity of their environment. There is no instance known to science in which any organism can increase in number indefinitely without coming to terms with physical limitations. If humans are exceptions, they are truly unique ones.

23. The passage is primarily about the
   (A) uniqueness of humans as a species
   (B) environmental limits to expansion of the human population
   (C) significant differences between humans and other species
   (D) biological requirements for human survival
   (E) pleasures of interacting with the environment

24. This passage is most likely to appear in:
   (A) an encyclopedia entry
   (B) a novel
   (C) an almanac
   (D) a memoir
   (E) a popular science article

25. In line 7, "coming to terms with" most nearly means
   (A) completing
   (B) encompassing
   (C) moving away from
   (D) adjusting to
   (E) conquering

GO ON TO THE NEXT PAGE.

In Europe in the eleventh century, peace and personal security were advanced by growth of the institution we know as "feudalism." In essence, feudalism was a means of carrying on some kind of government on a local basis where no organized state existed. Authority fell into the hands of persons usually called "counts." The count was the most important person of a region covering a few hundred square miles. To build up his own position and strengthen himself for war against other counts, he would try to maintain control over the lesser nobles in his county and keep them from fighting each other. They became his vassals, and he became their "lord." The lord protected the vassals and assured them justice and firm tenure of their land. The vassal agreed to serve the lord as a soldier for a certain number of days in the year. The vassal also owed it to the lord to attend and advise him, to sit in his court in the judging of disputes. Lord and vassal were joined in a kind of contract. Each owed something to the other. It was out of this mutual or contractual character of feudalism that ideas of constitutional government later developed.

26. The passage is primarily about
    (A) the decline of Europe in the eleventh century
    (B) European feudal wars between counts and vassals
    (C) the use and abuse of contracts and constitutions
    (D) the rise of law courts in Europe
    (E) the nature and development of European feudalism

27. According to the passage, a lord was expected to
    (A) ensure the vassals' right to maintain their own land
    (B) provide workers for the vassals' land
    (C) sit in another lord's court
    (D) set up a constitutional government
    (E) abide by the decisions made by his vassals

28. The passage refers to all of the following aspects of eleventh-century Europe EXCEPT the
    (A) judging of disputes in court
    (B) lord-vassal relationship
    (C) place of religion in a feudal society
    (D) foreshadowing of constitutional government
    (E) division of land into counties

29. The passage implies that a vassal would no longer owe allegiance to a count who
    (A) disagreed with the vassal in a court dispute
    (B) forced the vassal to make war on another count
    (C) failed to protect the vassal's holdings
    (D) organized a state
    (E) made a contract with another vassal

30. The passage is most likely taken from
    (A) a psychology journal
    (B) a history textbook
    (C) a political campaign speech
    (D) the diary of a feudal lord
    (E) an advertisement for a European tour

GO ON TO THE NEXT PAGE.

Of all the land snails, none wears as bright a shell as "the gem of the Everglades"—the *Liguus fasciatus*.

They have no taste for leaves and do not harm the tree. Parading up and down a tree trunk, the tree snail scrapes off minute algae, fungi, and lichens with a rasplike tongue called a radula. The snail moves by rippling contractions of the muscles on the surface of its large "foot." Its head, located on the front of the foot, has two pairs of retractable tentacles.

Liguus is most active during late spring through early summer. At its snail's pace (up to 4 1/2 inches a minute) Liguus roams about 25 feet a day.

Little by little the snail secretes a calcareous substance that hardens into shell. During its first growing season, the snail adds two or three whorls to its shell; that amount is halved each following year until the shell is between 2 and 3 inches long. The average life span of a snail is 3 to 4 years.

31. The passage describes the snail's "foot" (line 5) as
    (A) calcareous
    (B) muscular
    (C) rasplike
    (D) bright
    (E) retractable

32. According to the passage, "radula" (line 4) is another name for the snail's
    (A) tongue
    (B) foot
    (C) head
    (D) shell
    (E) tentacles

33. The passage suggests that the age of a snail can be determined by the
    (A) hardness of its shell
    (B) color of its shell
    (C) slowness of its movements
    (D) length of its tentacles
    (E) number of whorls on its shell

34. All of the following are accurate descriptions of *Liguus fasciatus* EXCEPT that it
    (A) is a tree-climbing land snail
    (B) is called "the gem of the Everglades"
    (C) does not eat foliage
    (D) is harmful to trees
    (E) has a bright shell

35. The passage says that compared to other snails, *Liguus fasciatus*
    (A) grows the largest shell
    (B) lives the longest
    (C) has the most colorful shell
    (D) moves the fastest
    (E) has the most comfortable dwelling place

GO ON TO THE NEXT PAGE.

After graduating from the Chicago Medical College of Northwestern University, Dr. Daniel Hale Williams began practicing medicine in Chicago in 1883. A dedicated physician and skillful surgeon, Dr. Williams' reputation grew rapidly and both Black and White patients soon flocked to him.

Dr. Williams felt keenly the need for a hospital where Black interns, nurses, and physicians could train; in 1890 he launched a drive to found a hospital. Provident Hospital, incorporated early in 1891, was the first hospital in the United States founded or fully controlled by Blacks. Under Dr. Williams' exacting leadership, Provident set high standards, had an integrated staff and patients, built a good reputation, and soon became a mecca for Black interns, nurses, and patients from all over the United States.

It was at Provident that Dr. Williams performed the world's first successful heart surgery. On July 9, 1893, he boldly opened the chest and sewed the pericardial sac of a man who had been stabbed. Medical thinking of the day demanded that heart punctures be left, either to heal themselves or to prove fatal. Dr. Williams dared to do the unthinkable operation, risking his reputation and the hospital's to save the patient. The operation succeeded and the patient lived another twenty years. Operating without any of today's modern devices, techniques, and experience, Dr. Daniel Hale Williams took the first step that led to the spectacular heart transplants of many years later.

36. The author's primary purpose is to
    (A) describe the accomplishments of a brilliant doctor
    (B) persuade people to donate money for medical research
    (C) demonstrate how to establish a hospital
    (D) describe how to acquire medical expertise
    (E) indicate that heart transplants are safe

37. The passage implies that the kind of heart operation performed by Dr. Williams was
    (A) in keeping with medical practice of the 1890s
    (B) only successful on puncture wounds to the heart
    (C) not performed again for twenty years
    (D) a courageous undertaking
    (E) the first ever attempted with anesthesia

38. The author's tone can best be described as
    (A) informal
    (B) neutral
    (C) respectful
    (D) despondent
    (E) cautious

39. The passage is most likely taken from a
    (A) textbook on surgery
    (B) college catalog
    (C) doctor's diary
    (D) listing of medical colleges
    (E) book of biographical sketches

40. In line 8, "exacting" most nearly means
    (A) accurate
    (B) rough
    (C) critical
    (D) demanding
    (E) insightful

STOP

IF YOU FINISH BEFORE TIME IS CALLED, YOU MAY CHECK YOUR WORK ON THIS SECTION ONLY. DO NOT TURN TO ANY OTHER SECTION IN THE TEST.

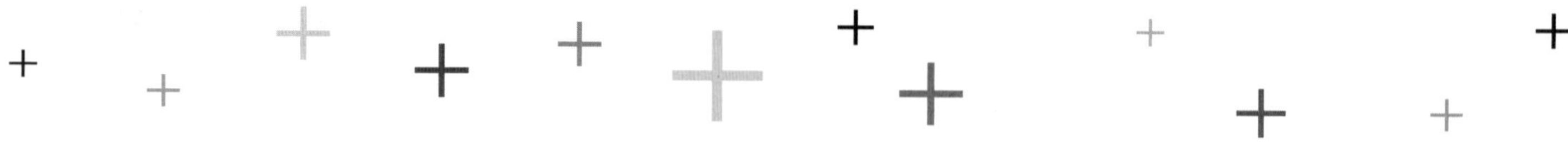

SECTION 3
60 Questions

This section consists of two different types of questions: synonyms and analogies. There are directions and a sample question for each type.

Synonyms
Each of the following questions consists of one word followed by five words or phrases. You are to select the one word or phrase whose meaning is closest to the word in capital letters.

Sample Question:

CHILLY:
(A) lazy
(B) nice
(C) dry
(D) cold
(E) sunny

1. CONVERSATION:
   (A) change
   (B) mixture
   (C) appointment
   (D) discussion
   (E) rotation
2. QUARANTINE:
   (A) isolation
   (B) disease
   (C) observation
   (D) therapy
   (E) banishment
3. PROPOSE:
   (A) bestow
   (B) overcome
   (C) question
   (D) suggest
   (E) reveal
4. ABUNDANT:
   (A) plentiful
   (B) repetitive
   (C) frantic
   (D) obvious
   (E) precious
5. INVESTIGATE:
   (A) conceal
   (B) accuse
   (C) examine
   (D) prove
   (E) capture
6. APPROPRIATE:
   (A) suitable
   (B) successful
   (C) professional
   (D) customary
   (E) competent
7. JEER:
   (A) refuse
   (B) block
   (C) scoff
   (D) desert
   (E) ignore
8. TRADITION:
   (A) technique
   (B) training
   (C) celebration
   (D) ancestry
   (E) custom

GO ON TO THE NEXT PAGE.

9. PERPETUAL:
   (A) swift
   (B) unending
   (C) tedious
   (D) complete
   (E) reckless

10. PRESTIGE:
   (A) bliss
   (B) wealth
   (C) haste
   (D) status
   (E) reward

11. MODIFY:
   (A) update
   (B) alter
   (C) transport
   (D) soften
   (E) exchange

12. WILY:
   (A) eager
   (B) frantic
   (C) random
   (D) flexible
   (E) cunning

13. ENVELOP:
   (A) send
   (B) wrap
   (C) design
   (D) hinder
   (E) change

14. CASCADE:
   (A) waterfall
   (B) iceberg
   (C) pageant
   (D) pinnacle
   (E) barrel

15. EXTRACT:
   (A) remove
   (B) breathe
   (C) overload
   (D) abandon
   (E) dissolve

16. PERFORATE:
   (A) detach
   (B) obstruct
   (C) replace
   (D) puncture
   (E) scrape

17. GIMMICK:
   (A) halting speech
   (B) devious trick
   (C) careless error
   (D) clever prank
   (E) sticky surface

18. DRUDGERY:
   (A) filth
   (B) nonsense
   (C) cheating
   (D) sadness
   (E) toil

19. ADVERSARY:
   (A) lawyer
   (B) celebration
   (C) opponent
   (D) criminal
   (E) contest

20. OBSCURE:
   (A) clumsy
   (B) stubborn
   (C) dainty
   (D) vague
   (E) harmful

GO ON TO THE NEXT PAGE.

21. TOLERATE:
   (A) allow
   (B) understand
   (C) donate
   (D) confront
   (E) encourage

22. STAUNCH:
   (A) putrid
   (B) violent
   (C) steadfast
   (D) obedient
   (E) plump

23. ARID:
   (A) sharp
   (B) breezy
   (C) dry
   (D) fresh
   (E) plain

24. HOODWINK:
   (A) gamble
   (B) sleep
   (C) deceive
   (D) steal
   (E) escape

25. MALFUNCTION:
   (A) disapproval
   (B) failure
   (C) exposure
   (D) scandal
   (E) falsehood

26. QUALM:
   (A) decree
   (B) obligation
   (C) captivity
   (D) violation
   (E) misgiving

27. VIGILANT:
   (A) alert
   (B) angry
   (C) patient
   (D) fearful
   (E) smart

28. SIMULATE:
   (A) pause
   (B) include
   (C) hinder
   (D) reform
   (E) feign

29. PREMONITION:
   (A) introduction
   (B) forewarning
   (C) discovery
   (D) conspiracy
   (E) opening

30. COLLABORATE:
   (A) pass sentence
   (B) settle down
   (C) forge ahead
   (D) work together
   (E) build up

GO ON TO THE NEXT PAGE.

Analogies

The following questions ask you to find relationships between words. For each question, select the answer choice that best completes the meaning of the sentence.

Sample Question:

Kitten is to cat as
(A) fawn is to colt
(B) puppy is to dog
(C) cow is to bull
(D) wolf is to bear
(E) hen is to rooster

Ⓐ ● Ⓒ Ⓓ Ⓔ

Choice (B) is the best answer because a kitten is a young cat just as a puppy is a young dog. Of all the answer choices, (B) states a relationship that is most like the relationship between kitten and cat.

---

31. Shoe is to moccasin as
    (A) glove is to leather
    (B) collar is to coat
    (C) fragrance is to nose
    (D) gem is to ruby
    (E) hair is to head

32. Chick is to egg as
    (A) dog is to litter
    (B) cat is to kitten
    (C) fish is to school
    (D) bat is to cave
    (E) moth is to cocoon

33. Strum is to banjo as
    (A) sit is to piano
    (B) hum is to tune
    (C) strike is to chord
    (D) blow is to trumpet
    (E) practice is to scale

34. Menu is to food as
    (A) glossary is to vocabulary
    (B) catalog is to merchandise
    (C) directory is to telephone
    (D) agenda is to meeting
    (E) roster is to team

35. Thank is to gratitude as
    (A) learn is to knowledge
    (B) threaten is to fear
    (C) promise is to honesty
    (D) allay is to anger
    (E) pardon is to mercy

36. Prospector is to gold as
    (A) soldier is to army
    (B) proofreader is to error
    (C) accountant is to bank
    (D) singer is to melody
    (E) chemist is to laboratory

37. Grid is to line as
    (A) comb is to tooth
    (B) square is to angle
    (C) net is to string
    (D) shoe is to lace
    (E) road is to curve

38. Clothe is to garment as
    (A) arm is to weapon
    (B) sell is to money
    (C) invite is to party
    (D) build is to house
    (E) hire is to skill

GO ON TO THE NEXT PAGE.

39. Modesty is to humble as
   (A) wealth is to generous
   (B) sorrow is to pathetic
   (C) doubt is to confident
   (D) courage is to valiant
   (E) optimism is to naive

40. Stomp is to step as
   (A) stand is to sit
   (B) lift is to move
   (C) shove is to push
   (D) dive is to fall
   (E) slap is to flinch

41. Chisel is to marble as
   (A) camera is to film
   (B) pencil is to paper
   (C) brush is to paint
   (D) footprint is to snow
   (E) trimmer is to hedge

42. Numeric is to number as
   (A) verbal is to word
   (B) chronic is to disease
   (C) female is to gender
   (D) acute is to angle
   (E) valid is to reason

43. Sundial is to clock as
   (A) scale is to weight
   (B) ruler is to yardstick
   (C) milestone is to speedometer
   (D) thermometer is to degree
   (E) abacus is to calculator

44. Immigrant is to country as
   (A) explorer is to frontier
   (B) employee is to occupation
   (C) convert is to religion
   (D) voter is to party
   (E) member is to club

45. Herald is to proclaim as
   (A) pupil is to teach
   (B) sentry is to guard
   (C) citizen is to vote
   (D) orphan is to adopt
   (E) outcast is to shun

46. Sand is to glass as
   (A) wood is to paper
   (B) cow is to milk
   (C) crust is to bread
   (D) stitch is to clothing
   (E) lead is to pencil

47. Rub is to friction as
   (A) pour is to liquid
   (B) squeeze is to pressure
   (C) throw is to distance
   (D) boil is to temperature
   (E) drop is to gravity

48. Reek is to odor as
   (A) shine is to light
   (B) wince is to pain
   (C) cook is to flavor
   (D) blare is to sound
   (E) gaze is to view

49. Shack is to mansion as
   (A) tent is to camp
   (B) locomotive is to train
   (C) kitchen is to restaurant
   (D) grocery is to market
   (E) jalopy is to limousine

50. Clamp is to hold as
   (A) ladder is to lean
   (B) nail is to pound
   (C) lever is to lift
   (D) board is to cut
   (E) cement is to mix

GO ON TO THE NEXT PAGE.

51. Chat is to converse as
    (A) browse is to look
    (B) win is to compete
    (C) listen is to obey
    (D) lend is to borrow
    (E) lull is to sleep

52. Atrocious is to bad as
    (A) infinite is to complete
    (B) gaunt is to thin
    (C) short is to small
    (D) visible is to legible
    (E) fancy is to plain

53. Fickle is to change as
    (A) broken is to repair
    (B) mute is to speak
    (C) hesitant is to fail
    (D) fretful is to worry
    (E) random is to predict

54. Evict is to residence as
    (A) besiege is to fortress
    (B) abandon is to ship
    (C) resign is to position
    (D) banish is to country
    (E) transfer is to school

55. Bashful is to socialize as
    (A) punctual is to begin
    (B) impatient is to wait
    (C) fearless is to harm
    (D) jealous is to envy
    (E) suspicious is to blame

56. Braggart is to boastful as
    (A) fanatic is to ardent
    (B) coward is to courageous
    (C) pessimist is to angry
    (D) nomad is to lonesome
    (E) miser is to wealthy

57. Remind is to remember as
    (A) learn is to understand
    (B) reject is to accept
    (C) convince is to believe
    (D) travel is to arrive
    (E) perform is to rehearse

58. Feeble is to vigor as
    (A) optional is to choice
    (B) notorious is to fame
    (C) profound is to depth
    (D) liberal is to freedom
    (E) awkward is to grace

59. Applaud is to approval as
    (A) achieve is to success
    (B) express is to emotion
    (C) salute is to command
    (D) renege is to promise
    (E) beckon is to invitation

60. Taboo is to permissible as
    (A) gruesome is to squeamish
    (B) stalwart is to robust
    (C) dispensable is to essential
    (D) pitiful is to sympathetic
    (E) prosperous is to wealthy

STOP

IF YOU FINISH BEFORE TIME IS CALLED, YOU MAY CHECK YOUR WORK ON THIS SECTION ONLY. DO NOT TURN TO ANY OTHER SECTION IN THE TEST.

SECTION 4
25 Questions

Following each problem in this section, there are five suggested answers. Work each problem in your head or in the blank space provided at the right of the page. Then look at the five suggested answers and decide which one is best.

Note: Figures that accompany problems in this section are drawn as accurately as possible EXCEPT when it is stated in a specific problem that its figure is not drawn to scale.

Sample Problem:

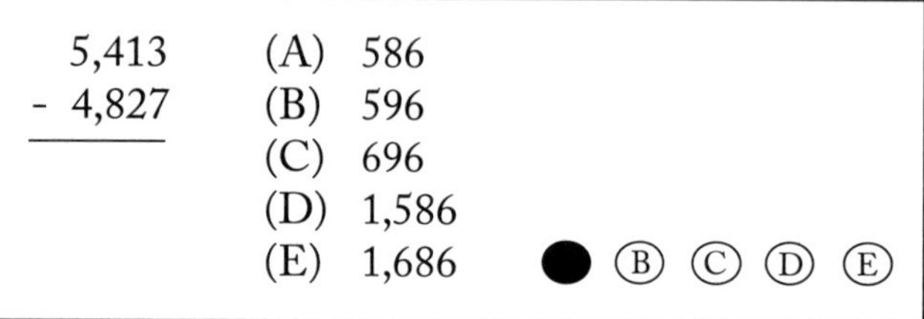
5,413
- 4,827

(A) 586
(B) 596
(C) 696
(D) 1,586
(E) 1,686

USE THIS SPACE FOR FIGURING.

1. If $2n = 12$, what is the value of n ?

   (A) 6
   (B) 10
   (C) 12
   (D) 14
   (E) 24

---

2. In the number 137.26, which of the following digits is in the tenths place?

   (A) 1
   (B) 2
   (C) 3
   (D) 6
   (E) 7

GO ON TO THE NEXT PAGE.

USE THIS SPACE FOR FIGURING.

3. Each week, Carmen saves 25% of her weekly allowance. Which of the following circle graphs best represents her savings?

(A) 

(B) 

(C) 

(D) 

(E) 

3, 6, 12, ...

4. In the sequence above, 3 is the first number and each number after the first is 2 times the preceding number. Which of the following is a number in the sequence?

(A) 30
(B) 60
(C) 144
(D) 192
(E) 248

GO ON TO THE NEXT PAGE.

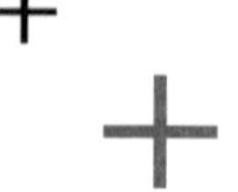

USE THIS SPACE FOR FIGURING.

5. What is the value of $\frac{1}{3} + \frac{2}{6} + \frac{3}{9}$?

   (A) $\frac{1}{27}$

   (B) $\frac{2}{3}$

   (C) $\frac{8}{9}$

   (D) $\frac{17}{18}$

   (E) 1

3, 4, 5, 1, 3, 6, 4, 6

6. Each of the numbers in the list above shows the number of hours of TV that Ling watched per week over the course of 8 weeks. What is the mean number of hours of TV Ling watched per week?

   (A) 1
   (B) 2
   (C) 3
   (D) 4
   (E) 5

---

7. If $\frac{2}{5}$ of a number n is 50, then $\frac{4}{5}$ of n is

   (A) 20
   (B) 40
   (C) 60
   (D) 80
   (E) 100

---

8. In triangle ABC shown, if $AB = BC$, what is the perimeter of the triangle?

   (A) 11
   (B) 15
   (C) 16
   (D) 17
   (E) 30

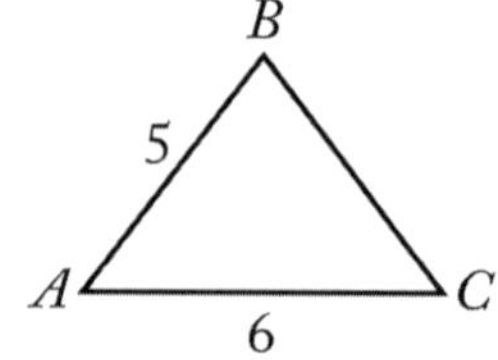

GO ON TO THE NEXT PAGE.

9. Of the following, which is closest to 79.6 – 2.12 ?
   (A) 50
   (B) 60
   (C) 68
   (D) 70
   (E) 78

USE THIS SPACE FOR FIGURING.

---

10. It takes Marcia 80 minutes to hike uphill on a trail from her car to the campsite and $\frac{1}{4}$ of that time to hike downhill to her car from the campsite. What is the time it takes, in minutes, to hike to her car from the campsite?
    (A) 20
    (B) 40
    (C) 100
    (D) 120
    (E) 320

---

11. Which of the following can be used to create the figure shown without overlap?

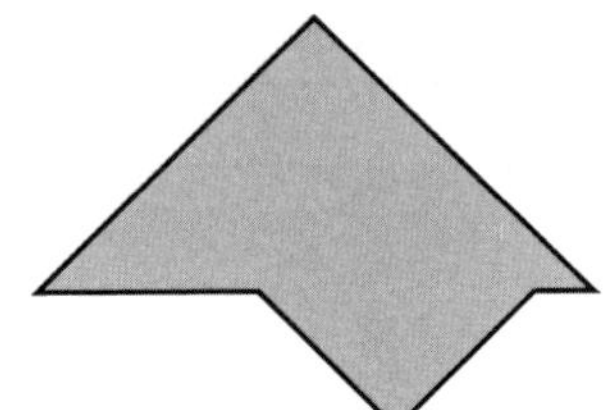

(A) 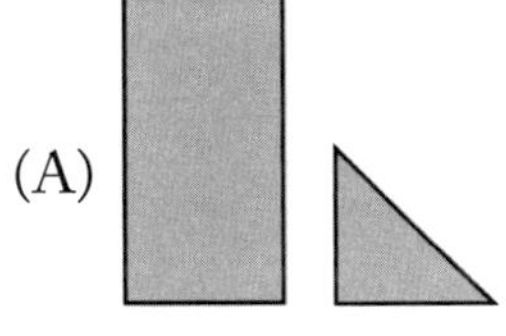

(B) 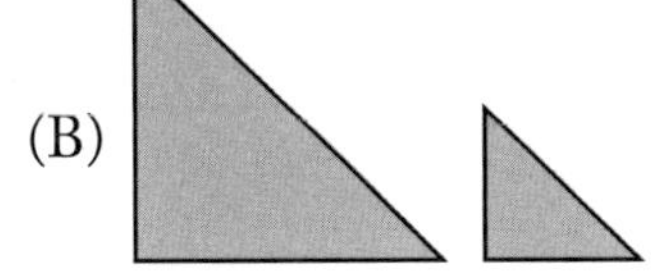

(C) 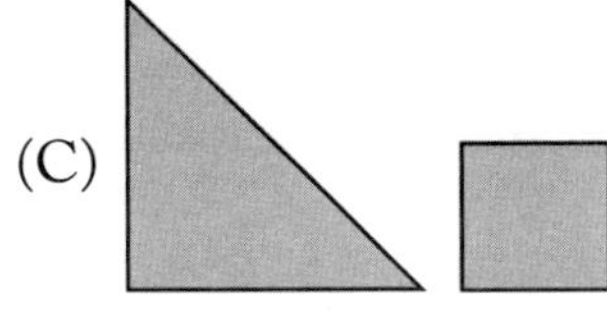

(D) 

(E) 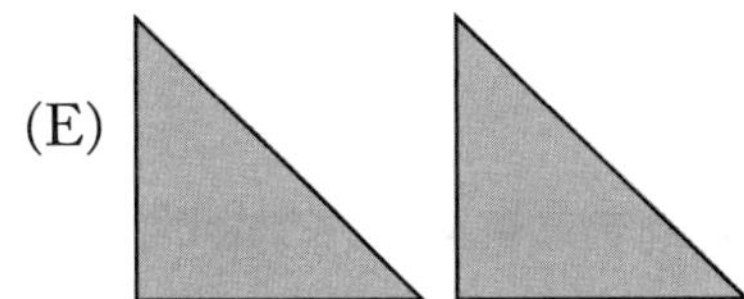

GO ON TO THE NEXT PAGE.

USE THIS SPACE FOR FIGURING.

12. Sarah has 8 stamps and Elsa has 20. How many stamps must Elsa give Sarah so that both Sarah and Elsa have the same number of stamps?

(A) 3
(B) 6
(C) 7
(D) 8
(E) 10

---

13. Which of the following is less than $\frac{1}{2}$?

(A) $\frac{2}{6}$
(B) $\frac{5}{10}$
(C) $\frac{7}{14}$
(D) $\frac{10}{18}$
(E) $\frac{12}{24}$

---

14. What is the greatest common factor of 36 and 72 ?

(A) 6
(B) 9
(C) 12
(D) 36
(E) 72

---

15. There are x fish for sale in a pet store, and 12 of them are goldfish. In terms of x, how many of the fish in the pet store are <u>not</u> goldfish?

(A) $\frac{x}{12}$
(B) $\frac{12}{x}$
(C) $12 - x$
(D) $x - 12$
(E) $x + 12$

GO ON TO THE NEXT PAGE.

USE THIS SPACE FOR FIGURING.

16. What is the value of $93 - 3 + 12 \div 3$?
    (A) 34
    (B) 81
    (C) 86
    (D) 88
    (E) 94

---

17. Nodí has read $\frac{1}{6}$ of a book. If he has read 24 pages of the book, how many more pages must he read to finish the book?
    (A) 4
    (B) 20
    (C) 28
    (D) 120
    (E) 144

---

18. What is 10.9 times 0.4 ?
    (A) 0.436
    (B) 4.36
    (C) 43.6
    (D) 436
    (E) 4,360

---

19. In a group of 100 high school students, $\frac{1}{5}$ of the students are ninth graders, and $\frac{1}{4}$ of the other students are tenth graders. How many of the students in the group are neither ninth graders nor tenth graders?
    (A) 20
    (B) 40
    (C) 60
    (D) 75
    (E) 80

GO ON TO THE NEXT PAGE.

USE THIS SPACE FOR FIGURING.

20. What is the value of $\frac{20}{3}$ divided by 4 ?

(A) $\frac{3}{80}$

(B) $\frac{3}{5}$

(C) $\frac{5}{3}$

(D) $\frac{15}{4}$

(E) $\frac{80}{3}$

---

21. Chaim has $4,500 in a savings account. If last year he had $5,000 in the savings account, by what percent did the money in the account decrease from last year to now?

(A) 11%
(B) 10%
(C) 9%
(D) 5%
(E) 1%

---

22. In the figure shown, line k intersects parallel lines l and m. What is the value of x ?

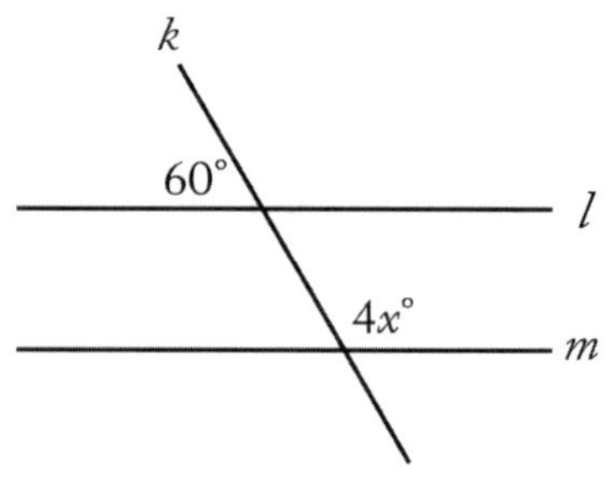

(A) 15
(B) 20
(C) 25
(D) 30
(E) 35

---

23. Which of the following is equivalent to $4(2x + 3 - x)$?

(A) $10x$
(B) $16x$
(C) $4x + 12$
(D) $7x + 3$
(E) $12x + 12$

GO ON TO THE NEXT PAGE.

USE THIS SPACE FOR FIGURING.

24. If $a = -2$ and $b = 3$, what is the value of $b - 4a$?
   (A) −5
   (B) −3
   (C) 2
   (D) 9
   (E) 11

---

25. The length of rectangle A is 6 times the length of rectangle B. The width of rectangle A is $\frac{4}{3}$ the width of rectangle B. If the area of rectangle A is x times the area of rectangle B, what is the value of x ?
   (A) $\frac{9}{2}$
   (B) 6
   (C) 8
   (D) $\frac{20}{3}$
   (E) 12

STOP

IF YOU FINISH BEFORE TIME IS CALLED, YOU MAY CHECK YOUR WORK ON THIS SECTION ONLY. DO NOT TURN TO ANY OTHER SECTION IN THE TEST.

THIS PAGE INTENTIONALLY LEFT BLANK.

Practice Test IV: Middle Level Answer Sheet

Be sure each mark completely fills the answer space.
Start with number 1 for each new section of the test.

Section 1

1 ⒶⒷⒸⒹⒺ	6 ⒶⒷⒸⒹⒺ	11 ⒶⒷⒸⒹⒺ	16 ⒶⒷⒸⒹⒺ	21 ⒶⒷⒸⒹⒺ
2 ⒶⒷⒸⒹⒺ	7 ⒶⒷⒸⒹⒺ	12 ⒶⒷⒸⒹⒺ	17 ⒶⒷⒸⒹⒺ	22 ⒶⒷⒸⒹⒺ
3 ⒶⒷⒸⒹⒺ	8 ⒶⒷⒸⒹⒺ	13 ⒶⒷⒸⒹⒺ	18 ⒶⒷⒸⒹⒺ	23 ⒶⒷⒸⒹⒺ
4 ⒶⒷⒸⒹⒺ	9 ⒶⒷⒸⒹⒺ	14 ⒶⒷⒸⒹⒺ	19 ⒶⒷⒸⒹⒺ	24 ⒶⒷⒸⒹⒺ
5 ⒶⒷⒸⒹⒺ	10 ⒶⒷⒸⒹⒺ	15 ⒶⒷⒸⒹⒺ	20 ⒶⒷⒸⒹⒺ	25 ⒶⒷⒸⒹⒺ

Section 2

1 ⒶⒷⒸⒹⒺ	9 ⒶⒷⒸⒹⒺ	17 ⒶⒷⒸⒹⒺ	25 ⒶⒷⒸⒹⒺ	33 ⒶⒷⒸⒹⒺ
2 ⒶⒷⒸⒹⒺ	10 ⒶⒷⒸⒹⒺ	18 ⒶⒷⒸⒹⒺ	26 ⒶⒷⒸⒹⒺ	34 ⒶⒷⒸⒹⒺ
3 ⒶⒷⒸⒹⒺ	11 ⒶⒷⒸⒹⒺ	19 ⒶⒷⒸⒹⒺ	27 ⒶⒷⒸⒹⒺ	35 ⒶⒷⒸⒹⒺ
4 ⒶⒷⒸⒹⒺ	12 ⒶⒷⒸⒹⒺ	20 ⒶⒷⒸⒹⒺ	28 ⒶⒷⒸⒹⒺ	36 ⒶⒷⒸⒹⒺ
5 ⒶⒷⒸⒹⒺ	13 ⒶⒷⒸⒹⒺ	21 ⒶⒷⒸⒹⒺ	29 ⒶⒷⒸⒹⒺ	37 ⒶⒷⒸⒹⒺ
6 ⒶⒷⒸⒹⒺ	14 ⒶⒷⒸⒹⒺ	22 ⒶⒷⒸⒹⒺ	30 ⒶⒷⒸⒹⒺ	38 ⒶⒷⒸⒹⒺ
7 ⒶⒷⒸⒹⒺ	15 ⒶⒷⒸⒹⒺ	23 ⒶⒷⒸⒹⒺ	31 ⒶⒷⒸⒹⒺ	39 ⒶⒷⒸⒹⒺ
8 ⒶⒷⒸⒹⒺ	16 ⒶⒷⒸⒹⒺ	24 ⒶⒷⒸⒹⒺ	32 ⒶⒷⒸⒹⒺ	40 ⒶⒷⒸⒹⒺ

Section 3

1 ⒶⒷⒸⒹⒺ	13 ⒶⒷⒸⒹⒺ	25 ⒶⒷⒸⒹⒺ	37 ⒶⒷⒸⒹⒺ	49 ⒶⒷⒸⒹⒺ
2 ⒶⒷⒸⒹⒺ	14 ⒶⒷⒸⒹⒺ	26 ⒶⒷⒸⒹⒺ	38 ⒶⒷⒸⒹⒺ	50 ⒶⒷⒸⒹⒺ
3 ⒶⒷⒸⒹⒺ	15 ⒶⒷⒸⒹⒺ	27 ⒶⒷⒸⒹⒺ	39 ⒶⒷⒸⒹⒺ	51 ⒶⒷⒸⒹⒺ
4 ⒶⒷⒸⒹⒺ	16 ⒶⒷⒸⒹⒺ	28 ⒶⒷⒸⒹⒺ	40 ⒶⒷⒸⒹⒺ	52 ⒶⒷⒸⒹⒺ
5 ⒶⒷⒸⒹⒺ	17 ⒶⒷⒸⒹⒺ	29 ⒶⒷⒸⒹⒺ	41 ⒶⒷⒸⒹⒺ	53 ⒶⒷⒸⒹⒺ
6 ⒶⒷⒸⒹⒺ	18 ⒶⒷⒸⒹⒺ	30 ⒶⒷⒸⒹⒺ	42 ⒶⒷⒸⒹⒺ	54 ⒶⒷⒸⒹⒺ
7 ⒶⒷⒸⒹⒺ	19 ⒶⒷⒸⒹⒺ	31 ⒶⒷⒸⒹⒺ	43 ⒶⒷⒸⒹⒺ	55 ⒶⒷⒸⒹⒺ
8 ⒶⒷⒸⒹⒺ	20 ⒶⒷⒸⒹⒺ	32 ⒶⒷⒸⒹⒺ	44 ⒶⒷⒸⒹⒺ	56 ⒶⒷⒸⒹⒺ
9 ⒶⒷⒸⒹⒺ	21 ⒶⒷⒸⒹⒺ	33 ⒶⒷⒸⒹⒺ	45 ⒶⒷⒸⒹⒺ	57 ⒶⒷⒸⒹⒺ
10 ⒶⒷⒸⒹⒺ	22 ⒶⒷⒸⒹⒺ	34 ⒶⒷⒸⒹⒺ	46 ⒶⒷⒸⒹⒺ	58 ⒶⒷⒸⒹⒺ
11 ⒶⒷⒸⒹⒺ	23 ⒶⒷⒸⒹⒺ	35 ⒶⒷⒸⒹⒺ	47 ⒶⒷⒸⒹⒺ	59 ⒶⒷⒸⒹⒺ
12 ⒶⒷⒸⒹⒺ	24 ⒶⒷⒸⒹⒺ	36 ⒶⒷⒸⒹⒺ	48 ⒶⒷⒸⒹⒺ	60 ⒶⒷⒸⒹⒺ

Section 4

1 ⒶⒷⒸⒹⒺ	6 ⒶⒷⒸⒹⒺ	11 ⒶⒷⒸⒹⒺ	16 ⒶⒷⒸⒹⒺ	21 ⒶⒷⒸⒹⒺ
2 ⒶⒷⒸⒹⒺ	7 ⒶⒷⒸⒹⒺ	12 ⒶⒷⒸⒹⒺ	17 ⒶⒷⒸⒹⒺ	22 ⒶⒷⒸⒹⒺ
3 ⒶⒷⒸⒹⒺ	8 ⒶⒷⒸⒹⒺ	13 ⒶⒷⒸⒹⒺ	18 ⒶⒷⒸⒹⒺ	23 ⒶⒷⒸⒹⒺ
4 ⒶⒷⒸⒹⒺ	9 ⒶⒷⒸⒹⒺ	14 ⒶⒷⒸⒹⒺ	19 ⒶⒷⒸⒹⒺ	24 ⒶⒷⒸⒹⒺ
5 ⒶⒷⒸⒹⒺ	10 ⒶⒷⒸⒹⒺ	15 ⒶⒷⒸⒹⒺ	20 ⒶⒷⒸⒹⒺ	25 ⒶⒷⒸⒹⒺ

Section 5

1 ⒶⒷⒸⒹⒺ	5 ⒶⒷⒸⒹⒺ	9 ⒶⒷⒸⒹⒺ	13 ⒶⒷⒸⒹⒺ
2 ⒶⒷⒸⒹⒺ	6 ⒶⒷⒸⒹⒺ	10 ⒶⒷⒸⒹⒺ	14 ⒶⒷⒸⒹⒺ
3 ⒶⒷⒸ			
4 ⒶⒷⒸⒹⒺ	8 ⒶⒷⒸⒹⒺ	12 ⒶⒷⒸⒹⒺ	16 ⒶⒷⒸⒹⒺ

Experimental Section – See page 9 for details.

THIS PAGE INTENTIONALLY LEFT BLANK.

Writing Sample

Schools would like to get to know you better through a story you tell or an essay you write. If you choose to write a story, use the sentence presented in A to begin. Make sure that your story has a beginning, middle, and end. If you choose to write a personal essay, base your essay on the topic presented in B. Please fill in the circle next to your choice.

Ⓐ I looked around and thought, "What am I doing here?"

Ⓑ What was one of the most difficult choices you've ever had to make? Describe the situation and explain the outcome.

Use this page and the next page to complete your writing sample.

Continue on next page

THIS PAGE INTENTIONALLY LEFT BLANK.

SECTION 1
25 Questions

Following each problem in this section, there are five suggested answers. Work each problem in your head or in the blank space provided at the right of the page. Then look at the five suggested answers and decide which one is best.

Note: Figures that accompany problems in this section are drawn as accurately as possible EXCEPT when it is stated in a specific problem that its figure is not drawn to scale.

Sample Problem:

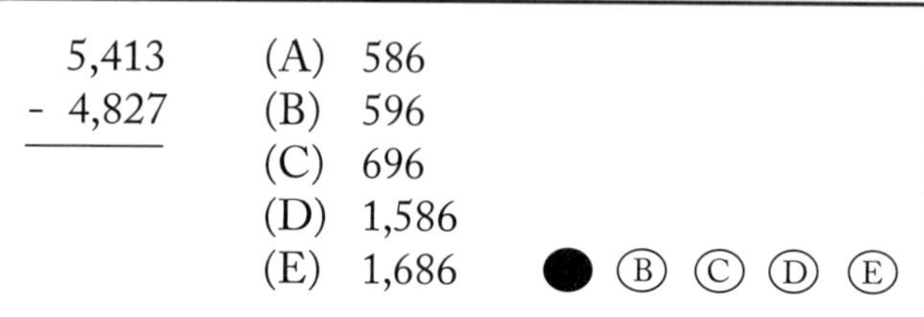

USE THIS SPACE FOR FIGURING.

1. What is the value of $\frac{4}{1} + \frac{5}{10} + \frac{2}{100} + \frac{7}{1{,}000}$?

(A) 45.27
(B) 4.527
(C) 4.5027
(D) 4.0527
(E) 0.4527

---

2. What is the perimeter of the triangle shown?

(A) 4
(B) 6
(C) 9
(D) 12
(E) 13

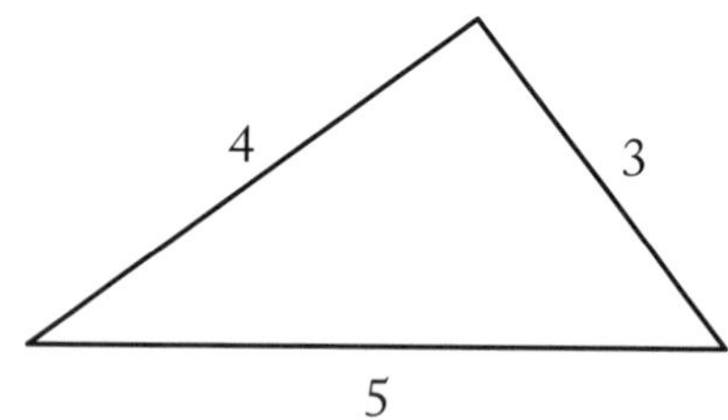

---

3. If $\frac{1}{3}$ of a number equals 24, which of the following equals $\frac{2}{3}$ of the number?

(A) 48
(B) 36
(C) 32
(D) 16
(E) 12

GO ON TO THE NEXT PAGE.

USE THIS SPACE FOR FIGURING.

4. According to the table, how many days was the temperature in Rapid City greater than or equal to 40°F ?
   (A) 9
   (B) 10
   (C) 11
   (D) 19
   (E) 20

Temperatures in April 2019 in Rapid City, South Dakota

Average Daily Temperature	Number of Days
20°F through 29°F	3
30°F through 39°F	7
40°F through 49°F	9
50°F through 59°F	10
60°F through 69°F	1

---

5. Simplify: $\frac{3}{7} \times \frac{50}{9} \times \frac{21}{5}$
   (A) $\frac{1}{10}$
   (B) $\frac{9}{10}$
   (C) $\frac{10}{9}$
   (D) 10
   (E) 90

---

6. For rectangle $ABCD$, what is the value of x ?
   (A) 15
   (B) 30
   (C) 60
   (D) 90
   (E) 150

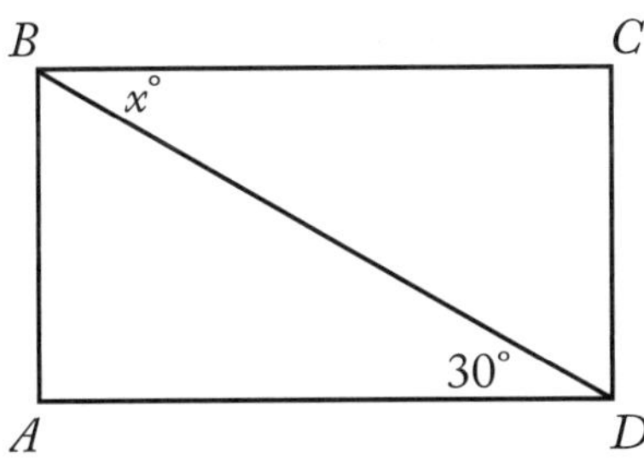

GO ON TO THE NEXT PAGE.

USE THIS SPACE FOR FIGURING.

7. A sequence is generated by repeating the six shapes above, in that order. What are the 42nd and 43rd shapes in the sequence?

(A)

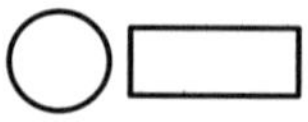

(B)

(C)

(D)

(E)

---

8. Which of the following routes from Padua to Radnor to Skillman is shortest?

(A)

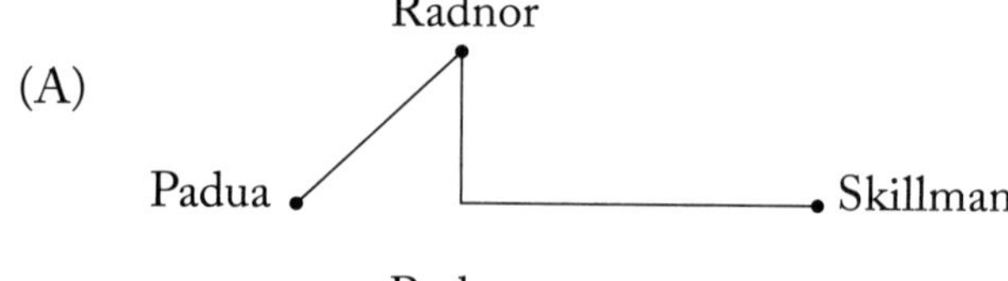

(B)

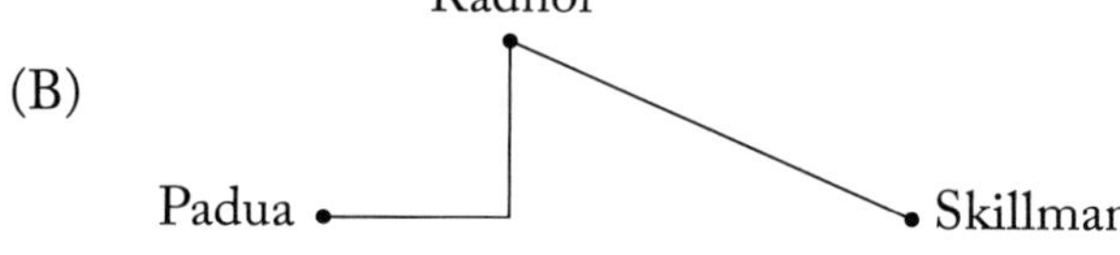

(C)

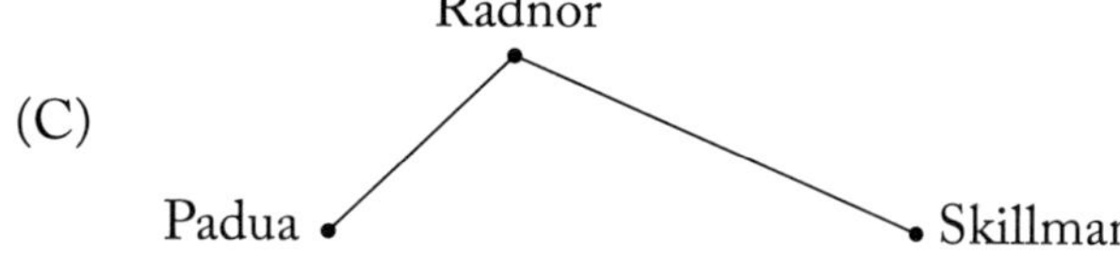

(D)

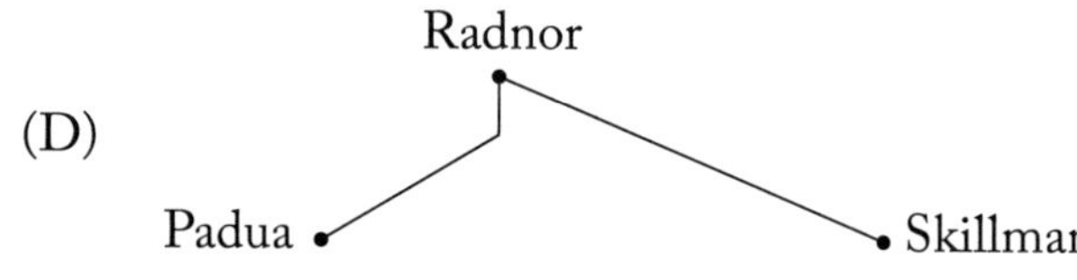

(E)

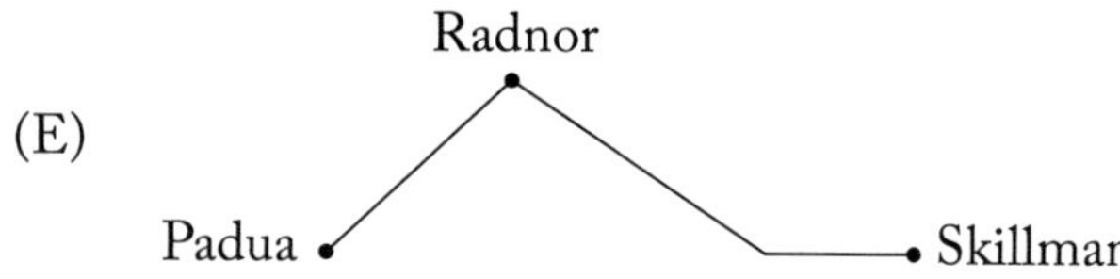

GO ON TO THE NEXT PAGE.

USE THIS SPACE FOR FIGURING.

9. Which of the following is NOT equal to $9 \times 8 \times 7 \times 6$?
   (A) 72×42
   (B) 56×54
   (C) 42×56
   (D) 36×84
   (E) 28×108

---

10. At a bakery on Tuesday, $\frac{1}{5}$ of the customers each bought a pie with cookie crust. Of the customers who bought a pie with cookie crust, $\frac{2}{3}$ bought a pie with pudding filling. What fraction of the customers bought a pie with cookie crust and pudding filling?
   (A) $\frac{2}{15}$
   (B) $\frac{3}{8}$
   (C) $\frac{3}{10}$
   (D) $\frac{7}{15}$
   (E) $\frac{13}{15}$

$$4 - 2y > -12$$

11. Of the following, which is the greatest possible integer value of y that satisfies the inequality above?
   (A) 9
   (B) 7
   (C) 3
   (D) 1
   (E) -5

GO ON TO THE NEXT PAGE.

USE THIS SPACE FOR FIGURING.

12. Anya is exactly 4 years older than her two 6-year old twin brothers. Every year on their birthday, Anya and the twins each receive a birthday cake, and the number of candles on each cake is equal to the age of the child who receives it. How many candles will be needed for their birthday cakes next year?

(A) 16
(B) 19
(C) 22
(D) 25
(E) 29

---

13. What is $7 \div \frac{14}{21}$?

(A) $\frac{1}{3}$
(B) $\frac{2}{21}$
(C) 3
(D) $\frac{14}{3}$
(E) $\frac{21}{2}$

---

14. When the beads in a bag were distributed equally to some children, there were 3 beads left over. If there were 84 beads in the bag, which of the following could be the number of children?

(A) 9
(B) 8
(C) 7
(D) 6
(E) 5

---

15. A rectangular solid has length 5 inches, width 5 inches, and height 6 inches. What is the total surface area, in square inches, of the solid?

(A) 170
(B) 160
(C) 150
(D) 145
(E) 140

GO ON TO THE NEXT PAGE.

USE THIS SPACE FOR FIGURING.

16. Of the following, which is the best estimate of 7.809×101.02 ?
    (A) 78,100
    (B) 8,000
    (C) 7,800
    (D) 800
    (E) 700

---

17. At eight years old, Renee's height was 50 inches. At twelve years old, her height was 60 inches. What was the percent increase in Renee's height from when she was eight years old to when she was twelve years old?
    (A) 10%
    (B) 17%
    (C) 20%
    (D) 67%
    (E) 83%

---

18. Of 4 numbers, the least is 20 and the greatest is 42. Which of the following could be the mean of the 4 numbers?
    (A) 38
    (B) 36
    (C) 25
    (D) 24
    (E) 22

---

19. A cookie company packs 30 cookies in each box and 20 boxes in each case. In the morning, the company receives an order to pack and ship 8 cases of cookies. By noon, all but one of the cases are completely packed. The number of cookies packed by noon falls within which of the following ranges?
    (A) Between 160 and 240
    (B) Between 240 and 500
    (C) Between 600 and 850
    (D) Between 4,200 and 4,800
    (E) Between 4,800 and 5,400

GO ON TO THE NEXT PAGE.

USE THIS SPACE FOR FIGURING.

20. If n is a positive whole number, of the following, which represents the greatest number?

(A) $\frac{n}{2} - \frac{n}{3}$
(B) $\frac{n}{3} - \frac{n}{2}$
(C) $\frac{n}{3} - \frac{n}{4}$
(D) $\frac{n}{4} - \frac{n}{3}$
(E) $\frac{n}{4} - \frac{n}{5}$

---

21. For a party, Mel bought 3 cups of chocolate ice cream for every 2 cups of vanilla ice cream. What fraction of the cups bought contained chocolate ice cream?

(A) $\frac{1}{2}$
(B) $\frac{1}{3}$
(C) $\frac{2}{3}$
(D) $\frac{2}{5}$
(E) $\frac{3}{5}$

---

22. If $3a + b = 12$, which of the following is equal to a ?

(A) $\frac{b}{3} - 4$
(B) $4 - b$
(C) $4 - \frac{b}{3}$
(D) $4 + \frac{b}{3}$
(E) $12 - \frac{b}{3}$

---

23. A train travels at an average rate of 90 meters per second. At this rate, how many kilometers will the train travel in 3 hours?

(A) 16.2
(B) 32.4
(C) 97.2
(D) 324
(E) 972

GO ON TO THE NEXT PAGE.

USE THIS SPACE FOR FIGURING.

24. Simplify: $(3ab + 2a + 1) - (-2ab + 2a - 1)$
    (A) $5ab$
    (B) $ab + 2$
    (C) $ab + 4a$
    (D) $5ab + 2$
    (E) $5ab + 4a$

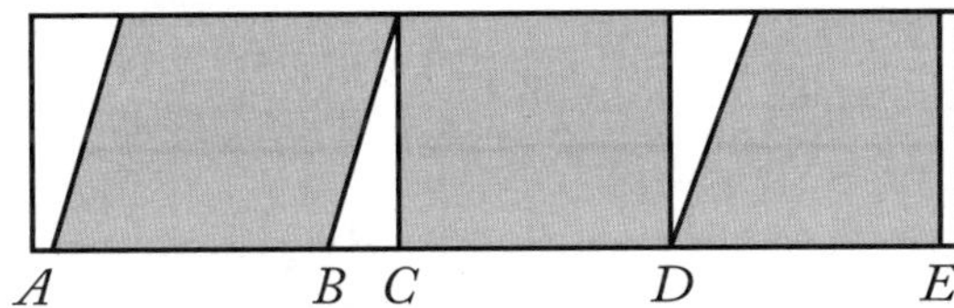

25. Inside the rectangle above is a shaded parallelogram, rectangle, and trapezoid. If $AB = CD = DE$, which of the following figures have the same area?
    (A) None of the figures
    (B) The parallelogram and the rectangle
    (C) The parallelogram and the trapezoid
    (D) The rectangle and the trapezoid
    (E) All of the figures

STOP

IF YOU FINISH BEFORE TIME IS CALLED, YOU MAY CHECK YOUR WORK ON THIS SECTION ONLY. DO NOT TURN TO ANY OTHER SECTION IN THE TEST.

SECTION 2
40 Questions

Read each passage carefully and then answer the questions about it. For each question, decide on the basis of the passage which one of the choices best answers the question.

The indescribable glory of the Gothic cathedral is its sculpture. The old churches are drenched with sculpture. It is estimated that the cathedral at Chartres, north of Paris, displays 10,000 carvings; they do not look as if they were added to the building like the frosted figures on a wedding cake, but as if they were a part of the building and as necessary as the arches and windows.

1. According to the passage, the outstanding feature of the cathedral at Chartres is the
   (A) age of its stonework
   (B) whiteness of the interior
   (C) location of the building
   (D) grandeur of its windows and arches
   (E) nature and number of its sculptures

2. The author indicates that the "carvings" (line 2) appear to be
   (A) purely decorative
   (B) stylistically varied
   (C) integral to the cathedral
   (D) too numerous to count
   (E) more beautiful than arches

3. The author uses the expression "frosted figures" (line 3) to create which literary device?
   (A) Onomatopoeia
   (B) Simile
   (C) Personification
   (D) Hyperbole
   (E) Oxymoron

GO ON TO THE NEXT PAGE.

"And now tell me about it." Mannering took notepaper from a drawer.

Sheila's glance strayed through the window and caught a little motorboat moored below. She braced herself and began to talk. He scribbled on the notepaper.

"And nobody knows about all this? Am I the first person you've managed to tell?"

She heard herself saying calmly, "I did say something to someone. One of your guests."

"One of my guests?" Mannering stood up.

He was gone—with frank haste. Sheila sprang to her feet. She had about two minutes. She picked up the telephone. Nothing happened. The instrument had been cut off. But somewhere in the castle there might be guests still. She ran to the door.

Locked. Sheila ran to the window, opened it and was on the terrace. There was a guard at either end, and these converged on her instantly. Sheila ran straight forward and leapt the balustrade.

She landed on a lower terrace, and the drop was sufficient to give her a nasty jar. But she scrambled up. There were shouts behind. She ran down the steps and jumped into the motorboat.

She realized that it had controls exactly like those of a car. She cast off.

4. The passage is primarily concerned with
   (A) a discovery
   (B) an escape
   (C) a rescue
   (D) a negotiation
   (E) a confession

5. Mannering leaves the room "with frank haste" (line 7) most likely because he wants to
   (A) give Sheila a chance to be alone
   (B) find the guest to whom Sheila had talked
   (C) say goodbye to his departing guests
   (D) find out why the telephone was cut off
   (E) move his motorboat out of sight

6. In the passage Sheila is portrayed as
   (A) resourceful
   (B) befuddled
   (C) negligent
   (D) dishonest
   (E) obedient

7. As it is used in line 13, "sufficient" most nearly means
   (A) loud enough
   (B) slow enough
   (C) mild enough
   (D) long enough
   (E) straight enough

8. The mood of the passage is best described as
   (A) somber
   (B) comical
   (C) tense
   (D) sedate
   (E) eerie

GO ON TO THE NEXT PAGE.

Sounds too high for humans to hear are audible to dogs. The upper limit of human hearing is about 20,000 hertz (cycles per second), of canine hearing about 40,000 hertz, and of mice hearing about 80,000 hertz. The lower limit of human hearing is about 125 hertz at normal levels of intensity. Are any animals able to hear even lower sounds than humans can?

It seems likely that all animals whose heads are larger than a human being's have this ability. Three investigators recently tested the hearing range of an Indian elephant. They found that Lois could not hear sounds higher than 12,000 hertz but could hear sounds as low as 16 hertz at levels of intensity that were inaudible to human beings. The investigators concluded that the range of hearing in animals is in inverse proportion, not to the size of the ear, but to the size of the skull, which is related to the distance between the ears.

9. The author uses the word "high" (line 1) in reference to
   (A) status
   (B) altitude
   (C) volume
   (D) pitch
   (E) emotion

10. According to the passage, the range of human hearing at normal levels of intensity is about
   (A) 16 to 125 hertz
   (B) 100 to 12,000 hertz
   (C) 125 to 20,000 hertz
   (D) 20,000 to 40,000 hertz
   (E) 40,000 to 80,000 hertz

11. In line 5, "this ability" refers to
   (A) making audible sounds
   (B) communicating with sounds
   (C) distinguishing high from low sounds
   (D) understanding human speech
   (E) hearing sounds below the human limit

12. It can be inferred from the passage that "Lois" (line 7) is the name of
   (A) an elephant
   (B) a canine subject
   (C) a human subject
   (D) an investigator
   (E) a recording device

13. According to the passage, an animal's range of hearing is proportionate to
   (A) the overall weight of the animal
   (B) the distance between the animal's ears
   (C) the size of the animal's ears
   (D) the range of sounds the animal produces
   (E) the volume of the animal's brain

GO ON TO THE NEXT PAGE.

There are several kinds of stories, but only one that is difficult to tell—the humorous. The humorous story is very different from the comic story. The humorous story depends for its effect upon the manner of the telling; the comic story upon the matter.

The humorous story may be spun out to great length, and wander around all it pleases, and arrive nowhere in particular, but the comic story must be brief and end with a point. The humorous story bubbles gently along; the other bursts.

The humorous story is strictly a work of art, and only an artist can tell it. No art is necessary in telling the comic story; anybody can do it. The humorous story is told gravely; the teller conceals that he or she even dimly suspects that there is anything funny about it.

The teller of a comic story tells you beforehand that it is funny, tells it with eager delight, and is the first person to laugh when the tale is told. And sometimes, if the story has had good success, the teller will gladly repeat the "nub" of it and glance around from face to face collecting applause, and then repeat it again. It is a pathetic thing to see.

Very often, of course, the rambling and disjointed humorous story finishes with a nub, point, snapper, or whatever you like to call it. Then the listener must be alert, for in many cases the teller will divert attention from that nub by dropping it in a carefully casual and indifferent way, with the pretense that he or she does not know it is a nub.

Artemus Ward used that trick a good deal; then when the audience belatedly caught the joke, he would look up with innocent surprise, as if wondering what they found to laugh at.

14. The primary purpose of the first four paragraphs (lines 1–13) is to
(A) distinguish humorous from comic stories
(B) outline the history of storytelling
(C) explain how to write a humorous story
(D) catalogue various kinds of stories
(E) analyze a story into its component parts

15. According to the passage, in comparison with a comic story, a humorous story is more
(A) condensed
(B) rambling
(C) instructive
(D) realistic
(E) absurd

16. According to the author, a humorous story should be told
(A) hurriedly
(B) sarcastically
(C) haltingly
(D) enthusiastically
(E) soberly

17. Another term for the "nub" (line 12) of a comic story is
(A) set-up
(B) tone
(C) punch line
(D) plot
(E) diversion

18. The author indicates that successful tellers of humorous stories often
(A) burst out unexpectedly with the snapper
(B) chuckle throughout the story
(C) clearly restate the point of the story
(D) focus attention on the nub of the story
(E) appear bewildered by the audience's laughter

GO ON TO THE NEXT PAGE.

Most caffeine research has focused on adults; less is known about the stimulant's possible effects on the young. Children seldom drink much coffee, but they can be exposed to significant amounts of caffeine in soft drinks and iced tea, especially relative to their body weight.

In a 1978 report, the Federation of American Societies for Experimental Biology (FASEB) reviewed estimates of caffeine intake among American youngsters. Adjusted for body weight, the average caffeine intake of the various age groups ranged from 36 to 58 percent of the average dose for adults. However, the top 10 percent in each age group had estimated intakes 3 to 10 times higher than the group average. Surprisingly, the highest intake occurred in the 1-to-5 age group.

The scientific committee of the FASEB expressed concern about possible behavioral effects of caffeine on children. "The estimated levels of caffeine intake at these ages are near those levels that are known to affect the central nervous system in adults," said the committee. But available evidence, they noted, was insufficient to judge whether such stimulation was a hazard.

Two subsequent studies at the National Institute of Mental Health offer some tentative evidence that caffeinism, or "coffee nerves," occurs in children as well as in adults. The studies each involved only about 20 boys and must be considered preliminary. But they appear to support the FASEB's suspicion that children who consume several caffeinated soft drinks daily experience jumpiness, insomnia, and other effects seen in adult coffee drinkers.

19. In line 7, "the top 10 percent" refers to
   (A) the oldest children studied
   (B) the healthiest children studied
   (C) the children who drank the most coffee
   (D) the children who exhibited the worst symptoms of caffeinism
   (E) the children who consumed the largest amounts of caffeine

20. The tone of the statement quoted in lines 10–11 is best described as
   (A) optimistic
   (B) humorous
   (C) combative
   (D) cautionary
   (E) sorrowful

21. The fourth paragraph (lines 13–17) answers which of the following questions?
   (A) How does the average intake of caffeine among children compare with that of adults?
   (B) What effects can caffeine have on children?
   (C) Why do adults and children exhibit similar symptoms of caffeinism?
   (D) What foods contain caffeine?
   (E) How much caffeine should children consume?

22. In the last paragraph (lines 13–17), the author implies that
   (A) the FASEB has overstated its claims about caffeine intake and behavioral consequences
   (B) the study conducted by the National Institute of Mental Health should have examined adults as well as children
   (C) more study is needed before research on the effects of caffeine on children can be considered conclusive
   (D) caffeine research conducted thus far is meaningless because of the small group of subjects
   (E) the effects of caffeine should be studied by medical doctors rather than by biologists

GO ON TO THE NEXT PAGE.

The dogs of London, Flush soon discovered, are strictly divided into different classes. Some are chained dogs, some run wild. Some take their airings in carriages and drink from purple jars; others are unkempt and uncollared and pick up a living in the gutter. Dogs, therefore, Flush began to suspect, differ; some are high, others low; and his suspicions were confirmed by snatches of talk held in passing with the dogs of Wimpole Street. "See that scallywag? A mere mongrel! . . . By gad, that's a fine Spaniel. One of the best in Britain! . . . Pity his ears aren't a shade more curly . . . There's a topknot for you! . . ."

Flush knew before the summer had passed that there is no equality among dogs; there are high dogs and low dogs. Which then was he? No sooner had Flush got home than he examined himself carefully in the looking-glass. Heaven be praised, he was a fine specimen! His head was smooth; his eyes were prominent but not goggled; his feet were feathered with long hair; he was the equal of the best-bred cocker in Wimpole Street. He noted with approval the purple jar from which he drank—such are the privileges of rank; he bent his head quietly to have the chain fixed to his collar—such are its penalties. When about this time Miss Barrett observed him staring in the glass, she was mistaken. He was a philosopher, she thought, meditating the difference between appearance and reality. On the contrary, he was an aristocrat considering his points.

23. In the first paragraph, "the dogs of Wimpole Street" (lines 5–6) are portrayed as
   (A) unkempt
   (B) snobbish
   (C) courteous
   (D) reckless
   (E) clever

24. According to the passage, which trait does Flush have that makes him high class?
   (A) Curly ears
   (B) A shiny coat
   (C) A topknot
   (D) Goggled eyes
   (E) Feathered feet

25. It can be inferred from the passage that after examining himself in the looking glass Flush felt a sense of
   (A) superiority
   (B) accomplishment
   (C) anxiety
   (D) outrage
   (E) shame

26. According to the passage, one of the "penalties" (line 14) Flush faces is being deprived of
   (A) food
   (B) shelter
   (C) affection
   (D) freedom
   (E) grooming

27. According to the passage, when Miss Barrett saw Flush looking in a mirror, she thought he was
   (A) vain
   (B) spying
   (C) contemplative
   (D) confused
   (E) distraught

28. The tone of the passage is best described as
   (A) foreboding
   (B) impassioned
   (C) melancholy
   (D) apologetic
   (E) fanciful

GO ON TO THE NEXT PAGE.

The Chickasaws were fierce warriors who once inhabited northeast Mississippi. Though fewer in number, they commanded respect from their neighbors, the Choctaws. The folklore of both tribes agreed that they had long ago been one people who had crossed the Mississippi River together, always traveling in obedience to a magic pole which pointed the way they should go. Perhaps, ironically, they originally came from that Oklahoma territory to which they were later exiled.

One Choctaw legend has it that the united people crossed the river at the Fourth Bluff, where a quarrel arose. One faction walked out of the council and thus acquired the name "Chickasaws" or "Rebels." Another Choctaw story keeps the people united until they reached the Yazoo River, where they built a sacrificial mound known as Nunih Wai-ya. The Chickasaw version is that they separated before crossing the Mississippi and that the Chickasaws then proceeded eastward till the magic pole stood upright near Tuscumbia, Alabama. Three years later the whimsical pole again leaned eastward and the tribe journeyed to the Atlantic Ocean, where evidence of their presence still exists near Savannah, Georgia. But a plague struck, the tribe was decimated, and the people retreated to Tuscumbia, where the rash pole stood meekly upright till it rotted.

29. The passage represents the Chickasaws as
   (A) formidable in war
   (B) oppressed by their enemies
   (C) living under a curse
   (D) disdainful of tradition
   (E) hospitable to strangers

30. According to the passage, the Chickasaws first crossed the Mississippi River because they
   (A) were fleeing a plague
   (B) had outgrown their homeland
   (C) had quarreled with their neighbors
   (D) were in search of a lost tribe
   (E) were following supernatural guidance

31. According to the passage, Nunih Wai-ya was
   (A) a fortress
   (B) a battle monument
   (C) an abandoned city
   (D) a place of worship
   (E) a burial site

32. Throughout the passage, the author uses which literary device to describe the "magic pole"?
   (A) Simile
   (B) Personification
   (C) Alliteration
   (D) Understatement
   (E) Onomatopoeia

33. The passage indicates that the Chickasaws
   (A) rebelled against the Choctaws before crossing the Mississippi River
   (B) grew in number after crossing the Mississippi River
   (C) stole the magic pole from the Choctaws
   (D) reached the Atlantic Ocean during the course of their travels
   (E) were exiled finally to a location near Savannah, Georgia

GO ON TO THE NEXT PAGE.

In my dreams, however strange it may sound, I dream at the same time of children and of an independent life, which should be both comfortable and beautiful. The question of woman's fate interests me tremendously. This interest lives in me somehow fundamentally; it is called forth neither by writing nor conversation, but has taken root in me of its own accord.

Is it necessary to add that I believe with all my heart and mind that women have absolutely equal rights with men, because I consider them in no wise men's intellectual inferior?

This year I have added to the books on social subjects, some that are concerned with the feminist question, and I shall read them with great enjoyment.

Of course, comparatively speaking, women have not asserted themselves up to now as capable individuals. There are many empty coquettes as well as spiritual nonentities among them, but, all the same, it is of note that now in all professions women appear who work on a level with men.

Are there also no empty-headed men? Oh many! Do not men themselves encourage the defects of women by considering them only as amusing playthings? I speak, of course, in general. There are exceptions but, taken on an average, they are in the minority.

Does the education of woman prepare her for the serious tasks of life? The evil of this education is rooted far back in the centuries. Give women scope and opportunity, and they will be no worse than men.

Yes, woman must have all the rights, and in time she can earn them fully. At present we have still many women who are satisfied with their empty lives, but if we raise the standard, and improve the social conditions of her life, woman will also rise. Even now there are many among them who would be capable of leading a conscious existence successfully. Give them that possibility. When people criticize a woman in my presence, I never feel at ease, and I realize that they are wrong, but I have not the courage to dispute with them; I lack arguments and only mentally say to myself, "Wait!"

34. The author uses the word "strange" (line 1) to describe

(A) an unfamiliar landscape
(B) an eccentric personality
(C) a supernatural occurrence
(D) a seeming contradiction
(E) a foreign language

35. According to the passage, the author's interest in the fate of women is the result of

(A) an education rooted far back in the centuries
(B) her extensive reading of feminist literature
(C) her dissatisfaction with her own life
(D) the kinship she feels with professional women
(E) a spontaneous inner urge

GO ON TO THE NEXT PAGE.

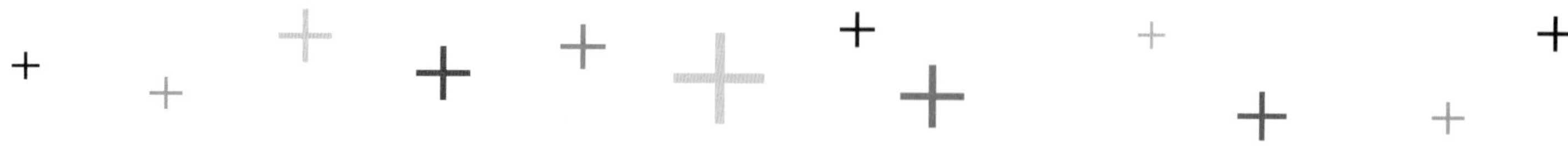

36. The author implies that a person's "rights" (line 6) are based on
    (A) property
    (B) intelligence
    (C) ancestry
    (D) occupation
    (E) gender

37. The author uses the expression "Of course" (line 9) to
    (A) acknowledge a shortcoming
    (B) convey an expectation
    (C) accept a proposal
    (D) draw an inference
    (E) confirm a principle

38. The author indicates that if given "scope and opportunity" (line 17), women will
    (A) be as successful as men
    (B) make better leaders than men
    (C) be more adept in business than men
    (D) take jobs away from men
    (E) oppress men as they have been oppressed

39. The author indicates that she does not challenge people who criticize women primarily because she
    (A) secretly agrees with the criticisms
    (B) is waiting for someone else to speak out
    (C) knows that she is too young to voice her opinions
    (D) has been told not to interfere
    (E) feels she cannot do so successfully

40. Throughout the passage, the author conveys her beliefs by means of
    (A) similes
    (B) poetic imagery
    (C) rhetorical questions
    (D) hyperbole
    (E) anecdotes

STOP

IF YOU FINISH BEFORE TIME IS CALLED, YOU MAY CHECK YOUR WORK ON THIS SECTION ONLY. DO NOT TURN TO ANY OTHER SECTION IN THE TEST.

SECTION 3
60 Questions

This section consists of two different types of questions: synonyms and analogies. There are directions and a sample question for each type.

Synonyms
Each of the following questions consists of one word followed by five words or phrases. You are to select the one word or phrase whose meaning is closest to the word in capital letters.

Sample Question:

CHILLY:
(A) lazy
(B) nice
(C) dry
(D) cold
(E) sunny

---

1. ASTONISHED:
(A) aged
(B) talented
(C) plump
(D) surprised
(E) tired

2. NOMINATE:
(A) understand
(B) pamper
(C) bargain
(D) excuse
(E) propose

3. CERTIFY:
(A) appoint temporarily
(B) substitute willingly
(C) confirm officially
(D) replace unconditionally
(E) allow hesitantly

4. PRECAUTION:
(A) optimism
(B) safeguard
(C) removal
(D) confidence
(E) delicacy

5. SEQUENCE:
(A) motion to adjourn
(B) plan of attack
(C) order of succession
(D) room for growth
(E) point of reference

6. FUMBLE:
(A) depart hastily
(B) destroy completely
(C) move unnecessarily
(D) handle clumsily
(E) react instinctively

7. CAPSIZE:
(A) occupy
(B) protect
(C) free
(D) inspire
(E) overturn

8. HOAX:
(A) problem
(B) omission
(C) force
(D) excess
(E) fraud

GO ON TO THE NEXT PAGE.

9. BRAWL:
   (A) sneak attack
   (B) noisy fight
   (C) defiant attitude
   (D) impolite refusal
   (E) sudden drop

10. MEDDLE:
   (A) encounter
   (B) surround
   (C) outline
   (D) deflect
   (E) interfere

11. SWELTERING:
   (A) uncomfortably hot
   (B) intensely boring
   (C) unusually dirty
   (D) extremely sad
   (E) very painful

12. CIRCUMFERENCE:
   (A) separation from
   (B) area under
   (C) distance around
   (D) path through
   (E) placement opposite

13. DETAIN:
   (A) prepare
   (B) disturb
   (C) separate
   (D) delay
   (E) grow

14. LUBRICATE:
   (A) dissolve
   (B) illuminate
   (C) grease
   (D) dampen
   (E) twist

15. CANDOR:
   (A) frankness
   (B) sacrifice
   (C) quantity
   (D) illusion
   (E) sympathy

16. DIMINISHED:
   (A) basic
   (B) reduced
   (C) joined
   (D) vertical
   (E) repeated

17. TRIVIAL:
   (A) delightful
   (B) unseen
   (C) illegal
   (D) unimportant
   (E) tangled

18. EVOLVE:
   (A) endure
   (B) evict
   (C) develop
   (D) launch
   (E) permit

19. IRRITATE:
   (A) confirm
   (B) debate
   (C) annoy
   (D) protect
   (E) applaud

20. BLOCKADE:
   (A) make preparations
   (B) assume command
   (C) take captive
   (D) prevent passage
   (E) ignore warnings

GO ON TO THE NEXT PAGE.

21. RETROSPECT:
    (A) hindsight
    (B) retreat
    (C) supervision
    (D) memorization
    (E) tribute

22. CONFER:
    (A) proceed
    (B) increase
    (C) consult
    (D) evade
    (E) agree

23. EXPENDITURE:
    (A) amount inherited
    (B) property sold
    (C) cash borrowed
    (D) goods donated
    (E) money paid out

24. IMPROMPTU:
    (A) compulsory
    (B) unplanned
    (C) punctual
    (D) vigorous
    (E) illicit

25. WITHER:
    (A) shrivel
    (B) endure
    (C) flee
    (D) tremble
    (E) decide

26. CONGENIAL:
    (A) nervous
    (B) courageous
    (C) modest
    (D) pitiable
    (E) friendly

27. MESMERIZE:
    (A) deceive
    (B) frustrate
    (C) spellbind
    (D) recall
    (E) dishevel

28. HOSPITABLE:
    (A) cordial
    (B) parallel
    (C) weak
    (D) useful
    (E) diseased

29. VIGILANT:
    (A) heavy
    (B) menacing
    (C) alert
    (D) sane
    (E) handsome

30. HAPHAZARD:
    (A) careless
    (B) harmful
    (C) powerless
    (D) unconvincing
    (E) mysterious

GO ON TO THE NEXT PAGE.

Analogies

The following questions ask you to find relationships between words. For each question, select the answer choice that best completes the meaning of the sentence.

Sample Question:

Kitten is to cat as
(A) fawn is to colt
(B) puppy is to dog
(C) cow is to bull
(D) wolf is to bear
(E) hen is to rooster

Choice (B) is the best answer because a kitten is a young cat just as a puppy is a young dog. Of all the answer choices, (B) states a relationship that is most like the relationship between kitten and cat.

---

31. Goose is to flock as
    (A) rabbit is to bunny
    (B) wolf is to pack
    (C) duck is to litter
    (D) turtle is to tortoise
    (E) child is to parent

32. Bowling is to lane as
    (A) baseball is to bat
    (B) basketball is to court
    (C) diamond is to field
    (D) soccer is to ball
    (E) tennis is to racquet

33. Skin is to potato as
    (A) stalk is to celery
    (B) pit is to olive
    (C) pole is to bean
    (D) vine is to cucumber
    (E) shell is to almond

34. Courthouse is to law as
    (A) church is to religion
    (B) jail is to crime
    (C) bank is to vault
    (D) library is to collection
    (E) restaurant is to server

35. Needle is to sew as
    (A) blanket is to crochet
    (B) thread is to snip
    (C) hair is to braid
    (D) loom is to weave
    (E) craft is to embroider

36. Dim is to dark as
    (A) chilly is to snowy
    (B) warm is to hot
    (C) quiet is to noisy
    (D) stormy is to windy
    (E) icy is to slippery

37. Nod is to approval as
    (A) ask is to favor
    (B) blink is to eye
    (C) wave is to greeting
    (D) jump is to exercise
    (E) laugh is to joke

38. Closet is to clothing as
    (A) lobby is to hall
    (B) floor is to carpet
    (C) pantry is to food
    (D) paper is to pencil
    (E) attic is to roof

GO ON TO THE NEXT PAGE.

39. Bright is to lightning as
    (A) loud is to thunder
    (B) steep is to hill
    (C) strong is to odor
    (D) temperate is to weather
    (E) stationary is to cloud

40. Drum is to stick as
    (A) nail is to hammer
    (B) log is to saw
    (C) grass is to mower
    (D) ball is to tee
    (E) bolt is to nut

41. Dessert is to meal as
    (A) sand is to shore
    (B) cream is to milk
    (C) finale is to performance
    (D) plant is to root
    (E) medicine is to symptom

42. Joking is to serious as
    (A) smug is to justified
    (B) deceptive is to honest
    (C) suspicious is to guilty
    (D) angry is to provoked
    (E) insulting is to impolite

43. Driver is to bus as
    (A) engineer is to train
    (B) passenger is to airplane
    (C) commuter is to taxi
    (D) balloonist is to parachute
    (E) pedestrian is to sidewalk

44. Music is to composer as
    (A) money is to cashier
    (B) drama is to audience
    (C) photography is to model
    (D) merchandise is to buyer
    (E) apparel is to designer

45. Glue is to paper as
    (A) pour is to oil
    (B) stitch is to thread
    (C) wind is to clock
    (D) weld is to metal
    (E) dig is to ditch

46. Veteran is to soldier as
    (A) professor is to scholar
    (B) lecturer is to scientist
    (C) alumnus is to student
    (D) dentist is to physician
    (E) litigator is to lawyer

47. Letter is to write as
    (A) brush is to paint
    (B) knife is to cut
    (C) picture is to draw
    (D) fatigue is to sleep
    (E) heat is to burn

48. Chapter is to book as
    (A) student is to faculty
    (B) experiment is to laboratory
    (C) story is to author
    (D) juice is to glass
    (E) course is to curriculum

49. Sandal is to shoe as
    (A) pullover is to sweater
    (B) pocket is to jeans
    (C) robe is to pajamas
    (D) button is to jacket
    (E) hood is to raincoat

50. Cane is to walk as
    (A) hair is to comb
    (B) lens is to see
    (C) door is to open
    (D) knee is to bend
    (E) plow is to push

GO ON TO THE NEXT PAGE.

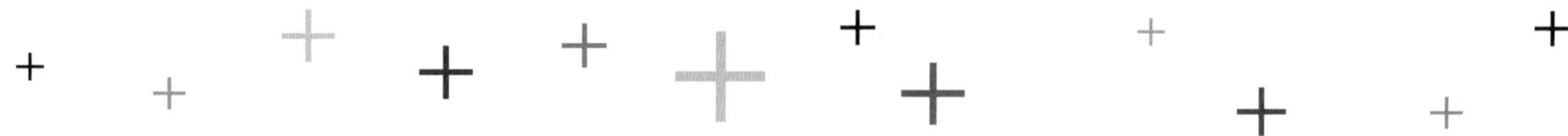

51. Celestial is to sky as
    (A) distant is to star
    (B) terrestrial is to alien
    (C) solar is to sun
    (D) liquid is to water
    (E) atmospheric is to cloud

52. Moth is to fabric as
    (A) termite is to wood
    (B) corn is to scarecrow
    (C) snake is to venom
    (D) butterfly is to cocoon
    (E) mosquito is to picnic

53. Sonnet is to poem as
    (A) salt is to shaker
    (B) foot is to shoe
    (C) chimney is to roof
    (D) steak is to chop
    (E) cedar is to wood

54. Spontaneous is to forethought as
    (A) immature is to youth
    (B) explosive is to fire
    (C) erroneous is to mistake
    (D) accidental is to intent
    (E) elementary is to education

55. Eminent is to obscurity as
    (A) joyous is to frivolity
    (B) brilliant is to education
    (C) deficient is to enhancement
    (D) hasty is to immediacy
    (E) affluent is to poverty

56. Magnify is to large as
    (A) speak is to silent
    (B) lift is to heavy
    (C) acquire is to greedy
    (D) elevate is to high
    (E) carry is to portable

57. Thesaurus is to word as
    (A) bibliography is to title
    (B) science is to experiment
    (C) printer is to ink
    (D) symphony is to orchestra
    (E) dictionary is to book

58. Surgeon is to operate as
    (A) chef is to serve
    (B) orator is to speak
    (C) singer is to compose
    (D) therapist is to injure
    (E) attorney is to investigate

59. Moor is to boat as
    (A) pave is to tar
    (B) tether is to horse
    (C) steer is to wheel
    (D) sink is to leak
    (E) load is to truck

60. Nimble is to acrobat as
    (A) verbose is to speaker
    (B) literate is to scholar
    (C) eloquent is to monarch
    (D) cynical is to philosopher
    (E) popular is to friend

STOP

IF YOU FINISH BEFORE TIME IS CALLED, YOU MAY CHECK YOUR WORK ON THIS SECTION ONLY. DO NOT TURN TO ANY OTHER SECTION IN THE TEST.

SECTION 4
25 Questions

Following each problem in this section, there are five suggested answers. Work each problem in your head or in the blank space provided at the right of the page. Then look at the five suggested answers and decide which one is best.

Note: Figures that accompany problems in this section are drawn as accurately as possible EXCEPT when it is stated in a specific problem that its figure is not drawn to scale.

Sample Problem:

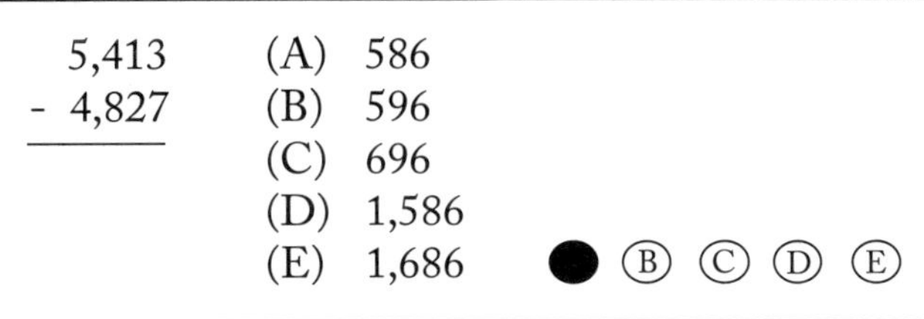

USE THIS SPACE FOR FIGURING.

1. A comic book artist can draw 2 comic book pages per day. At this rate, what is the total number of pages the artist can draw in 30 days?

   (A) 60
   (B) 45
   (C) 32
   (D) 28
   (E) 15

---

2. If $7 - n = 7 + n$, what is the value of n ?

   (A) -7
   (B) 0
   (C) $\frac{1}{7}$
   (D) 1
   (E) 14

---

3. Tony and Marion together have \$15. If Tony has x dollars, which of the following gives the number of dollars Marion has?

   (A) $\frac{15}{x}$
   (B) $15x$
   (C) $x - 15$
   (D) $15 + x$
   (E) $15 - x$

GO ON TO THE NEXT PAGE.

USE THIS SPACE FOR FIGURING.

4. Compute: 3.1 + 73.48 + 0.075
   (A) 10.523
   (B) 74.54
   (C) 76.33
   (D) 76.655
   (E) 77.655

5. A sheet of 35-cent stamps has 6 rows of stamps and 4 stamps in each row. What is the cost of 2 sheets of these stamps?
   (A) $16.80
   (B) $10.40
   (C) $8.40
   (D) $7.00
   (E) $4.20

6. For the parallelogram shown, what is the value of x ?

   (A) 100
   (B) 80
   (C) 60
   (D) 40
   (E) 10

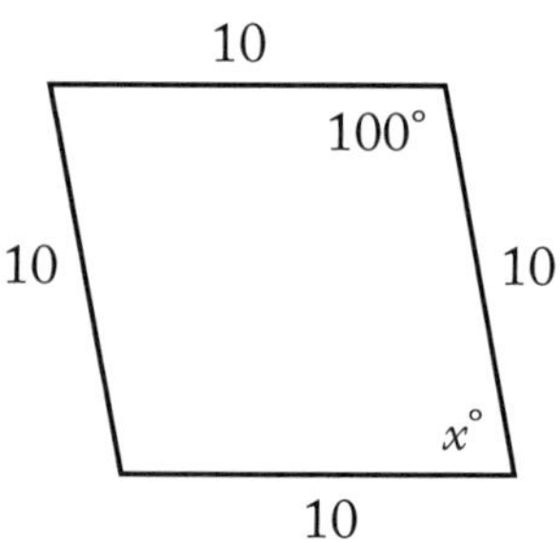

7. A mass of 400 grams is equivalent to how many kilograms?
   (A) 40
   (B) 25
   (C) 4
   (D) 2.5
   (E) 0.4

8. Each month, Dwayne reads 2 fiction books and 1 nonfiction book, and Kristina reads 1 fiction book and 2 nonfiction books. At this rate, how many more fiction books will Dwayne read than Kristina will read in one year?
   (A) 0
   (B) 1
   (C) 6
   (D) 12
   (E) 24

GO ON TO THE NEXT PAGE.

USE THIS SPACE FOR FIGURING.

9. Which of the following fractions is least?

(A) $\frac{4}{7}$

(B) $\frac{26}{51}$

(C) $\frac{79}{160}$

(D) $\frac{112}{224}$

(E) $\frac{210}{410}$

---

10. A light bulb manufacturer expects that in each batch of 10,000 light bulbs produced, 14 will be defective. In a recent batch of 10,000 light bulbs, it was found that 29% of the expected number of defective light bulbs were defective. Of the following, which is the best estimate for the number of defective light bulbs in this batch?

(A) 4
(B) 6
(C) 8
(D) 30
(E) 40

---

11. If $r = 6$, $s = 3$, and $t = 2$, what is the value of $\frac{r^2 - st}{s}$?

(A) 2
(B) 3
(C) 10
(D) 22
(E) 34

---

12. The recipe for a cake that serves 6 people requires 1.25 pounds of butter. How many $\frac{1}{4}$-pound sticks of butter will be required to make enough cakes to serve 18 people?

(A) 10
(B) 12
(C) 15
(D) 20
(E) 30

GO ON TO THE NEXT PAGE.

USE THIS SPACE FOR FIGURING.

13. For integers n, which of the following must be divisible by 3 ?

I. $24n - 6$
II. $27(n - 6)$
III. $36n + 4$

(A) None
(B) I and II only
(C) I and III only
(D) II and III only
(E) I, II, and III

---

14. The figure is a cylinder sliced in half. Of the following, which is the best estimate for the volume of the figure?

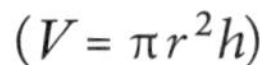
$(V = \pi r^2 h)$

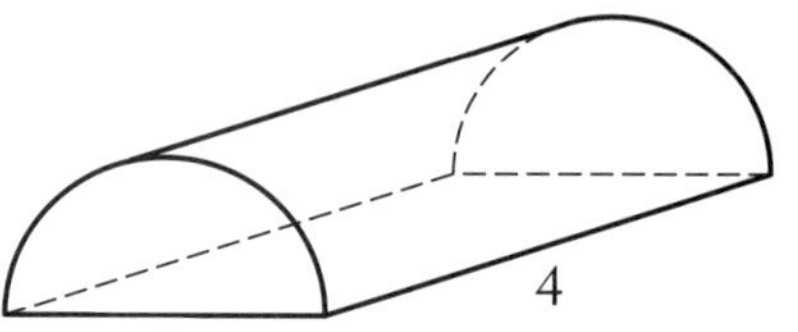

(A) 6
(B) 12
(C) 24
(D) 36
(E) 48

---

15. The first number in a sequence is 42, and each number after the first is 5 more than the preceding number. Which of the following is a number in the sequence?

(A) 143
(B) 158
(C) 180
(D) 201
(E) 237

---

16. There are 20 pieces of identically wrapped candies in a box, of which 8 are chocolate, 4 are mint, 3 are licorice, and the rest are vanilla. If Mike selects a piece of candy at random, what is the probability that he will select a vanilla candy?

(A) $\frac{1}{20}$
(B) $\frac{1}{5}$
(C) $\frac{1}{4}$
(D) $\frac{1}{3}$
(E) $\frac{3}{4}$

GO ON TO THE NEXT PAGE.

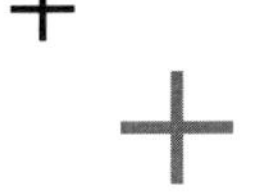

USE THIS SPACE FOR FIGURING.

17. What is 8,000 ÷ 40 ÷ 20 ÷ 10 ?
    (A) 1
    (B) 100
    (C) 400
    (D) 1,600
    (E) 4,000

---

18. Which of the following is true for all obtuse triangles?
    (A) The sides must be the same length.
    (B) The sides must be different lengths.
    (C) One of the interior angles must be a right angle.
    (D) Two of the interior angles must be acute angles.
    (E) All of the interior angles must be obtuse angles.

---

19. Calculate: 2 + 4(20 + 5)
    (A) 87
    (B) 102
    (C) 125
    (D) 150
    (E) 200

---

20. Which of the following will NOT produce the same result as 32,400 × 0.25 ?
    (A) $32{,}400 \times \frac{1}{4}$
    (B) 32,400 ÷ 4
    (C) $32{,}400 \times \frac{1}{25}$
    (D) 324 × 25
    (E) (32,400 × 25) ÷ 100

GO ON TO THE NEXT PAGE.

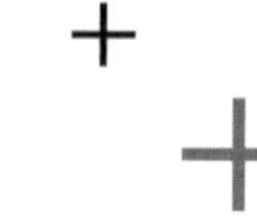

USE THIS SPACE FOR FIGURING.

21. Of the following, which is the best estimate for how much greater the total dollar sales were for drinks and popcorn than the total dollar sales were for hot dogs in the graph?

(A) \$200
(B) \$250
(C) \$300
(D) \$1,050
(E) \$1,350

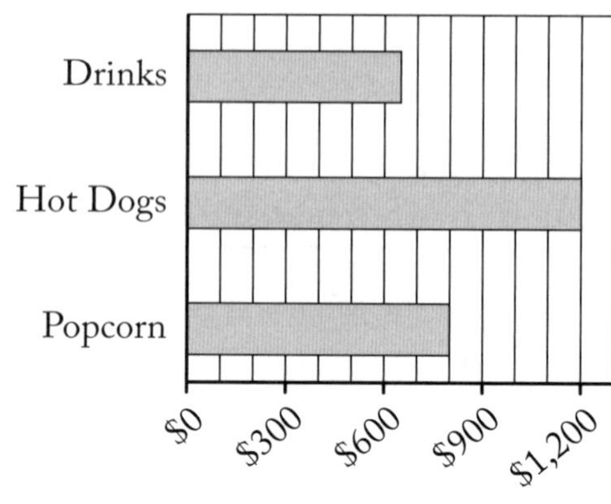

---

22. Of the following, which is closest to $\sqrt{50} + \sqrt{120}$?

(A) 9
(B) 13
(C) 18
(D) 85
(E) 170

---

23. Square *PQRS* shown contains two shaded squares. If the areas of the shaded squares are 25 and 9, respectively, what is the area of the square *PQRS* ?

(A) 32
(B) 34
(C) 61
(D) 64
(E) 68

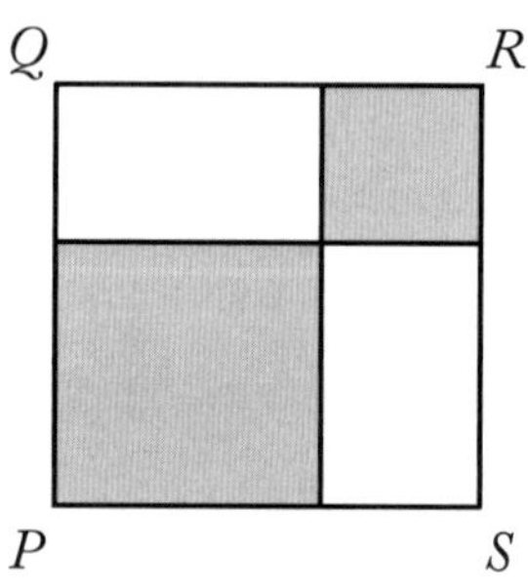

GO ON TO THE NEXT PAGE.

USE THIS SPACE FOR FIGURING.

24. What is the result when $-\frac{7}{5}$ is subtracted from $\frac{11}{3}$?

(A) $-\frac{76}{15}$

(B) $\frac{9}{4}$

(C) $\frac{18}{15}$

(D) $\frac{34}{15}$

(E) $\frac{76}{15}$

---

25. In the figure, how many non-overlapping segments equal in length to segment $\overline{OP}$ are there on segment $\overline{PQ}$?

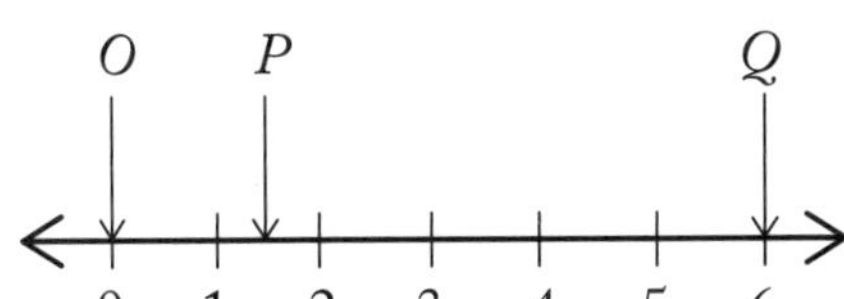

(A) One

(B) Three
(C) Four
(D) Five
(E) Six

STOP

IF YOU FINISH BEFORE TIME IS CALLED, YOU MAY CHECK YOUR WORK ON THIS SECTION ONLY. DO NOT TURN TO ANY OTHER SECTION IN THE TEST.

THIS PAGE INTENTIONALLY LEFT BLANK.

Evaluating Your
Middle Level SSAT

How Did You Do?

When you have completed the practice tests, give yourself a pat on the back, and then take a few moments to think about your performance.

- Did you leave many questions unanswered?
- Did you run out of time?
- Did you read the directions carefully?

Based on your understanding of how well you performed, review the particular test sections that gave you difficulty.

Scoring the Practice Tests

In order to calculate your "raw score" (right, wrong, and omitted answers) for each test section, use the answer keys on pages 218–229. *The Official Study Guide for the Middle Level SSAT* contains practice tests, not "retired" forms of the test. These tests are intended to familiarize you with the format, content, and timing of the actual test. These tests do not provide you with a score as if you were taking the actual SSAT.

Computing Your Raw Score

1. Using the Practice Test Answer Keys found on pages 218–229, check your answer sheet against the list of correct answers.

2. Mark your answer for each test question in the "Your Answer" column. Next, give yourself a ✓ in the "C" column for each correct answer, a 0 for each wrong answer in the "W" column, and a — for each question omitted in the "O" column.

Correct Answer	Your Answer	C ✓	W 0	O –
1. A	A	✓		
2. B	C		0	
3. C				–
4. C	C	✓		
5. D	D	✓		

3. Add the total number of correct answers and enter the number in the "Total # Correct" box; add the number of 0s and enter in the "Total # Wrong" box. (It is not necessary to add the number of omits. You can use that information to go back and review those questions and to make sure that you understand all answers.)

4. Raw scores are calculated by using the following system:
   - One point is given for each correct answer.
   - No points are added or subtracted for questions omitted.
   - One fourth of a point is subtracted for each incorrect answer.

5. Divide the number of wrong answers in the "Total # Wrong" box by 4 and enter the number in the "# Wrong ÷ 4" box. For example, if you had 32 right and 19 wrong, then your raw score is 32 minus one fourth of 19, which equals 27.25 (32 - 4.75 = 27.25).

6. Round the result in box 3 to the nearest whole integer. Put the integer in Box 4. For example, round 27.25 to 27.

7. The integer in Box 4 is the raw score on the section.

8. Repeat this procedure for each simulated test section that you have taken.

Total # Correct:	1
Total # Wrong:	
# Wrong ÷ 4:	2
Box 1 - Box 2	3
Round Box 3 to nearest whole integer:	4
Raw Score:	

Answer Key

Middle Level Practice Test I : QUANTITATIVE (Sections 1 and 4)

For each question, mark ✓ if correct (C), **0** if wrong (W), or **–** if omitted (O).

Correct Answer	Your Answer	C ✓	W **0**	O **–**
Section 1				
1. A				
2. B				
3. E				
4. B				
5. E				
6. D				
7. C				
8. B				
9. A				
10. D				
11. B				
12. E				
13. A				
14. C				
15. E				
16. D				
17. D				
18. E				
19. B				
20. D				
21. B				
22. A				
23. D				
24. A				
25. E				
Subtotal				

Correct Answer	Your Answer	C ✓	W **0**	O **–**
Section 4				
1. E				
2. B				
3. C				
4. A				
5. A				
6. B				
7. D				
8. E				
9. B				
10. D				
11. C				
12. D				
13. C				
14. A				
15. C				
16. E				
17. B				
18. D				
19. D				
20. B				
21. C				
22. B				
23. A				
24. D				
25. B				
Subtotal				

Total # Correct:	1
Total # Wrong:	
# Wrong ÷ 4:	2
Box 1 - Box 2	3
Round Box 3 to nearest whole integer:	4

Quantitative Raw Score:	

Box 4

Quantitative Estimated Scaled Score:	

See Table on page 230

Answer Key

Middle Level Practice Test I : READING (Section 2)

For each question, mark ✓ if correct (C), **0** if wrong (W), or **–** if omitted (O).

Correct Answer	Your Answer	C ✓	W **0**	O **–**
1. B				
2. C				
3. D				
4. E				
5. A				
6. C				
7. A				
8. B				
9. D				
10. D				
11. E				
12. E				
13. D				
14. B				
15. A				
16. C				
17. A				
18. B				
19. C				
20. D				
Subtotal				

Correct Answer	Your Answer	C ✓	W **0**	O **–**
21. E				
22. D				
23. B				
24. A				
25. C				
26. E				
27. C				
28. D				
29. B				
30. A				
31. B				
32. B				
33. E				
34. C				
35. A				
36. C				
37. B				
38. A				
39. B				
40. D				
Subtotal				

Total # Correct:	1
Total # Wrong:	
# Wrong ÷ 4:	2
Box 1 - Box 2	3
Round Box 3 to nearest whole integer:	4

Reading Raw Score:	

Box 4

Reading Estimated Scaled Score:	

See Table on page 230

Answer Key

Middle Level Practice Test I : VERBAL (Section 3)

For each question, mark ✓ if correct (C), **0** if wrong (W), or **–** if omitted (O).

Correct Answer	Your Answer	C ✓	W **0**	O **–**
1. E				
2. B				
3. A				
4. D				
5. A				
6. C				
7. A				
8. B				
9. E				
10. D				
11. C				
12. D				
13. C				
14. A				
15. E				
16. C				
17. D				
18. A				
19. D				
20. A				
21. D				
22. A				
23. C				
24. B				
25. D				
26. E				
27. A				
28. E				
29. C				
30. B				
Subtotal				

Correct Answer	Your Answer	C ✓	W **0**	O **–**
31. B				
32. C				
33. A				
34. C				
35. B				
36. E				
37. D				
38. A				
39. B				
40. A				
41. D				
42. C				
43. E				
44. D				
45. A				
46. A				
47. E				
48. E				
49. D				
50. A				
51. D				
52. C				
53. B				
54. C				
55. E				
56. D				
57. A				
58. E				
59. B				
60. D				
Subtotal				

Total # Correct:	1
Total # Wrong:	
# Wrong ÷ 4:	2
Box 1 - Box 2	3
Round Box 3 to nearest whole integer:	4

Verbal Raw Score:	

Box 4

Verbal Estimated Scaled Score:	

See Table on page 230

Answer Key

Middle Level Practice Test II : QUANTITATIVE (Sections 1 and 4)

For each question, mark ✓ if correct (C), **0** if wrong (W), or **–** if omitted (O).

Correct Answer	Your Answer	C ✓	W **0**	O **–**
Section 1				
1. C				
2. B				
3. E				
4. A				
5. B				
6. D				
7. B				
8. C				
9. E				
10. D				
11. C				
12. B				
13. A				
14. D				
15. D				
16. E				
17. B				
18. E				
19. E				
20. A				
21. D				
22. B				
23. A				
24. C				
25. A				
Subtotal				

Correct Answer	Your Answer	C ✓	W **0**	O **–**
Section 4				
1. C				
2. A				
3. D				
4. B				
5. C				
6. E				
7. B				
8. E				
9. D				
10. C				
11. A				
12. D				
13. D				
14. A				
15. E				
16. C				
17. E				
18. A				
19. B				
20. A				
21. D				
22. E				
23. E				
24. B				
25. C				
Subtotal				

Total # Correct:	1
Total # Wrong:	
# Wrong ÷ 4:	2
Box 1 - Box 2	3
Round Box 3 to nearest whole integer:	4

Quantitative Raw Score:	

Box 4

Quantitative Estimated Scaled Score:	

See Table on page 230

Answer Key

Middle Level Practice Test II : READING (Section 2)

For each question, mark ✓ if correct (C), **0** if wrong (W), or **–** if omitted (O).

Correct Answer	Your Answer	C ✓	W **0**	O **–**
1. C				
2. D				
3. B				
4. D				
5. E				
6. C				
7. A				
8. E				
9. D				
10. C				
11. A				
12. D				
13. A				
14. B				
15. E				
16. E				
17. D				
18. B				
19. A				
20. E				
Subtotal				

Correct Answer	Your Answer	C ✓	W **0**	O **–**
21. D				
22. E				
23. B				
24. C				
25. B				
26. B				
27. A				
28. C				
29. A				
30. E				
31. D				
32. B				
33. E				
34. D				
35. C				
36. B				
37. D				
38. C				
39. E				
40. A				
Subtotal				

Total # Correct:	1
Total # Wrong:	
# Wrong ÷ 4:	2
Box 1 - Box 2	3
Round Box 3 to nearest whole integer:	4

Reading Raw Score:	

Box 4

Reading Estimated Scaled Score:	

See Table on page 230

Answer Key

Middle Level Practice Test II : VERBAL (Section 3)

For each question, mark ✓ if correct (C), **0** if wrong (W), or **–** if omitted (O).

Correct Answer	Your Answer	C ✓	W **0**	O **–**
1. B				
2. A				
3. E				
4. C				
5. B				
6. D				
7. C				
8. C				
9. E				
10. D				
11. D				
12. A				
13. D				
14. A				
15. E				
16. B				
17. D				
18. B				
19. E				
20. D				
21. A				
22. C				
23. B				
24. C				
25. B				
26. C				
27. D				
28. E				
29. B				
30. A				
Subtotal				

Correct Answer	Your Answer	C ✓	W **0**	O **–**
31. E				
32. A				
33. E				
34. D				
35. A				
36. B				
37. D				
38. E				
39. C				
40. A				
41. D				
42. B				
43. C				
44. A				
45. C				
46. E				
47. C				
48. A				
49. C				
50. D				
51. E				
52. A				
53. E				
54. C				
55. A				
56. C				
57. B				
58. B				
59. E				
60. C				
Subtotal				

Total # Correct:	1
Total # Wrong:	
# Wrong ÷ 4:	2
Box 1 - Box 2	3
Round Box 3 to nearest whole integer:	4

Verbal Raw Score:	

Box 4

Verbal Estimated Scaled Score:	

See Table on page 230

Answer Key

Middle Level Practice Test III : QUANTITATIVE (Sections 1 and 4)

For each question, mark ✓ if correct (C), **0** if wrong (W), or **–** if omitted (O).

Correct Answer	Your Answer	C ✓	W **0**	O **–**
Section 1				
1. D				
2. A				
3. B				
4. D				
5. E				
6. C				
7. C				
8. D				
9. C				
10. B				
11. C				
12. A				
13. B				
14. D				
15. E				
16. E				
17. C				
18. E				
19. A				
20. C				
21. B				
22. B				
23. A				
24. E				
25. D				
Subtotal				

Correct Answer	Your Answer	C ✓	W **0**	O **–**
Section 4				
1. A				
2. B				
3. A				
4. D				
5. E				
6. D				
7. E				
8. C				
9. E				
10. A				
11. B				
12. B				
13. A				
14. D				
15. D				
16. E				
17. D				
18. B				
19. C				
20. C				
21. B				
22. D				
23. C				
24. E				
25. C				
Subtotal				

Total # Correct:	1
Total # Wrong:	
# Wrong ÷ 4:	2
Box 1 - Box 2	3
Round Box 3 to nearest whole integer:	4

Quantitative Raw Score:	

Box 4

Quantitative Estimated Scaled Score:	

See Table on page 230

Answer Key

Middle Level Practice Test III : READING (Section 2)

For each question, mark ✓ if correct (C), **0** if wrong (W), or **–** if omitted (O).

Correct Answer	Your Answer	C ✓	W 0	O –
1. B				
2. C				
3. B				
4. A				
5. A				
6. E				
7. C				
8. A				
9. E				
10. B				
11. D				
12. D				
13. B				
14. E				
15. A				
16. C				
17. E				
18. D				
19. A				
20. B				
Subtotal				

Correct Answer	Your Answer	C ✓	W 0	O –
21. D				
22. C				
23. B				
24. E				
25. D				
26. E				
27. A				
28. C				
29. C				
30. B				
31. B				
32. A				
33. E				
34. D				
35. C				
36. A				
37. D				
38. C				
39. E				
40. D				
Subtotal				

Total # Correct:	1
Total # Wrong:	
# Wrong ÷ 4:	2
Box 1 - Box 2	3
Round Box 3 to nearest whole integer:	4

Reading Raw Score:	

Box 4

Reading Estimated Scaled Score:	

See Table on page 230

Answer Key

Middle Level Practice Test III : VERBAL (Section 3)

For each question, mark ✓ if correct (C), **0** if wrong (W), or **–** if omitted (O).

Correct Answer	Your Answer	C ✓	W **0**	O **–**
1. D				
2. A				
3. D				
4. A				
5. C				
6. A				
7. C				
8. E				
9. B				
10. D				
11. B				
12. E				
13. B				
14. A				
15. A				
16. D				
17. B				
18. E				
19. C				
20. D				
21. A				
22. C				
23. C				
24. C				
25. B				
26. E				
27. A				
28. E				
29. B				
30. D				
Subtotal				

Correct Answer	Your Answer	C ✓	W **0**	O **–**
31. D				
32. E				
33. D				
34. B				
35. E				
36. B				
37. C				
38. A				
39. D				
40. C				
41. E				
42. A				
43. E				
44. C				
45. B				
46. A				
47. B				
48. D				
49. E				
50. C				
51. A				
52. B				
53. D				
54. D				
55. B				
56. A				
57. C				
58. E				
59. E				
60. C				
Subtotal				

Total # Correct:	1
Total # Wrong:	
# Wrong ÷ 4:	2
Box 1 - Box 2	3
Round Box 3 to nearest whole integer:	4

Verbal Raw Score:	

Box 4

Verbal Estimated Scaled Score:	

See Table on page 230

Answer Key

Middle Level Practice Test IV : QUANTITATIVE (Sections 1 and 4)

For each question, mark ✓ if correct (C), **0** if wrong (W), or **–** if omitted (O).

Correct Answer	Your Answer	C ✓	W **0**	O **–**
Section 1				
1. B				
2. D				
3. A				
4. E				
5. D				
6. B				
7. B				
8. C				
9. C				
10. A				
11. B				
12. D				
13. E				
14. A				
15. A				
16. D				
17. C				
18. B				
19. D				
20. A				
21. E				
22. C				
23. E				
24. D				
25. B				
Subtotal				

Correct Answer	Your Answer	C ✓	W **0**	O **–**
Section 4				
1. A				
2. B				
3. E				
4. D				
5. A				
6. B				
7. E				
8. D				
9. C				
10. A				
11. C				
12. C				
13. B				
14. A				
15. E				
16. C				
17. A				
18. D				
19. B				
20. C				
21. B				
22. C				
23. D				
24. E				
25. B				
Subtotal				

Total # Correct:	1
Total # Wrong:	
# Wrong ÷ 4:	2
Box 1 - Box 2	3
Round Box 3 to nearest whole integer:	4

Quantitative Raw Score:	

Box 4

Quantitative Estimated Scaled Score:	

See Table on page 230

Answer Key

Middle Level Practice Test IV : READING (Section 2)

For each question, mark ✓ if correct (C), **0** if wrong (W), or **–** if omitted (O).

Correct Answer	Your Answer	C ✓	W **0**	O **–**
1. E				
2. C				
3. B				
4. B				
5. B				
6. A				
7. D				
8. C				
9. D				
10. C				
11. E				
12. A				
13. B				
14. A				
15. B				
16. E				
17. C				
18. E				
19. E				
20. D				
Subtotal				

Correct Answer	Your Answer	C ✓	W **0**	O **–**
21. B				
22. C				
23. B				
24. E				
25. A				
26. D				
27. C				
28. E				
29. A				
30. E				
31. D				
32. B				
33. D				
34. D				
35. E				
36. B				
37. A				
38. A				
39. E				
40. C				
Subtotal				

Total # Correct:	1
Total # Wrong:	
# Wrong ÷ 4:	2
Box 1 - Box 2	3
Round Box 3 to nearest whole integer:	4

Reading Raw Score:	

Box 4

Reading Estimated Scaled Score:	

See Table on page 230

Answer Key

Middle Level Practice Test IV : VERBAL (Section 3)

For each question, mark ✓ if correct (C), **0** if wrong (W), or **–** if omitted (O).

Correct Answer	Your Answer	C ✓	W **0**	O **–**
1. D				
2. E				
3. C				
4. B				
5. C				
6. D				
7. E				
8. E				
9. B				
10. E				
11. A				
12. C				
13. D				
14. C				
15. A				
16. B				
17. D				
18. C				
19. C				
20. D				
21. A				
22. C				
23. E				
24. B				
25. A				
26. E				
27. C				
28. A				
29. C				
30. A				
Subtotal				

Correct Answer	Your Answer	C ✓	W **0**	O **–**
31. B				
32. B				
33. E				
34. A				
35. D				
36. B				
37. C				
38. C				
39. A				
40. A				
41. C				
42. B				
43. A				
44. E				
45. D				
46. C				
47. C				
48. E				
49. A				
50. B				
51. C				
52. A				
53. E				
54. D				
55. E				
56. D				
57. A				
58. B				
59. B				
60. B				
Subtotal				

Total # Correct:	1
Total # Wrong:	
# Wrong ÷ 4:	2
Box 1 - Box 2	3
Round Box 3 to nearest whole integer:	4

Verbal Raw Score:	

Box 4

Verbal Estimated Scaled Score:	

See Table on page 230

Equating Raw Scores to Scaled Scores

Scores are first calculated by awarding one point for each correct answer and subtracting one quarter of one point for each incorrect answer. These scores are called raw scores. Raw scores can vary from one edition of the test to another due to differences in difficulty among editions. Score equating is used to adjust for these differences. Even after these adjustments, no single test score provides a perfectly accurate estimate of your proficiency.

Because *The Official Study Guide for the Middle Level SSAT* contains practice tests and not "retired" forms of the test, there are no norm group data associated with these forms, and calculations of exact scaled scores or specific percentile rankings are not possible. But the following chart will give you an estimate of where your scaled scores might fall within each of the three scored sections: verbal, quantitative/math, and reading.

Table: Middle Level Estimated SSAT Scaled Scores

Raw Score	Estimated Verbal Scaled Score	Estimated Quantitative Scaled Score	Estimated Reading Scaled Score
60	710		
55	710		
50	707	710	
45	695	692	
40	677	674	710
35	656	656	701
30	635	638	671
25	617	619	641
20	596	599	614
15	575	578	587
10	551	554	557
5	528	530	524
0	506	506	497
-5	479	479	458

These are estimated scaled scores based on the raw-to-scaled conversion of many forms, and a student's score can vary when taking the test.

Notes

Notes

Notes

Notes

Notes

Notes

Notes

Notes

Notes

Notes